SOURCE
The Prentice Hall
ENGINEERING SOURCE

# Introduction to MathCAD®

## Ronald W. Larsen

*Montana State University*

**Prentice Hall**
Upper Saddle River, NJ 07458

**Library of Congress Cataloging-In-Publication Data**

Larsen, Ronald W.

Introduction to MathCAD

   p. cm.—(Prentice Hall modular series for engineering)

Includes index.

ISBN: 0-13-937493-0

1. Computer graphics.   2. MathCAD (Computer file).

II. Title.   III. Series.

T585.D6327     1999

831 '.44936' 6798--dc21            98-54617

                                 CIP

Editor-in-chief: **MARCIA HORTON**
Acquisitions editor: **ERIC SVENDSEN**
Director of production and manufacturing: **DAVID W. RICCARDI**
Managing editor: **EILEEN CLARK**
Editorial/Production Supervision: **ROSE KERNAN**
Cover director: **JAYNE CONTE**
Creative Director: **AMY ROSEN**
Manufacturing buyer: **PAT BROWN**
Editorial assistant: **GRIFFIN CABLE**

The author and publisher of this book have used their best efforts in
preparing this book. These efforts include the development, research,
and testing of the theories and programs to determine their effective-
ness. The author and publisher shall not be liable in any event for inci-
dental or consequential damages in connection with, or arising out of,
the furnishing, performance, or use of these programs.

Printed in the United States of America

10 9 8 7 6 5 4 3 2

Printed with Corrections, July 1999.

ISBN 0-13-937493-0

Prentice-Hall International (UK) Limited, *London*
Prentice-Hall of Australia Pty. Limited, *Sydney*
Prentice-Hall Canada, Inc., *Toronto*
Prentice-Hall Hispanoamericana, S.A., *Mexico*
Prentice-Hall of India Private Limited, *New Delhi*
Prentice-Hall of Japan, Inc., *Tokyo*
Simon & Schuster Asia Pte., Ltd., *Singapore*
Editora Prentice-Hall do Brazil, Ltda., *Rio de Janeiro*

# About ESource

### The Challenge

Professors who teach the Introductory/First-Year Engineering course popular at most engineering schools have a unique challenge—teaching a course defined by a changing curriculum. The first-year engineering course is different from any other engineering course in that there is no real cannon that defines the course content. It is not like Engineering Mechanics or Circuit Theory where a consistent set of topics define the course. Instead, the introductory engineering course is most often defined by the creativity of professors and students, and the specific needs of a college or university each semester. Faculty involved in this course typically put extra effort into it, and it shows in the uniqueness of each course at each school.

Choosing a textbook can be a challenge for unique courses. Most freshmen require some sort of reference material to help them through their first semesters as a college student. But because faculty put such a strong mark on their course, they often have a difficult time finding the right mix of materials for their course and often have to go without a text, or with one that does not really fit. Conventional textbooks are far too static for the typical specialization of the first-year course. How do you find the perfect text for your course that will support your students educational needs, but give you the flexibility to maximize the potential of your course?

### ESource—The Prentice Hall Engineering Source
### http://emissary.prenhall.com/esource

Prentice Hall created ESource—The Prentice-Hall Engineering Source—to give professors the power to harness the full potential of their text and their freshman/first year engineering course. In today's technologically advanced world, why settle for a book that isn't perfect for your course? Why not have a book that has the exact blend of topics that you want to cover with your students?

More then just a collection of books, ESource is a unique publishing system revolving around the ESource website—http://emissary.prenhall.com/esource/. ESource enables you to put your stamp on your book just as you do your course. It lets you:

*Control*    You choose exactly what chapters or sections are in your book and in what order they appear. Of course, you can choose the entire book if you'd like and stay with the authors original order.

*Optimize*    Get the most from your book and your course. ESource lets you produce the optimal text for your students needs.

*Customize*   You can add your own material anywhere in your text's presentation, and your final product will arrive at your bookstore as a professionally formatted text.

### ESource Content

All the content in ESource was written by educators specifically for freshman/first-year students. Authors tried to strike a balanced level of presentation, one that was not either too formulaic and trivial, but not focusing heavily on advanced topics that most introductory students will not encounter until later classes. A developmental editor reviewed the books and made sure that every text was written at the appropriate level, and that the books featured a balanced presentation. Because many professors do not have extensive time to cover these topics in the classroom, authors prepared each text with the idea that many students would use it for self-instruction and independent study. Students should be able to use this content to learn the software tool or subject on their own.

While authors had the freedom to write texts in a style appropriate to their particular subject, all followed certain guidelines created to promote the consistency a text needs. Namely, every chapter opens with a clear set of objectives to lead students into the chapter. Each chapter also contains practice problems that tests a student's skill at performing the tasks they have just learned. Chapters close with extra practice questions and a list of key terms for reference. Authors tried to focus on motivating applications that demonstrate how engineers work in the real world, and included these applications throughout the text in various chapter openers, examples, and problem material. Specific Engineering and Science **Application Boxes** are also located throughout the texts, and focus on a specific application and demonstrating its solution.

Because students often have an adjustment from high school to college, each book contains several **Professional Success Boxes** specifically designed to provide advice on college study skills. Each author has worked to provide students with tips and techniques that help a student better understand the material, and avoid common pitfalls or problems first-year students often have. In addition, this series contains an entire book titled *Engineering Success* by Peter Schiavone of the University of Alberta intended to expose students quickly to what it takes to be an engineering student.

### Creating Your Book

Using ESource is simple. You preview the content either on-line or through examination copies of the books you can request on-line, from your PH sales rep, or by calling(1-800-526-0485). Create an on-line outline of the content you want in the order you want using ESource's simple interface. Either type or cut and paste your own material and insert it into the text flow. You can preview the overall organization of the text you've created at anytime (please note, since this preview is immediate, it comes unformatted.), then press another button and receive an order number for your own custom book . If you are not ready to order, do nothing—ESource will save your work. You can come back at any time and change, re-arrange, or add more material to your creation. You are in control. Once you're finished and you have an ISBN, give it to your bookstore and your book will arrive on their shelves six weeks after the order. Your custom desk copies with their instructor supplements will arrive at your address at the same time.

To learn more about this new system for creating the perfect textbook, go to **http://emissary.prenhall.com/esource/**. You can either go through the on-line walkthrough of how to create a book, or experiment yourself.

### Community

ESource has two other areas designed to promote the exchange of information among the introductory engineering community, the Faculty and the Student Centers. Created and maintained with the help of Dale Calkins, an Associate Professor at the University of Washington, these areas contain a wealth of useful information and tools. You can preview outlines created by other schools and can see how others organize their courses. Read a monthly article discussing important topics in the curriculum. You can post your own material and share it with others, as well as use what others have posted in your own documents. Communicate with our authors about their books and make suggestions for improvement. Comment about your course and ask for information from others professors. Create an on-line syllabus using our custom syllabus builder. Browse Prentice Hall's catalog and order titles from your sales rep. Tell us new features that we need to add to the site to make it more useful.

### Supplements

Adopters of ESource receive an instructor's CD that includes solutions as well as professor and student code for all the books in the series. This CD also contains approximately **350 Powerpoint Transparencies** created by Jack Leifer—of University South Carolina—Aiken. Professors can either follow these transparencies as pre-prepared lectures or use them as the basis for their own custom presentations. In addition, look to the web site to find materials from other schools that you can download and use in your own course.

# Titles in the ESource Series

**Introduction to Unix**
*0-13-095135-8*
*David L. Schwartz*

**Introduction to Maple**
*0-13-095-133-1*
*David L. Schwartz*

**Introduction to Word**
*0-13-254764-3*
*David C. Kuncicky*

**Introduction to Excel**
*0-13-254749-X*
*David C. Kuncicky*

**Introduction to Mathcad**
*0-13-937493-0*
*Ronald W. Larsen*

**Introduction to AutoCAD, R. 1.4**
*0-13-011001-9*
*Mark Dix*

**Introduction to the Internet, 2/e**
*0-13-011037-X*
*Scott D. James*

**Design Concepts for Engineers**
*0-13-081369-9*
*Mark N. Horenstein*

**Engineering Design—A Day in the Life of Four Engineers**
*0-13-660242–8*
*Mark N. Horenstein*

**Engineering Ethics**
*0-13-784224-4*
*Charles B. Fledderman*

**Engineering Success**
*0-13-080859-8*
*Peter Schiavone*

**Mathematics Review**
*0-13-011501-0*
*Peter Schiavone*

**Introduction to ANSI C**
*0-13-011854-0*
*Dolores Etter*

**Introduction to C++**
*0-13-011855-9*
*Dolores Etter*

**Introduction to MATLAB**
*0-13-013149-0*
*Dolores Etter*

**Introduction to Engineering and Problem Solving**
*0-13-908435-5*
*Dolores Etter*

**Introduction to FORTRAN 90**
*0-13-013146-6*
*Larry Nyhoff & Sanford Leestma*

# About the Authors

No project could ever come to pass without a group of authors who have the vision and the courage to turn a stack of blank paper into a book. The authors in this series worked diligently to produce their books, provide the building blocks of the series.

**Delores M. Etter** is a Professor of Electrical and Computer Engineering at the University of Colorado. Dr. Etter was a faculty member at the University of New Mexico and also a Visiting Professor at Stanford University. Dr. Etter was responsible for the Freshman Engineering Program at the University of New Mexico and is active in the Integrated Teaching Laboratory at the University of Colorado. She was elected a Fellow of the Institute of Electrical and Electronic Engineers for her contributions to education and for her technical leadership in digital signal processing. IN addition to writing best-selling textbooks for engineering computing, Dr. Etter has also published research in the area of adaptive signal processing.

**Sanford Leestma** is a Professor of Mathematics and Computer Science at Calvin College, and received his Ph.D from New Mexico State University. He has been the long time co-author of successful textbooks on Fortran, Pascal, and data structures in Pascal. His current research interests are in the areas of algorithms and numerical compuitation.

**Larry Nyhoff** is a Professor of Mathematics and Computer Science at Calvin College. After doing bachelors work at Calvin, and Masters work at Michigan, he received a Ph.D. from Michigan State and also did graduate work in computer science at Western Michigan. Dr. Nyhoff has taught at Calvin for the past 34 years—mathematics at first and computer science for the past several years. He has co-authored several computer science textbooks

since 1981 including titles on Fortran and C++, as well as a brand new title on Data Structures in C++.

***Acknowledgments:*** We express our sincere appreciation to all who helped in the preparation of this module, especially our acquisitions editor Alan Apt, managing editor Laura Steele, development editor Sandra Chavez, and production editor Judy Winthrop. We also thank Larry Genalo for several examples and exercises and Erin Fulp for the Internet address application in Chapter 10. We appreciate the insightful review provided by Bart Childs. We thank our families—Shar, Jeff, Dawn, Rebecca, Megan, Sara, Greg, Julie, Joshua, Derek, Tom, Joan; Marge, Michelle, Sandy, Lori, Michael—for being patient and understanding. We thank God for allowing us to write this text.

**Mark Dix** began working with AutoCAD in 1985 as a programmer for CAD Support Associates, Inc. He helped design a system for creating estimates and bills of material directly from AutoCAD drawing databases for use in the automated conveyor industry. This system became the basis for systems still widely in use today. In 1986 he began collaborating with Paul Riley to create AutoCAD training materials, combining Riley's background in industrial design and training with Dix' s background in writing, curriculum development, and programming. Dix and Riley have created tutorial and teaching methods for every AutoCAD release since Version 2.5. Mr. Dix has a Master of Arts in Teaching from Cornell University and a Masters of Education from the University of Massachusetts. He is currently the Director of Dearborn Academy High School in Arlington, Massachusetts.

**Paul Riley** is an author, instructor, and designer specializing in graphics and design for multimedia. He is a founding partner of CAD Support Associates, a contract service and professional training organization for computer-aided design. His 15 years of business experience and 20 years of teaching experience are supported by degrees in education and computer science. Paul has taught AutoCAD at the University of Massachusetts at Lowell and is presently teaching AutoCAD at Mt. Ida College in Newton, Massachusetts. He has developed a program, Computer-Aided Design for Professionals that is highly regarded by corporate clients and has been an ongoing success since 1982.

**David I. Schwartz** is a Lecturer at SUNY-Buffalo who teaches freshman and first-year engineering, and has a Ph.D from SUNY-Buffalo in Civil Engineering. Schwartz originally became interested in Civil engineering out of an interest in building grand structures, but has also pursued other academic interests including artificial intelligence and applied mathematics. He became interested in Unix and Maple through their application to his research, and eventually jumped at the chance to teach these subjects to students. He tries to teach his students to become incremental learners and encourages frequent practice to master a subject, and gain the maturity and confidence to tackle other subjects independently. In his spare time, Schwartz is an avid musician and plays drums in a variety of bands.

*Acknowledgments:* I would like to thank the entire School of Engineering and Applied Science at the State University of New York at Buffalo for the opportunity to teach not only my students, but myself as well; all my EAS140 students, without whom this book would not be possible—thanks for slugging through my lab packets; Andrea Au, Eric Svendsen, and Elizabeth Wood at Prentice Hall for advising and encouraging me as well as wading through my blizzard of e-mail; Linda and Tony for starting the whole thing in the first place; Rogil Camama, Linda Chattin, Stuart Chen, Jeffrey Chottiner, Roger Christian, Anthony Dalessio, Eugene DeMaitre, Dawn Halvorsen, Thomas Hill, Michael Lamanna, Nate "X" Patwardhan, Durvejai Sheobaran, "Able" Alan Somlo, Ben Stein, Craig Sutton, Barbara Umiker, and Chester "JC" Zeshonski for making this book a reality; Ewa Arrasjid, "Corky" Brunskill, Bob Meyer, and Dave Yearke at "the Department Formerly Known as ECS" for all their friendship, advice, and respect; Jeff, Tony, Forrest, and Mike for the interviews; and, Michael Ryan and Warren Thomas for believing in me.

**Ronald W. Larsen** is an Associate Professor in Chemical Engineering at Montana State University, and received his Ph.D from the Pennsylvania State University. Larsen was initially attracted to engineering because he felt it was a serving profession, and because engineers are often called on to eliminate dull and routine tasks. He also enjoys the fact that engineering rewards creativity and presents constant challenges. Larsen feels that teaching large sections of students is one of the most challenging tasks he has ever encountered because it enhances the importance of effective communication. He has drawn on a two year experince teaching courses in Mongolia through an interpreter to improve his skills in the classroom. Larsen sees software as one of the changes that has the potential to radically alter the way engineers work, and his book Introduction to Mathcad was written to help young engineers prepare to be productive in an ever-changing workplace.

*Acknowledgments:* To my students at Montana State University who have endured the rough drafts and typos, and who still allow me to experiment with their classes— my sincere thanks.

**Peter Schiavone** is a professor and student advisor in the Department of Mechanical Engineering at the University of Alberta. He received his Ph.D. from the University of Strathclyde, U.K. in 1988. He has authored several books in the area of study skills and academic success as well as numerous papers in scientific research journals.

Before starting his career in academia, Dr. Schiavone worked in the private sector for Smith's Industries (Aerospace and Defence Systems Company) and Marconi Instruments in several different areas of engineering including aerospace, systems and software engineering. During that time he developed an interest in engineering research and the applications of mathematics and the physical sciences to solving real-world engineering problems.

His love for teaching brought him to the academic world. He founded the first Mathematics Resource Center at the University of Alberta: a unit designed specifically to teach high school students the necessary survival skills in mathematics and the physical sciences required for first-year engineering. This led to the Students' Union Gold Key award for outstanding contributions to the University and to the community at large.

Dr. Schiavone lectures regularly to freshman engineering students, high school teachers, and new professors on all aspects of engineering success, in particular, maximizing students' academic performance. He wrote the book *Engineering Success* in order to share with you the *secrets of success in engineering study*: the most effective, tried and tested methods used by the most successful engineering students.

*Acknowledgments:* I'd like to acknowledge the contributions of: Eric Svendsen, for his encouragement and support; Richard Felder for being such an inspiration; the many students who shared their experiences of first-year engineering—both good and bad; and finally, my wife Linda for her continued support and for giving me Conan.

**Scott D. James** is a staff lecturer at Kettering University (formerly GMI Engineering & Management Institute) in Flint, Michigan. He is currently pursuing a Ph.D. in Systems Engineering with an emphasis on software engineering and computer-integrated manufacturing. Scott decided on writing textbooks after he found a void in the books that were available. "I really wanted a book that showed how to do things in good detail but in a clear and concise way. Many of the books on the market are full of fluff and force you to dig out the really important facts." Scott decided on teaching as a profession after several years in the computer industry. "I thought that it was really important to know what it was like outside of

academia. I wanted to provide students with classes that were up to date and provide the information that is really used and needed."

*Acknowledgments:* Scott would like to acknowledge his family for the time to work on the text and his students and peers at Kettering who offered helpful critique of the materials that eventually became the book.

**David C. Kuncicky** is a native Floridian. He earned his Baccalaureate in psychology, Master's in computer science, and Ph.D. in computer science from Florida State University. He is also the author of *Excel 97 for Engineers*. Dr. Kuncicky is the Director of Computing and Multimedia Services for the FAMU-FSU College of Engineering. He also serves as a faculty member in the Department of Electrical Engineering. He has taught computer science and computer engineering courses for the past 15 years. He has published research in the areas of intelligent hybrid systems and neural networks. He is actively involved in the education of computer and network system administrators and is a leader in the area of technology-based curriculum delivery.

*Acknowledgments:* Thanks to Steffie and Helen for putting up with my late nights and long weekends at the computer. Thanks also to the helpful and insightful technical reviews by the following people: Jerry Ralya, Kathy Kitto of Western Washington University, Avi Singhal of Arizona State University, and Thomas Hill of the State University of New York at Buffalo. I appreciate the patience of Eric Svendsen and Rose Kernan of Prentice Hall for gently guiding me through this project. Finally, thanks to Dean C.J. Chen for providing continued tutelage and support.

**Mark Horenstein** is an Associate Professor in the Electrical and Computer Engineering Department at Boston University. He received his Bachelors in Electrical Engineering in 1973 from Massachusetts Institute of Technology, his Masters in Electrical Engineering in 1975

from University of California at Berkeley, and his Ph.D. in Electrical Engineering in 1978 from Massachusetts Institute of Technology. Professor Horenstein's research interests are in applied electrostatics and electromagnetics as well as microelectronics, including sensors, instrumentation, and measurement. His research deals with the simulation, test, and measurement of electromagnetic fields. Some topics include electrostatics in manufacturing processes, electrostatic instrumentation, EOS/ESD control, and electromagnetic wave propagation.

Professor Horenstein designed and developed a class at Boston University, which he now teaches entitled Senior Design Project (ENG SC 466). In this course, the student gets real engineering design experience by working for a virtual company, created by Professor Horenstein, that does real projects for outside companies—almost like an apprenticeship. Once in "the company" (Xebec Technologies), the student is assigned to an engineering team of 3-4 persons. A series of potential customers are recruited, from which the team must accept an engineering project. The team must develop a working prototype deliverable engineering system that serves the need of the customer. More than one team may be assigned to the same project, in which case there is competition for the customer's business.

*Acknowledgements:* Several individuals contributed to the ideas and concepts presented in Design Principles for Engineers. The concept of the Peak Performance design competition, which forms a cornerstone of the book, originated with Professor James Bethune of Boston University. Professor Bethune has been instrumental in conceiving of and running Peak Performance each year and has been the inspiration behind many of the design concepts associated with it. He also provided helpful information on dimensions and tolerance. Several of the ideas presented in the book, particularly the topics on brainstorming and teamwork, were gleaned from a workshop on engineering design help bi-annually by Professor Charles Lovas of Southern Methodist University. The principles of estimation were derived in part from a freshman engineering problem posed by Professor Thomas Kincaid of Boston University.

I would like to thank my family, Roxanne, Rachel, and Arielle, for giving me the time and space to think about and write this book. I also appreciate Roxanne's inspiration and help in identifying examples of human/machine interfaces.

Dedicated to Roxanne, Rachel, and Arielle

**Charles B. Fleddermann** is a professor in the Department of Electrical and Computer Engineering at the University of New Mexico in Albuquerque, New Mexico. He is a third generation engineer—his grandfather was a civil engineer and father an aeronautical engineer—so "engineering was in my genetic makeup." The genesis of a book on engineering ethics was in the ABET requirement to incorporate ethics topics into the undergraduate engineering curriculum. "Our department decided to have a one-hour seminar course on engineering ethics, but there was no book suitable for such a course." Other texts were tried the first few times the course was offered, but none of them presented ethical theory, analysis, and problem solving in a readily accessible way. "I wanted to have a text which would be concise, yet would give the student the tools required to solve the ethical problems that they might encounter in their professional lives."

# Reviewers

ESource benefited from a wealth of reviewers who on the series from its initial idea stage to its completion. Reviewers read manuscripts and contributed insightful comments that helped the authors write great books. We would like to thank everyone who helped us with this project.

## Concept Document

Naeem Abdurrahman- University of Texas, Austin
Grant Baker- University of Alaska, Anchorage
Betty Barr- University of Houston
William Beckwith- Clemson University
Ramzi Bualuan- University of Notre Dame
Dale Calkins- University of Washington
Arthur Clausing- University of Illinois at Urbana-Champaign
John Glover- University of Houston
A.S. Hodel- Auburn University
Denise Jackson- University of Tennessee, Knoxville
Kathleen Kitto- Western Washington University
Terry Kohutek- Texas A&M University
Larry Richards- University of Virginia
Avi Singhal- Arizona State University
Joseph Wujek- University of California, Berkeley
Mandochehr Zoghi- University of Dayton

## Books

Stephen Allan- Utah State University
Naeem Abdurrahman - University of Texas Austin
Anil Bajaj- Purdue University
Grant Baker - University of Alaska - Anchorage
Betty Barr - University of Houston

William Beckwith - Clemson University
Haym Benaroya- Rutgers University
Tom Bledsaw- ITT Technical Institute
Tom Bryson- University of Missouri, Rolla
Ramzi Bualuan - University of Notre Dame
Dan Budny- Purdue University
Dale Calkins - University of Washington
Arthur Clausing - University of Illinois
James Devine - University of South Florida
Patrick Fitzhorn - Colorado State University
Dale Elifrits- University of Missouri, Rolla
Frank Gerlitz - Washtenaw College
John Glover - University of Houston
John Graham - University of North Carolina-Charlotte
Malcom Heimer - Florida International University
A.S. Hodel - Auburn University
Vern Johnson- University of Arizona
Kathleen Kitto - Western Washington University
Robert Montgomery- Purdue University
Mark Nagurka- Marquette University
Ramarathnam Narasimhan- University of Miami
Larry Richards - University of Virginia
Marc H. Richman - Brown University
Avi Singhal-Arizona State University
Tim Sykes- Houston Community College
Thomas Hill- SUNY at Buffalo
Michael S. Wells - Tennessee Tech University
Joseph Wujek - University of California - Berkeley
Edward Young- University of South Carolina
Mandochehr Zoghi - University of Dayton

# Contents

# 6 MATHCAD'S SYMBOLIC MATH CAPABILITIES

# 7 NUMERICAL TECHNIQUES

# 1

# Mathcad: The Engineer's Scratch Pad

## 1.1 INTRODUCTION TO MATHCAD

Mathcad[1] is an equation-solving software package that has proven to have a wide range of applicability to engineering problems. Mathcad's ability to display equations the same way you would write them on paper makes a Mathcad worksheet easy to read. For example, if you wanted to calculate the mass of water in a storage tank, you might solve the problem on paper like this:

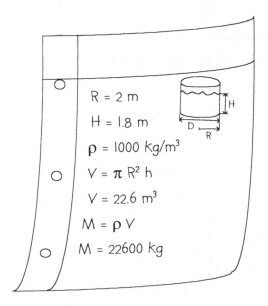

R = 2 m

H = 1.8 m

$\rho = 1000 \text{ kg/m}^3$

$V = \pi R^2 h$

$V = 22.6 \text{ m}^3$

$M = \rho V$

$M = 22600 \text{ kg}$

[1] Mathcad is a registered trademark of Mathsoft, Inc. All examples in this text were developed using Mathcad 7.

## OBJECTIVES

*After reading this chapter, you should be able to:*

- To begin to show you how Mathcad solves problems.
- To describe the unique features that make Mathcad a valuable tool for engineers and scientists, especially Mathcad's value as:
  —A design tool.
  —A mathematical problem solver.
  —A unit converter.
  —A good way to present your results.
- To let you know what to expect from the text, the objectives, and a typical chapter layout.
- To introduce some conventions that will be used in this text.

The same calculation in Mathcad might look like this:

$$R := 2 \cdot m$$

$$H := 1.8 \cdot m$$

$$\rho := 1000 \cdot \frac{kg}{m^3}$$

$$V := \pi \cdot R^2 \cdot H$$

$$V = 22.6 \cdot m^3$$

$$M := \rho \cdot V$$

$$M = 2.26 \cdot 10^4 \cdot kg$$

One of the nicest features of Mathcad is its ability to solve problems much the same way people do, rather than making your solution process fit the program's way of doing things. For example, you could also solve this problem in a spreadsheet by entering the constants and the equations for volume and mass into various cells:

|   | A | B | C |
|---|---|---|---|
| 1 | R: | 2 | |
| 2 | H: | 1.8 | |
| 3 | Rho: | 1000 | |
| 4 | | | |
| 5 | V: | 22.6 | |
| 6 | M: | 22619 | |
| 7 | | | |

In the C programming language, the problem might be solved with the following program:

```
#include stdio.h
#include math.h

main()
{
      float R, H, Rho, V, M;

      R = 2;
      H = 1.8;
      V = 3.1416 * pow(R,2) * H;
      M = Rho * V;
      printf("V = %f \n M = %f", V, M);
}
```

While spreadsheets and programming languages can produce the solution, Mathcad's presentation of the solution is much more like the way people solve equations on paper. This makes Mathcad easier for you to use. It also makes it easier for others to read and understand your results.

*Work to develop communication skills as well as technical skills.*

An engineer's job is to find a solution to someone's problem. Finding the solution requires good technical skills, but the solution must *always* be communicated to other people. An engineer's communication skills are just as important as her or his technical skills.

Because Mathcad's worksheets are easy to read, they can help you communicate your results to others. You can improve the readability of your worksheets by:

- Performing your calculations in an orderly way—plan your work.
- Adding comments to your worksheet.
- Using units on your variables.

The last two items will be discussed in more detail in the next chapter.

Mathcad's user interface is an important feature, but Mathcad has other features that make it excel as a design tool; a mathematical problem solver, a unit converter, and a communicator of results.

## 1.2  MATHCAD AS A DESIGN TOOL

A Mathcad worksheet is a collection of variable definitions, equations, text regions, and graphs displayed on the screen in pretty much the same fashion you would write them on paper. A big difference between a Mathcad worksheet and your paper scratch pad is *automatic recalculation.* If you make a change to any of the definitions or equations in your worksheet, the rest of the worksheet is automatically updated. This makes it easy to do the "what if" calculations that are so common in engineering. For example, What if the water level rises to 2.8 m? Would the mass in the tank exceed the tank's maximum design value of 40,000 kg?

To answer these questions, simply edit the definition of H in the Mathcad worksheet. The rest of the equations are automatically updated and the new result is displayed:

$$R := 2 \cdot m$$
$$H := 2.8 \cdot m$$
$$\rho := 1000 \cdot \frac{kg}{m^3}$$
$$V := \pi \cdot R^2 \cdot H$$
$$V = 35.2 \cdot m^3$$
$$M := \rho \cdot V$$
$$M = 3.52 \cdot 10^4 \cdot kg$$

From this calculation, we see that even at a height of 2.8 m, the mass in the tank is still within the design specifications.

The ability to develop a worksheet for a particular case and then vary one or more parameters to observe their impact on the calculated results makes a Mathcad worksheet a valuable tool for evaluating multiple designs.

Mathcad has another feature, called a QuickPlot, that is very useful for visualizing functions, and this can also speed the design process. With a QuickPlot, you simply create a graph, put the function on the *y*-axis, and place a dummy variable on the *x*-axis. Mathcad evaluates the function for a range of values and displays the graph. For example, if you want to see what the hyperbolic sine function looks like, use a Quick-Plot, such as the following:

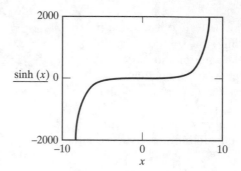

QuickPlots are discussed in more detail in later chapters—we'll use them a lot.

## 1.3 MATHCAD AS A MATHEMATICAL PROBLEM SOLVER

Mathcad has the ability to solve problems numerically (computing a value) or symbolically (working with the variables directly). It has a large collection of built-in functions for trigonometric calculations, statistical calculations, data analysis (e.g., regression), and matrix operations. Mathcad can calculate derivatives and evaluate integrals, and it can handle many differential equations. It can work with imaginary numbers and handle Laplace transforms. Iterative solutions are tedious by hand, but very straightforward in Mathcad. In summary, while it is possible to come up with problems that are beyond Mathcad's capabilities, Mathcad can handle the bulk of an engineer's day-to-day calculations, and do them very well.

Some of these features, like Laplace transforms and functions for solving differential equations, are beyond the scope of this text, but many of Mathcad's commonly used features and functions will be presented and used.

## 1.4 MATHCAD AS A UNIT CONVERTER

Mathcad allows you to build units into most equations. (There are a couple of restrictions, which will be discussed in the next chapter.) Allowing Mathcad to handle the chore of getting all the values converted to a consistent set of units can be a major time-saver. For example, if the storage tank's radius had been measured in feet and the depth in inches, then

$$R = 6.56 \text{ ft (equivalent to 2 m)}$$
$$H = 70.87 \text{ in (equivalent to 1.8 m)}$$

We could convert the feet and inches to meters ourselves, or let Mathcad do it as shown here:

$$R := 6.56 \cdot \text{ft}$$
$$H := 70.87 \cdot \text{in}$$
$$\rho := 1000 \cdot \frac{\text{kg}}{\text{m}^3}$$

$$V := \pi \cdot R^2 \cdot H$$
$$V = 22.609 \cdot m^3$$
$$M := \rho \cdot V$$
$$M = 22609 \cdot kg$$

*Note:* The mass is slightly lower here than in the first example because of rounding of the R and H values.

For complicated problems, and when your input values have many different units, Mathcad's ability to handle the unit conversions is a very nice feature.

## 1.5  MATHCAD FOR PRESENTING RESULTS

Engineering and science are both fields in which a person's computed results have little meaning unless they are given to someone else. A circuit design has to be passed along to a manufacturer, for example. Getting the results in a useful form can often take as long as computing the results. This is an area where Mathcad can help speed up the process.

Practicing engineers use spreadsheets for many routine calculations, but spreadsheets can be frustrating because they only display the calculated results while hiding the equations. If someone gives you a spreadsheet printout, it probably shows only numbers, and you have to take their word for the equations or ask for a copy of the spreadsheet file. If you dig into the spreadsheet to see the equations, they are still somewhat cryptic because they typically use cell references (e.g., B12) rather than variable names.

Computer program listings make it clear how the results were calculated, and recognizable variable names can be used, but long equations on a single line can still be difficult to decipher. Mathcad's ability to show the equations and the results the way people are used to reading them makes a Mathcad worksheet a good way to give your results to someone else. If there is a question about a result, the solution method is obvious. Mathcad's ability to print equations in the order we would write them, but with typeset quality, is a bonus.

Still, there are times when you need to get your results into a more formal report. Mathcad helps out in that area too. Equations and results (e.g., values, matrices, graphs) on a Mathcad worksheet can be inserted (via copy and paste operations) into other software programs, such as word processors. You don't have to retype the equations in the word processor, which can be a major time-saver. This compatibility with other software also means you can get a matrix from Mathcad into a spreadsheet, or create a Mathcad matrix from a column of values in a spreadsheet. These features will be described in much more detail later.

## 1.6  MATHCAD'S PLACE IN AN ENGINEER'S TOOL KIT

Spreadsheets, programming languages, and mathematical problem solvers all have their place, and the tools you will use routinely will depend on where your career takes you, or perhaps vice versa. There is no single "right" tool for most problems, but Mathcad seems a logical choice when the requirements of the problem align with Mathcad's strengths. These strengths include:

- Equations that are displayed in very readable form.
- The ability to work with units.

- A symbolic math capability.
- An iterative solution capability.
- An extensive function library.

Deciding on which software product to use requires an understanding of the various products. For example:

- Spreadsheets can solve equations requiring iteration, but the process is much easier to follow in Mathcad.
- Mathcad can handle lists of numbers (e.g., analyses of experimental data sets), but columns of numbers fit well into the strengths of a spreadsheet.
- Spreadsheets cannot handle symbolic mathematics, so Mathcad (or Maple, or Mathematica)[2] must be used for this type of work.

Hopefully, this text will demonstrate Mathcad's capabilities, and it will help you learn where this package fits in your tool kit.

## 1.7 OBJECTIVES OF THIS TEXT

The first objective is to teach you how to use Mathcad to solve engineering problems. The second objective is to show the wide range of career areas open to engineers and to demonstrate how Mathcad fits into all these areas. Finally, the third objective is to address a few of the challenges and opportunities that the next generation of engineers will face. With these objectives in mind, a typical chapter will include the following:

- An introduction to one of the expanding fields of engineering.
- Information on Mathcad, initially using simple examples for clarity.
- Practice! boxes—an opportunity for you to try Mathcad's features for yourself using quick and easy problems.
- Application boxes, showing how Mathcad can be used to solve real problems.

At the end of each chapter there are several homework problems, some related to the challenges and opportunities mentioned. The following themes will appear throughout the text:

- *Global warming,* an issue the next generation of engineers will have to address.
- *Biomedical engineering,* a potential opportunity for future engineers.
- *Optics,* an old field that is expanding rapidly into new areas.
- *Risk analysis,* a necessary and challenging part of many engineering activities.
- *Total recycle:* Can we eliminate waste products entirely? It's being tried.
- *Composite materials,* engineered materials that require the skills of a variety of engineering disciplines and that have the potential to change the way we do a lot of things.

---

[2] Maple is product of Waterloo Maple Inc. 57 Erb Street W. Waterloo, Ontario Canada. Mathematica is produced by Wolfram Research, Inc., Champaign, IL.

## 1.8 CONVENTIONS USED IN THIS TEXT

| | |
|---|---|
| `Stdev(v)` | Function names and variable names in text are shown in a different font. |
| [Ctrl-6] | Keystrokes are shown in brackets. This example indicates that the control key and 6 key should be pressed simultaneously. |
| File / Save As | Menu selections are listed with the main menu item and sub-menu items separated by "/". |
| $A := \pi \cdot r^2$ | Mathcad examples are shown in Times New Roman font and are indented. |
| *Keyword* | Keywords are shown in italics the first time they are used. |

# 2

# Mathcad Fundamentals

## GLOBAL WARMING

The *greenhouse effect* is an atmospheric phenomenon in which a buildup of greenhouse gases (carbon dioxide, methane, et al.) increases the amount of infrared radiation from the earth that is reflected back to the earth. If the concentration of greenhouse gases in the atmosphere increases, the result is increased surface temperature, or *global warming*.

Our world's problem with global warming is hotly debated, but there are a few points that are generally agreed upon:

1. The concentration of greenhouse gases (principally $CO_2$) in our atmosphere is increasing.

2. The average surface temperature of our planet is slowly increasing.

3. The greenhouse effect could cause global warming.

It is the likelihood and significance of the potential problem that is being questioned. The worst-case scenario melts back polar ice packs, floods coastal cities around the world, and changes climates, turning America's grain belt (for example) into a desert. Best-case scenarios have

## SECTIONS

- 2.1 The Mathcad Workplace
- 2.2 Determining the Order of Solving Equations in Mathcad
- 2.3 Four Different Kinds of Equal Signs!
- 2.4 Entering an Equation
- 2.5 Working with Units
- 2.6 Entering and Editing Text
- 2.7 A Simple Editing Session
- Summary

## OBJECTIVES

*After reading this chapter, you should be able to:*

- To learn to work with Mathcad:
  - How the Mathcad workspace is laid out.
  - How to enter an equation.
  - How to display a result.
  - How to control the order in which Mathcad evaluates equations.
- To learn how Mathcad handles unit conversions.
- To learn to enter and format text in a Mathcad worksheet.

atmospheric $CO_2$ concentrations leveling off as the earth's ecosystem responds to the changing atmospheric conditions, and the problem goes away. The science is likely to be debated for many years to come. Even then, we may decide that we simply cannot know for certain what will happen. But even if we cannot know, that does not imply that we should not act—uncertainty does not justify inaction if there is a real possibility of catastrophe. This has led the leaders of the world's industrialized nations to commit to reducing their nations' emissions of $CO_2$. Because of this, global warming has become a very real problem for engineers and one that may well be a significant part of your career.

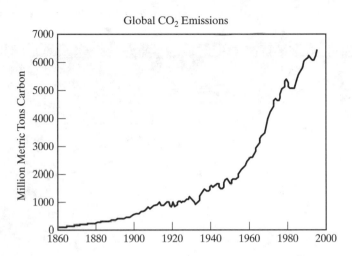

### Historical Perspective

Energy has been a major contributor to economic growth ever since the Industrial Revolution, and much of that energy has come from fossil fuels. One such result has been increased emissions of greenhouse gases into the atmosphere. Because there are many greenhouse gases, the total emissions are often reported in terms of carbon only.

The accompanying graph looks a lot like an exponential growth curve with a few perturbations. For example, 1918 to 1945 was a period of reduced growth in $CO_2$ emissions that coincides with World Wars I and II and the Great Depression. There's a bump around 1980 that coincides with a worldwide recession. Finally, there's a flat spot in the early 1990s that is being attributed to emission reductions in eastern Europe following the collapse of the Soviet Union.

There is good evidence that hard times coincide with reduced $CO_2$ emissions. Many people are concerned that attempting to reduce $CO_2$ emissions may bring about hard times. Finding ways to reduce emissions while maintaining economic growth will require some very creative solutions. But finding creative solutions is what engineering is all about.

*Practice, Practice, Practice!*
This does not mean that you should perform the same tasks over and over again (you're not trying to improve manual dexterity), but you can take conceptual information in a textbook and make it your own by putting it into practice.

The fastest way to learn Mathcad is to use it. Try working through the examples in this text on a computer. There are "Practice!" boxes throughout the text that have been designed to help you learn what Mathcad can do—to help you put this new knowledge into practice.

## 2.1 THE MATHCAD WORKPLACE

When you start Mathcad, on your screen you should see the following:

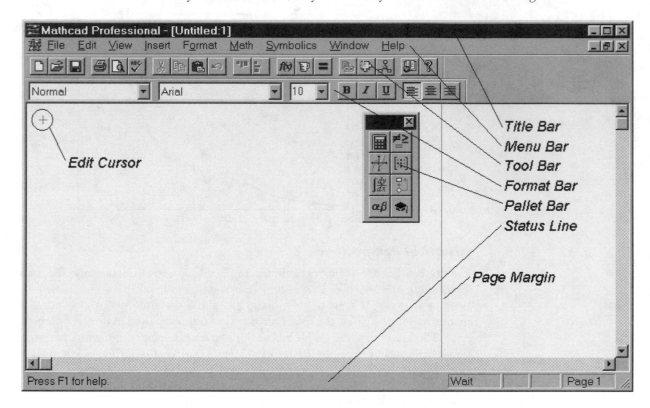

(The exact appearance of the screen depends upon the version of Mathcad you are using, and the options that have been selected. Some of these options will be described in this chapter.) The screen examples in this text are from version 7 of Mathcad.)

Several of the bars near the top of the screen should be pretty familiar to Windows users. The Title Bar and Menu Bar are common to most Windows applications. Many of the most common menu commands are also available as buttons on the Tool Bar. The Font Bar is very similar to that used by most word processors, but it displays the font type and size only when you are actually editing text or equations. The bold, italic, and underline buttons on the Font Bar apply to text only.

When you enter an equation or some text, it is initially formatted using a predefined *style*. There are separate styles defined for constants, variables, and text. You can change the formatting of selected text or an equation that you have selected by using the Format Bar, or you can change the formatting of all constants, variables, or text by redefining their respective styles. You access the styles by using the Format menu.

The *Math Palette,* or Palette Toolbar[1] (shown floating, but it can be moved to other locations on the screen), is unique to Mathcad and provides access to a variety of useful mathematical symbols and functions. Clicking on any of the buttons on the Palette Toolbar brings up another Palette. For example, clicking the Matrix Palette button displays the Matrix Palette—a collection of functions that are useful for performing matrix operations. The Mathcad Palettes available from the Palette Toolbar include the following:

- Arithmetic Palette.
- Evaluation and Boolean Palette.
- Graph Palette.
- Vector and Matrix Palette.
- Calculus Palette.
- Programming Palette.
- Greek Symbol Palette.
- Symbolic Keyword Palette.

The majority of the workspace is a blank, white space called the *worksheet.* This is the area available for you to enter your equations, text, graphs, etc. The worksheet scrolls if you need more space.

There is a small crosshair cursor displayed on the worksheet. This is the *edit cursor,* and it indicates where the next equation or text region will be displayed. Clicking the mouse anywhere on the worksheet moves the edit cursor to the mouse pointer's location. If the edit cursor is located between two equations, you can add lines between the equations by pressing [Enter], or delete lines between the equations by pressing [Delete].

## 2.2 DETERMINING THE ORDER OF SOLVING EQUATIONS IN MATHCAD

It is usually very important to solve a set of equations in a particular order. In Mathcad, you use the placement of equations on the worksheet to control the order of their solution. Mathcad evaluates equations from left to right and top to bottom. When two

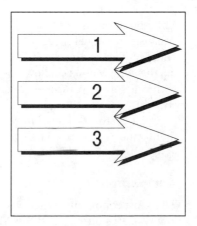

---

[1] The "palettes" in version 7 of Mathcad are called "toolbars" in version 8. They provide access to the same functions and operators in both versions.

equations are side by side on the worksheet, the equation on the left will be evaluated first, then the equation on the right. When there are no more equations to evaluate on a line, Mathcad moves down the worksheet and continues evaluating equations from left to right.

Some equations take a lot more space on the screen than others, so how do you determine which equation will be evaluated first? Mathcad assigns each equation an *anchor point* on the screen. The anchor point is located to the left of the first character in the equation, at the character baseline. You can ask Mathcad to display the anchor points by selecting Regions from the View Menu (View/Regions). When View/Regions is on, the background of the worksheet is dimmed, and the equation regions appear as bright boxes. The anchor point is indicated by a black dot and is displayed only when you click inside a region. (The following figure is a composite made from two screen images—you will only see one anchor point at a time in Mathcad.)

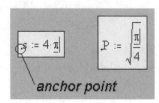

In this figure, the equation on the left would be evaluated first, since the anchor points are the same distance from the top of the worksheet. But the anchor point on the s is to the left of the anchor point on the P. For simple variable definitions, like the s and P definitions shown here the anchor point is always located at the bottom-left corner of the variable name.

## 2.3   FOUR DIFFERENT KINDS OF EQUAL SIGNS!

In high school algebra, you learned that the equal sign indicates that the left and right sides of an equation are equal. Then, in a programming course, you may have seen a statement such as:

$$\text{COUNT} = \text{COUNT} + 1$$

This statement is never an algebraic equality, but it is a valid programming statement because the equal sign, in a programming context, means assignment, not algebraic equality. That is, the result of the calculation on the right side is assigned to the variable on the left. Mathcad allows both types of usage (algebraic equality and assignment) within a single worksheet, but different types of equal signs are used to keep things straight.

In Mathcad, four different symbols are available to represent equality or assignment (more if you count the "symbolic evaluation" and programming "temporary assignment" symbols). Fortunately, some are used less often than others.

### Assignment :=

The most commonly used *assignment operator* is :=, which is entered by using the colon key [ : ]. It is often called the "define as equal to" operator. This type of equal sign was used to assign values to variables s and P in the previous figure.

### Display the Value
### (Variable, Result of a Calculation) =

Once a variable has been assigned a value (either directly or by means of a calculation), you can display the value by using the plain equal sign [ = ]. Displaying a value is the only usage of the plain equal sign in Mathcad; it is never used for assignment or algebraic equality. To display the value of the calculated variable s, you first define the equation used to compute s and then display the result using the equal sign. For example, we might have

$$s := 4 \cdot \pi$$
$$s = 12.566$$

You can also display a calculated result without assigning it to a variable. This displays the result of the calculation, but you cannot use the result in further calculations without assigning the result to a variable. An example is

$$4 \cdot \pi = 12.566$$

### Symbolic Equality =

The *symbolic equality* is used to indicate that the combination of variables on the left side of an equation is equal to the combination of variables on the right side of an equation—the high school algebra meaning of the equal sign. The symbolic equality is displayed as a heavy boldface equal sign in Mathcad and is entered by pressing [Ctrl - =]. (Press the control and equal keys simultaneously.) An example of a formula using this operation is

$$P \cdot V = n \cdot R \cdot T$$

The symbolic equality is used to show a relationship between variables. There is no assignment of a value to any variable when the symbolic equality is used. This type of equal sign is used for symbolic math and when solving equations using iterative methods.

### Global Assignment ≡

There is one way to override the left-to-right, top-to-bottom evaluation order in Mathcad, and that is to use a *global assignment*. Mathcad actually evaluates a worksheet in two passes. In the first pass, all global assignment statements are evaluated (left to right and top to bottom). Then, in the second pass, all other equations are evaluated. Defining a variable using a global assignment equal sign has the same effect as putting the equation at the top of the worksheet, since both cause the statement to be evaluated first.

Global assignments are not used a lot, but it is fairly common to use them for unit definitions. For example, Mathcad already knows what a year (yr) is, but you could define a new unit, the decade, in terms of years as

$$\text{Decade} \equiv 10 \cdot \text{yr}$$

*Note:* You could also define the decade by using the regular assignment operator, :=. It is common, but not required, to use global assignment for units.

**PRACTICE!**

What will Mathcad display as the value of x for each of these examples? (Try each in a separate worksheet.)

**a.** Use of "define as equal to" . . .

$y := 3$

$x := y$

$x =$

**b.** Use of a symbolic equality . . .

$y = 3$

$x := y$

$x =$

**c.** With units . . .

$y := 3 \cdot cm$

$x := y$

$x =$

**d.** Use of a "global define as equal to" . . .

$x := y$

$x =$

$y \equiv 3$

## 2.4 ENTERING AN EQUATION

To enter an equation, you simply position the edit cursor (crosshair) where you want the equation to go, and start typing. (Whenever Mathcad is waiting for you to type in the workspace, it waits in *equation edit mode* so you can easily enter a new equation.) To enter the defining equation for the variable s, you would type [ s ] [ : ] [ 4 ] [ ° ] [Ctrl-Shift-p][Enter].[2] To see the result of this calculation, move the cursor to the right and/or down, and type [ s ] [ = ]. Mathcad will display the result after the equal sign.

$$s := 4 \cdot \pi$$
$$s = 12.566$$

### Predefined Variables

Pi is such a commonly used value, that it comes as a *predefined variable* in Mathcad. You can get the $\pi$ symbol either from the Greek Symbols Palette or by pressing [Ctrl-Shift-p], the shortcut used in the previous paragraph. Pi comes predefined in Mathcad to have a value of 3.14159265. . . . You can redefine pi (or any other predefined variable) simply by building it into a new definition:

$$\pi := 7$$
$$s := 4 \cdot \pi$$
$$s = 28$$

However, redefining a commonly used constant is usually not a good idea.

---

[2] The keyboard shortcut for pi is [Ctrl-Shift-p] in version 8 of Mathcad, and [Ctrl-p] in version 7.

Four common predefined values in Mathcad are $\pi$, e, g, and %. These are entered by using [Ctrl-Shift-p],[3] [ e ], [ g ], and [ % ], respectively.

### Exponents

Use the caret symbol [ ^ ] or [Shift-6] to enter an exponent in an equation. The right-hand side of the equation for the area of a circle would be entered as [Ctrl-Shift-p] [ ° ] [ r ] [ ^ ] [ 2 ], which gives.

$$Area := \pi \cdot r^2$$

Note that once Mathcad has moved the cursor up so you can enter the exponent, it *stays* in the exponent. That is, if you were to enter a plus sign after the 2 in the preceding equation, you would be adding to the 2 (the exponent), not to the $r^2$. If you need to add something to the $r^2$, you must first select a portion of the equation and then enter the plus sign.

*Note:* Mathcad uses standard mathematical *operator precedence rules:* exponentiation before multiplication and division, and multiplication and division before addition and subtraction. Parentheses can be used to ensure that an equation is evaluated in the desired order.

*Entering Nondecimal Values*    To enter a hexadecimal value when defining a variable, simply add the letter h after the value. Hexadecimal values can contain the digits 0 through 9, and the letters a through f. No decimal points are allowed. Similarly, octal values can be used in variable definitions simply by adding the letter o after the value. Only digits 0 through 7 may be used. Version 8 of Mathcad allows binary values to be entered by adding a b at the end of the value (consisting of zeroes and ones only). Version 7 does not support binary values.

| | | |
|---|---|---|
| A := 12 | A = 12 | decimal |
| B := 12o | B = 10 | octal |
| C := 12h | C = 18 | hexadecimal |
| D := 1011b | D = 11 | binary (Mathcad 8 only) |

To see a result expressed as an octal, hexadecimal or binary[4] value, double-click the value and change the *radix* of the displayed result on the Format Result dialog.[5]

| | |
|---|---|
| E := 201 | E = 201 |
| | E = 311o |
| | E = 0c9h |
| | E = 11001001b |

### Selecting Part of an Equation

If you want to compute the surface area of a cylinder, you need to add the areas of the circles on each end ($2\pi r^2$) and the area of the side of the cylinder ($2\pi rL$). After entering the exponent on the first term, you need to add another piece to the equation. If you don't select the $r^2$ before entering the plus sign, you will end up adding to the exponent, as shown in the following equation:

$$A_{cyl} := 2 \cdot \pi \cdot r^{2 + 2 \cdot \pi \cdot r}$$

---

[3] Ibid.

[4] Binary values are supported in Mathcad 8 only.

[5] In version 7 of Mathcad it is called the Format Number dialog.

This is obviously not what we want. Right after entering the 2 in the $r^2$, you need to press the [Space] key once to select the $r^2$. (Mathcad will indicate the selected portion of the equation with an underline. There is also a vertical line, called the *insert bar*, that shows where the next typed character will go.) After you enter the exponent, the worksheet should look like this:

$$A_{cyl} := 2 \cdot \pi \cdot r^{2|}$$

After you enter the exponent and press [Space], the worksheet should look like this:

$$A_{cyl} := 2 \cdot \pi \cdot r^{2}$$

The underline beneath the $r^2$ indicates that the next operation will be applied to the entire selected region, which is what we want—we want to add $(2\pi r L)$ to the selected region. The final result is:

$$A_{cyl} := 2 \cdot \pi \cdot r^2 + 2 \cdot \pi \cdot r \cdot L$$

*Note:* You might think you should select the entire term, $2 \cdot \pi \cdot r^2$, instead of just the $r^2$. That would work. You would just press [Space] two more times to select the $\pi$ and the 2. To reduce the number of keystrokes required to enter an equation, Mathcad keeps multiplied variables together when you add to the collection. This is just a convenience; it is handy, but does take some getting used to.

## PRACTICE!

What does Mathcad display when you enter the following key sequences?

**a.** [P][ ° ][V][Ctrl =][n][ ° ][R][ ° ][T]

**b.** [P][ : ][n][ ° ][R][ ° ][T][/][V]

**c.** [P][ : ][n][ ° ][R][ ° ][T][Space][Space][Space][/][V]

**d.** [r][ : ][k][1][ ° ][C][A][^][2][ - ][k][2][ ° ][C][B]

**e.** [r][ : ][k][1][ ° ][C][A][^][2][Space][ - ][k][2][ ° ][C][B]

### Text Subscripts and Index Subscripts

The "cyl" in the variable name $A_{cyl}$ presented earlier is slightly lower than the A—this is an example of a *text subscript*. Mathcad will allow the use of a text subscript as part of a variable name, which can be useful when naming related variables. For example, the areas of a circle, sphere, and cylinder might be indicated as $A_{circle}$, $A_{sphere}$, and $A_{cyl}$, respectively. The variable name $A_{cyl}$ was entered as [ A ] [.] [ c ] [ y ] [ l ], where the period was used to indicate that a text subscript follows.

The *index subscript,* which may look similar to the text subscript, is used for an entirely different purpose. Index subscripts indicate a particular element of an array, (a vector or matrix). The first element of an array is called element zero in Mathcad. For example, if you have a three-element array called $Z$, containing the values 2, 5, and 7, i.e.,

$$Z := \begin{bmatrix} 2 \\ 5 \\ 7 \end{bmatrix}$$

then the value of element zero of array z is 2. The zero element can be accessed individually using an index subscript, as

$$Z_0 = 2$$

While it looks similar to a text subscript, an index subscript is entered differently and has a different meaning than a text subscript. The preceding index subscript was entered as [ Z ] [ [ ] [0 ], where [ [ ] means the left-square-bracket key.

**PRACTICE!**

What does Mathcad display when you enter the following key sequences?

**a.** [r][.][A][ : ][k][.][0][ * ][C][.][A][^][2]—this expression has a *text* subscript on k

**b.** [r][.][A][ : ][k][ [ ][0][ * ][C][.][A][^][2]—this expression has an *index* subscript on k

**c.** [r][.][A][ : ][k][ [ ][0][space][ * ][C][.][A][^][2]

### Changing a Value or Variable Name

If you click in the middle of a value or variable name, a vertical insert bar (cursor) will be displayed. The insert bar indicates where any edits will take place. You can use the left- and right-arrow keys to move the bar. The delete key will remove the character to the right of the insert bar, while the backspace key will remove the character to the left.

Not all characters that are entered are displayed by Mathcad, but they can still be deleted. For example, the [.] used to enter a text subscript is not shown on the screen, but if you position the insert bar at the beginning of the subscript text and press [Backspace], the [.] will be removed, and the subscript will become regular text.

For example, if the ideal gas constant (0.08206 liter atm/mole K) had been entered incorrectly as 0.08506, you would click next to the 5, as in the following figure:

$$R_{gas} := 0.085|06$$

Then press [Backspace] to remove the 5, and press [ 2 ] to enter the correct value. The final result would look like this:

$$R_{gas} := 0.08206$$

### Changing an Operator

When you need to edit an *operator*, such as changing a symbolic equality (=) to an assignment operator ( := ), you click just to the right of the operator itself. This puts the insert bar just to the right of the operator:

$$s = |4 \cdot \pi$$

Then, press [Backspace] to delete the operator:

$$s \; |4 \cdot \pi$$

Then enter the new operator, [ : ]:

$$s := 4 \cdot \pi$$

For a slightly more complicated example, we will use the equation for the surface area of a cylinder. The following equation is incorrectly entered with a minus sign between the two terms on the right side:

$$A_{cyl} := 2 \cdot \pi \cdot r^2 - 2 \cdot \pi \cdot r \cdot L$$

To change the minus sign to a plus sign, click on the 2 to the right of the minus sign. (If the insert bar appears on the right side of the 2, press [Insert] to move it to the left side of the 2. This procedure is illustrated in the following figure:

$$A_{cyl} := 2 \cdot \pi \cdot r^2 - 2 \cdot \pi \cdot r \cdot L$$

Then press [Backspace] to remove the minus sign (parentheses appear to keep the first term together during the edit),

$$A_{cyl} := \left(2 \cdot \pi \cdot r^2\right) 2 \cdot \pi \cdot r \cdot L$$

And finally, press [ + ] to insert the plus sign:

$$A_{cyl} := 2 \cdot \pi \cdot r^2 + 2 \cdot \pi \cdot r \cdot L$$

## 2.5  WORKING WITH UNITS

Mathcad supports units. Its ability to automatically handle unit conversions is a *very* nice feature for engineering calculations since the number of required unit conversions can be considerable. Mathcad handles units by storing all values in a base set of units (SI by default, but you can change it):

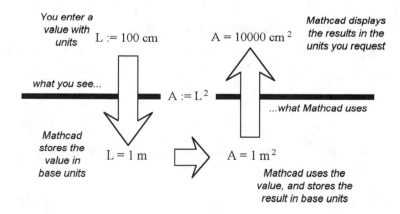

Values are converted from the units you enter to the base set before storing the value. Then, when a value is displayed, the conversions required to give the requested units are automatically performed. Mathcad's unit handling works very well for most situations, but it does have some limitations, which will be discussed shortly.

Mathcad supports the following *systems of units*:

- SI—default units (meter, kilogram, second, etc.).
- MKS—meter, kilogram, second.
- CGS—centimeter, gram, second.
- US—foot, pound, second.
- None—disables all built-in units, but user-defined units still work.

Within each system, certain *dimensions* are supported. But not all dimensions are supported in all systems. The following table shows the dimensions the various systems support in Mathcad:

| | SYSTEM | | | | |
| --- | --- | --- | --- | --- | --- |
| **DIMENSION** | SI | MKS | CGS | US | None |
| Mass | ✓ | ✓ | ✓ | ✓ | ✓ |
| Length | ✓ | ✓ | ✓ | ✓ | ✓ |
| Time | ✓ | ✓ | ✓ | ✓ | ✓ |
| Current | ✓ | no | no | no | no |
| Charge | no | ✓ | ✓ | ✓ | ✓ |
| Temperature | ✓ | ✓ | ✓ | ✓ | ✓ |
| Luminosity | ✓ | no | no | no | no |
| Substance | ✓ | no | no | no | no |

If you plan to work with luminosity (typical units; candelas) or substance (typical units; moles), then you probably want to use the default SI units. If these specialized units are not important to you, you have more system options available. You set the system of units to be used as base units from the menu bar: Math/Options . . ./ Unit System.

Some common unit abbreviations, by category, are

| | |
| --- | --- |
| Mass | kg, gm, lb |
| Length | m, cm, ft |
| Time | sec, hr |
| Current | amp |
| Charge | coul |
| Temperature | K, R |
| Substance | mole |
| Volume | liter, gal, galUK (Imperial gallon) |
| Force | N, dyne, lbf |
| Pressure | Pa, atm, torr, in_Hg, psi |
| Energy and Work | joule, erg, cal, BTU |
| Power | watt, kW, hp |

These units are only a small subset of the predefined units in Mathcad. A list of available units is always available by pressing [Ctrl-u]. You can select units from the list, or simply type the unit name (using Mathcad's abbreviation).

For example, you could find the area of a circle with a radius of 7 cm by using the following equations:

$$r := 7 \cdot cm$$
$$Area := \pi \cdot r^2$$

In the first line the 7 is multiplied by the unit name, 'cm'; then the area is computed on the second line. The result is displayed as

$$\boxed{Area\,| = 0.015 \cdot m^2} \quad \blacksquare$$

The box around this equation and the vertical bar at the right side of `Area` indicate that we haven't completed editing the equation; that is, we haven't pressed [Enter] yet. As soon as you press [ = ], Mathcad shows the value currently assigned to the variable `Area` in the base units (SI, by default). A *placeholder* is also shown to the right of the units (only while the equation is being edited), so that you can request that the value be displayed in different units. If you want the result displayed in cm², click on the place-holder and then enter [ c ] [ m ] [ ^ ] [ 2 ] [Enter]. The result is displayed in the requested units:

$$Area = 153.938 \cdot cm^2$$

You can put any defined (predefined, or defined as part of the worksheet) unit in that placeholder. If the units you enter have the wrong dimensions, Mathcad will make that apparent by showing you the "leftover" base units. For example, if you had placed 'atm' (atmospheres) in the placeholder, the dimensions would be quite wrong, and the displayed result would make this apparent:

$$Area = 1.519 \cdot 10^{-7} \cdot kg^{-1} \cdot m^3 \cdot s^2 \circ atm$$

### Defining a New Unit

New units are defined in terms of predefined units. For example, a commonly used unit of viscosity is the centipoise, or cP. The poise is predefined in Mathcad, but the centipoise is not. The new unit can be defined like this:

$$cP := \frac{poise}{100}$$

Once the new unit has been defined, it can be used throughout the rest of the worksheet. Here the viscosity of honey is defined as 10000 cP, and then the value is displayed by using another common unit for viscosity: Pascal·seconds.

$$visc_{honey} := 10000 \cdot cP$$
$$visc_{honey} = 10 \circ Pa \cdot s$$

**PRACTICE!**

Try these obvious unit conversions:

**a.** $100\ cm \rightarrow m$

**b.** $2.54\ cm \rightarrow in$

**c.** $454\ gm \rightarrow lb$

Now try these less obvious conversions:

**d.** $1\ hp \rightarrow kW$

**e.** $1\ liter \cdot atm \rightarrow joule$

**f.** $1\ joule \rightarrow watt$    This is an invalid conversion. How does Mathcad respond?

---

**PROFESSIONAL SUCCESS**

*First make sure your method [or design/computer code/ Mathcad worksheet] works correctly on a test case whose answer you know. Then try your method [design/ computer code/Mathcad worksheet] on a new problem.*

In the last Practice! box, you were asked to try Mathcad on some obvious cases before trying some less obvious ones. Testing against a known result is a standard procedure in engineering. If you get the right answer in the test case, you have increased confidence (not total confidence) that your method is working. If you get the wrong answer, it is a lot easier to find out what went wrong using the test problem than it is to try to fix the method and solve the real problem simultaneously.

You'll see this technique used throughout the text.

### Editing the Units on a Value or Result

Once you have entered units, simply edit the unit name to change them. Click on the unit name, delete characters as needed, and then type in the desired units.

### Limitations to Mathcad's Units Capabilities

- Mathcad's unit conversions must be multiplicative—no additive constants can be used in unit conversions. This means that Mathcad can convert Kelvins to °R (degrees Rankine), but cannot convert °C to Kelvins (add 273) or °C to °F (add 32). Similarly, Mathcad can handle absolute pressure conversions, but cannot automatically convert gauge pressures to absolute (add the barometric pressure).

- Some of Mathcad's built-in functions do not support, or do not fully support, units. For example, the linear regression function `linfit( )` does not accept values with units. The iterative solver (`given-find` solve block) does allow units, but if you are solving for two or more variables simultaneously, the variables must have the same units.

- Mathcad's built-in graphics always display the values in the base (stored) units.

- Only the SI system of units fully supports moles. In the other systems, Mathcad allows you to use the term "mole" as a unit, but does not consider it a dimension and does not display it when presenting units. This means that *you should use the SI system if you plan to work with moles.*

- The mole defined in Mathcad's SI system is the gram-mole. I like to make this obvious by defining a new unit, the gmol:

$$gmol := mole$$

You can define the other commonly used molar units as well:

$$kmol := 1000 \cdot mole$$
$$lbmol := 453.593 \cdot mole$$

With these definitions, Mathcad can convert between the various types of moles (but only if you are using the SI system of units.)

---

**APPLICATIONS: DETERMINING THE CURRENT IN A CIRCUIT**

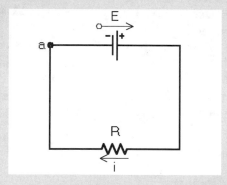

Consider a simple circuit containing a 9-volt battery and a 90-ohm resistor as shown in the diagram. What current would flow in the circuit? To solve this problem, you need to know Ohm's law,

$$V = iR,$$

and Kirchhoff's law of voltage,

*For a closed (loop) circuit, the algebraic sum of all changes in voltage must be zero.*

This is perhaps easier to understand if you consider the following analogy:

If you are hiking in the hills and you end up back at the same spot you started from (a loop trail), then the sum of the changes in elevation must be zero: You must end up at the same elevation at which you started.

The electrons moving through the circuit from point 'a' may have their electric potential (volts) increased (by the battery) or decreased (by the resistor), but if they end up back where they started from (in a loop circuit), they must end up with the same potential they started with.

We can use Kirchhoff's law to write an equation describing the voltage changes through the circuit. Starting at an arbitrary point 'a' and moving through the circuit in the direction of the current flow, the voltage is first raised by the battery ($V_B = E$), and then lowered by the resistor ($V_R$). These are the only two elements in the circuit, so

$$V_B - V_R = 0$$

by Kirchhoff's law. Now we know that the battery raises the electric potential by 9 volts, and Ohm's law relates the current flowing through the resistor (and the rest of the circuit) to the resistance, 90 ohms.

$$V_B - i\,R = 0$$

The Mathcad equations needed to calculate the current through the circuit look like this:

$$V_B := 9 \cdot \text{volt}$$

$$R := 90 \cdot \text{ohm}$$

$$i := \frac{V_B}{R}$$

$$i = 0.1 \circ \text{amp}$$

## 2.6 ENTERING AND EDITING TEXT

Mathcad defaults to equation edit mode, so if you just start typing, Mathcad will try to interpret your entry as an equation. If you type a series of letters and then a space, Mathcad will recognize that you are entering text and will switch to *text edit mode* and create a *text region*. Or, you can tell Mathcad you want to enter text by pressing the double-quote key [ " ].

To create a text region, position the edit cursor (crosshair) in the blank portion of the worksheet where you want the text to be placed, and then press [ " ] (double-quote key). A small rectangle with a vertical line (the insert bar) inside appears on the worksheet, indicating that you are creating a text region. The text region will automatically expand as you type, until you reach the page margin (the vertical line at the right side of the screen, shown in the next figure), and then the text will automatically wrap to the next line.

> This text region will expand until it reaches the page margin, then the text will automatically wrap...|

You can change the size or location of an existing text region by clicking on the text to select the region and display the border. Then, drag the border to move the box, or drag one of the handles to change the size of the box. If you change the width of a text region, the text will wrap as necessary to fit in the new width.

Once you have a block of text in a text region, you can select all or part of the text with the mouse and then use the formatting buttons on the Font Bar. These buttons allow you to make the font boldface, add italics, or underline the text. For example, to create a heading for some global-warming calculations, you might type in some text and then select "Global Warming":

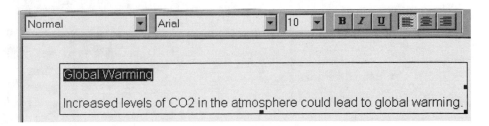

Then increase the font size of the selected text by using the Font Bar:

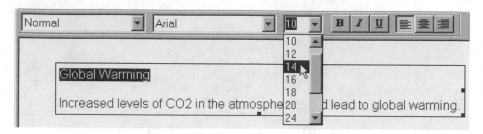

And finally, make the font in the heading boldface by using the Font Bar.

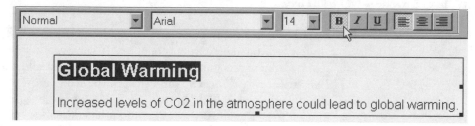

You can also create sub- or superscripts within the text region by selecting the characters to be raised or lowered. Next, using Format/Text . . .from the menu bar, select Subscript or Superscript from the Text Format dialog box as follows:

1.  Select the text to subscript:

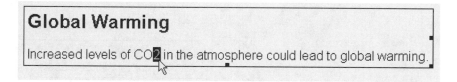

2.  Select Text . . . from the Format menu:

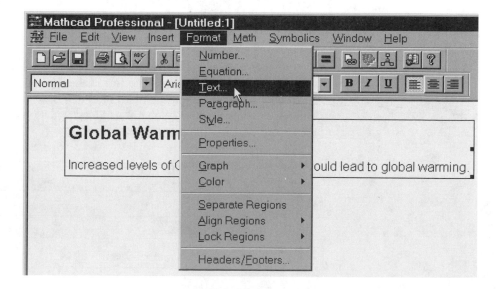

3.   Select Subscript on the Text Format dialog box:

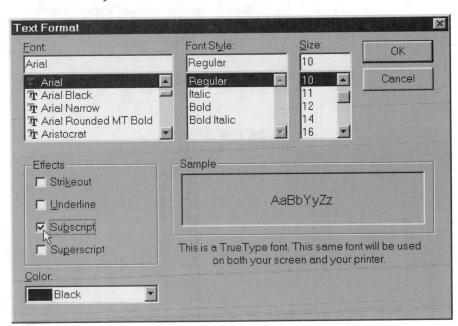

After these changes, the worksheet heading looks like this:

## Global Warming

Increased levels of $CO_2$ in the atmosphere could lead to global warming.

Mathcad gives you a great deal of control over the appearance of your text, and adding headings and notes to your worksheets can make them much easier for others to read and understand.

*Document your results.*

Taking the time to document your worksheets by adding headings and comments can have a big payoff later (sometimes years later), when you need to perform a similar calculation and want to refer to your worksheets to see how it was done.

The skills you develop and the knowledge you acquire in your academic and professional careers combine to form the resource base, or expertise, that you bring to a new job or project. But when your resource base gets stale, you can spend a lot of time relearning things you once knew. Plan ahead and make the relearning as easy as possible by making your worksheets easy to understand.

*Note:* If you want to make a change to all text regions—italicizing all the text so that it is easier to see the difference between your text regions and equations, for example—then change the *style* used with all text regions. To modify the text style sheet, select Format/Style . . ./Normal/Modify/Font from the menu bar. This will bring up a dialog box describing the Normal style (used for regular text.) If you click on the italic property and close the dialog box, all text created using the Normal style will be in italics. (Format changes to individual text boxes or selected characters override the style sheet. If you select one word in a text box and remove the italics using the format bar, that individual change would override the style sheet, and the italics would be removed for that word.)

### Sizing and Moving a Text or Equation Region

If you click outside of a region and drag the mouse into the region, Mathcad will show you the size and location of the region by drawing a line around it. For resizable regions, like text regions, Mathcad will also show three small black squares on the edges of the region, called handles. Grab a handle with the mouse, and drag it to change the size or shape of a region. (Some regions automatically resize, so they might snap back again when you release the handle.) To move a single selected region, move the mouse over the border until it changes to a hand symbol. While the hand symbol is displayed, drag the border (and the region) to the new location on the worksheet. If multiple regions are selected, dashed lines are drawn around each region. They cannot be resized, but they can be moved together by clicking inside any of the selected regions and dragging all the selected regions to a new location.

## 2.7 A SIMPLE EDITING SESSION

We will use one of the examples mentioned earlier, namely, determining the surface area of a cylinder, to demonstrate how to solve a simple problem using Mathcad. Even in this simple example, the following Mathcad features will be used:

- Text editing and formatting.
- Variable definitions ($r$ and $L$).
- Equation definition ($A_{cyl}$).
- Exponentiation ($r^2$).
- Displaying the result ( = ).
- Working with units.

### Problem Statement

Determine the surface area of a cylinder with a radius of 7 cm and a length of 21 cm.

The solution will be presented with a step-by-step commentary. For this simple example, the complete Mathcad worksheet will be shown as it develops at each step.

**STEP 1—USE A TEXT REGION TO DESCRIBE THE PROBLEM**

1. Position the edit cursor (crosshair) near the top of the blank worksheet and click the left mouse button.
2. Press [ " ] to create a text region.
3. Enter the problem statement.
4. Click outside of the text region when you are done entering text.

The result might look something like this. (Italic text is not the Mathcad default, but adding italics can help differentiate text regions from equations):

```
Problem Statement

Determine the surface area of a cylinder with a radius of 7 cm
and a length of 21 cm.
```

**STEP 2—ENTER THE KNOWN VALUES OF RADIUS AND LENGTH, WITH APPROPRIATE UNITS**

1. Position the edit cursor below the text region and near the left side of the worksheet. Click the left mouse button.
2. Define the value of r by typing [ r ] [ : ] [ 7 ] [ ° ] [ c ] [ m ] [Enter].
3. Similarly, position the edit cursor, and enter the value of L (21 cm).

The positions of the r and L equations are arbitrary, but they might look like the following:

```
Problem Statement

Determine the surface area of a cylinder with a radius of 7 cm
and a length of 21 cm.
```

$$r := 7 \cdot cm$$
$$L := 21 \cdot cm$$

**STEP 3— ENTER THE EQUATION FOR COMPUTING THE SURFACE AREA OF A CYLINDER**

1. Position the edit cursor below or to the right of the definitions of r and L.
2. Enter the area variable name $A_{cyl}$, by using a text subscript as [ A ] [.] [ c ] [ y ] [ l ].
3. Press [ : ] to indicate that you are defining the $A_{cyl}$ variable.
4. Enter the first term on the right side $(2\pi r^2)$ as [ 2 ] [ ° ] [Ctrl-Shift-p] [ ° ] [ r ] [ ^ ] [ 2 ].[6]
5. Press [Space] to select the $r^2$ in the $2\pi r^2$ term.
6. Press [ + ] to add to the selected term.
7. Enter the second term on the right side $(2\pi rL)$ as [ 2 ] [ ° ] [ r ] [ ° ] [ L ].
8. Press [Enter] to conclude the equation entry.

The result will look like this:

```
Problem Statement

Determine the surface area of a cylinder with a radius of 7 cm
and a length of 21 cm.
```

$$r := 7 \cdot cm$$
$$L := 21 \cdot cm$$
$$A_{cyl} := 2 \cdot \pi \cdot r^2 + 2 \cdot \pi \cdot r \cdot L$$

**STEP 4— DISPLAY THE RESULT IN THE DESIRED UNITS**

1. Position the edit cursor below or to the right of the $A_{cyl}$ equation.
2. Ask Mathcad to display the result of the calculation by typing [ A ] [.] [ c ] [ y ] [ l ] [ = ].
3. Click on the units placeholder (to the right of the displayed base units).
4. Enter the desired units (e.g., $cm^2$).
5. Press [Enter] to conclude the entry.

---

[6] The keyboard shortcut for pi is [Ctrl-Shift-p] in version 8 of Mathcad, and [Ctrl-p] in version 7.

The worksheet will look like this:

```
Problem Statement

Determine the surface area of a cylinder with a radius of 7 cm
and a length of 21 cm.
```

$$r := 7 \cdot cm$$

$$L := 21 \cdot cm$$

$$A_{cyl} := 2 \cdot \pi \cdot r^2 + 2 \cdot \pi \cdot r \cdot L$$

$$A_{cyl} = 1.232 \cdot 10^3 \cdot cm^2$$

**PRACTICE!**

Calculate the surface area and volume of

**a.** a cube 1 cm on a side.

**b.** a sphere with a radius of 7 cm.

Equations for the sphere are $A = 4 \pi r^2$ and $V = (4/3) \pi r^3$.

---

**APPLICATIONS: GLOBAL WARMING**

The Kyoto Accords of 1997 commit the United States and Canada to reducing $CO_2$ emissions to levels 7% below the 1990 baseline. European countries have committed to lower their emissions to 8% below the baseline. Developing nations such as India and China were asked to voluntarily lower their $CO_2$ emissions as well. Whether or not the various governments ratify the accords, there is now a strong worldwide emphasis on trying to reduce $CO_2$ emissions to delay or prevent global warming.

Carbon dioxide is extremely abundant on our planet, and the vast majority of the gaseous $CO_2$ produced each year is from natural sources: plant and animal respiration, aerobic decay of vegetation, and releases of $CO_2$ from the oceans. The planet also has considerable resources for removing $CO_2$ from the atmosphere, mostly by uptake into the oceans and plant photosynthesis. These natural sources and sinks for $CO_2$ are approximately in balance. The source of the increasing $CO_2$ in our atmosphere is human-made, or anthropogenic, $CO_2$. (See accompanying table.)

**The Global CO$_2$ Imbalance** (units are million metric tons of carbon per year)

| SOURCES | | SINK |
|---------|---|------|
| Natural | Anthropogenic | Natural |
| 150,000 | 7,100 | 154,000 |

*Source:* Intergovernmental Panel on Climate Change, *Climate Change 1995: The Science of Climate Change* (Cambridge, UK: Cambridge University Press, 1996), pp. 17–19, reported in *Emissions of Greenhouse Gases in the United States 1996*, Chapter 1, Energy Information Agency, U.S. Department of Energy.

Natural removal processes can handle all of the naturally produced $CO_2$ and a substantial part of the anthropogenic $CO_2$. But the excess $CO_2$ has nowhere to go and is building up in our atmosphere. In order to restore the balance, we must either reduce one or the other of the source terms, increase the sink term, or add another term to the equation (give the $CO_2$ someplace else to go.) The Kyoto solution focuses on reducing the anthropogenic source term to move towards balance.

The Kyoto Accords have made the 1997 emissions (estimates at the time of the Kyoto meeting) and the 1990 emissions data of primary significance. These data are summarized in following table:

### U.S. CO$_2$ Emissions Data

| CATEGORY | 1990 | 1997 (PREDICTED) |
|---|---|---|
| | Million Metric Tons Carbon | |
| Residential, Commercial | 459.9 | 528.3 |
| Industrial | 453.8 | 487.6 |
| Transportation | 432.1 | 484.5 |
| Total | 1345.8 | 1493.2 |

*Sources:* 1990 Data: *Emissions of Greenhouse Gases in the United States 1996,* Energy Information Agency, U.S. Department of Energy.
1997 Predictions: *Annual Energy Outlook 1998,* U.S. Department of Energy.

The global estimate for CO$_2$ emissions in 1990 is 6120 million metric tons of carbon.[7] We can use Mathcad to determine the percentage of global CO$_2$ emissions that came from the United States in 1990:

$$MMT \equiv 1 \cdot 10^6 \cdot tonne$$
*define unit: million metric ton*

$$CO2_{US} := 1345.8 \cdot MMT$$
*set U.S. emissions in 1990*

$$CO2_{Global} := 6120 \cdot MMT$$
*set global emissions in 1990*

[7] Greg Marl and Tom Boden, *Global, Regional, and National Annual Carbon Dioxide Emissions from Fossil-Fuel Burning and Cement Production: 1950–1994,* Environmental Sciences Division, Oak Ridge National Laboratory, Oak Ridge, TN.

$$\frac{CO2_{US}}{CO2_{Global}} = 0.22$$
*result expressed as fraction*

$$\frac{CO2_{US}}{CO2_{Global}} = 21.99 \circ \%$$
*result expressed as percentage*

In 1990, the United States emitted almost 22% of the world's anthropogenic (human-generated) CO$_2$, making it the world's largest emitter of this gas.

The U.S. is supposed to reduce CO$_2$ emissions to 7% below the 1990 level. We can see what this target means in terms of millions of metric tons of CO$_2$:

$$CO2_{target} := CO2_{US} - (0.07 \cdot CO2_{US})$$
$$CO2_{target} = 1251.6 \cdot MMT$$

And we can calculate the required reduction in CO$_2$ emissions by using the following equations:

$$CO2_{US97} := 1493.2 \cdot MMT$$
$$CO2_{reduction} := CO2_{US97} - CO2_{target}$$
$$CO2_{reduction} = 241.6 \circ MMT$$

This represents a 16.18% reduction in CO$_2$ emissions from the 1997 levels.

$$\frac{CO2_{reduction}}{CO2_{US97}} = 16.18 \cdot \%$$

The levels requested by the Kyoto Accords will be hard to achieve—but even if they are achieved, they will not "fix" the problem. This is only a beginning.

### Summary

In this chapter, we learned the basics of working with Mathcad: how the screen is laid out, how to enter equations and text, and how Mathcad handles units.

## MATHCAD SUMMARY

**FOUR KINDS OF EQUAL SIGNS:**

:=   Assigns a value or the result of a calculation to a variable.

=   Displays a value or the result of a calculation.

≡   Symbolic equality; shows the relationship between variables.

≡   Global assignment; these are evaluated before the rest of the worksheet is.

**PREDEFINED VARIABLES:**

π   3.141592 . . .          Press [Ctrl-Shift-p] or choose π from the Greek Symbols Palette.[8]

e   2.718281 . . .

g    9.8 m/s$^2$

%    multiplies the displayed value by 100
     and displays the percent symbol.

[8] The keyboard shortcut for pi is [Ctrl-Shift-p] in version 8 of Mathcad, and [Ctrl-p] in version 7.

**ENTERING EQUATIONS:**

+, −         addition and subtraction.

*, /         multiplication and division.          Press [Shift-8] for the multiplication
                                                    symbol.

^            exponentiation.                        Press [Shift-6] for the caret symbol.

[Space]      enlarges the currently selected region—used after typing in expo-
             nents and denominators.

[Insert]     moves the vertical edit cursor between the front and back of a
             selected region—used when you need to delete an operator to the
             left of a selected region.

[.]          text subscript.

[ [ ]        index subscript—used to indicate a particular element of an array.

**OPERATOR PRECEDENCE:**

^            exponentiation is performed before multiplication and division.

*, /         multiplication and division are performed before addition and subtraction.

+, −         addition and subtraction are performed last.

**TEXT REGIONS:**

[ " ]        Creates a text region—if you type in characters that include a space
             (i.e., two words), Mathcad will automatically create a text region around
             these characters.

# Problems

## 2.1  UNIT CONVERSIONS

a.  speed of light in a vacuum                        $2.998 \times 10^8$ m/sec to miles per hour.

b.  density of water at room temperature              62.3 lb/ft$^3$ to kg/m$^3$.

c.  density of water at 4°C                           1000 kg/m$^3$ to lb/gal.

d.  viscosity of water at room temperature (approx.)  0.01 poise to lb/ft sec.
                                                      0.01 poise to kg/m sec.

e.  ideal gas constant                               0.08206 L·atm/mole·K to
                                                      joules/mole·K.

*Note:* The "lb" in parts b), c) and d) is a pound mass, and "mole" in part e) is a gram mole.

## 2.2  RELATING FORCE AND MASS (BRIDGE—PART A)

This problem is the first in a series that introduces the concepts needed to design a suspension bridge. Fundamental to the design of the bridge is the relation between the mass of the deck and the force on the wires supporting the deck. The relationship between force and mass is called *Newton's law* and in physics courses is usually written as

$$F = m\,a$$

In engineering courses we often build in the gravitational constant, $g_c$, to help keep the units straight:

$$F = m\frac{a}{g_c}$$

Note that $g_c$ has a value of 1 (no units) in SI and a value of 32.174 ft · lb/lb$_f$ · s$^2$ in American engineering units. If the mass is being acted on by gravity, Newton's law can be written as

$$F = m\frac{g}{g_c}$$

where $g$ is the acceleration due to gravity: 9.8 m/s$^2$ or 32.174 ft/s$^2$.

*Note:* While the acceleration due to gravity, $g$, is predefined in Mathcad, $g_c$ is not. If you want to use $g_c$, it can easily be defined in your worksheet using the SI value and letting Mathcad take care of the unit conversions. The definition is simply

$$g_c := 1$$

a.  If a 150 kg mass is hung from a hook by a fine wire (of negligible mass), what force (N) is exerted on the hook?
b.  If the mass in part a were suspended by two wires, the force on the hook would be unchanged, but the tension in each wire would be halved. If the duty rating on the wire states that the tension in any wire should not exceed 300 N, how many wires should be used to support the mass?

Related Bridge Problems: 2.2, 3.7, 3.8, 3.9, 3.10

## 2.3 SPRING CONSTANTS

Springs are so common that we hardly even notice them, but if you are designing a component that needs a spring, you have to know enough about them to specify them correctly. Common springs obey *Hooke's law* (if they are not overstretched), which simply states that the spring extension, $x$ ( the amount of stretch) is linearly related to the force exerted on the spring, $F$.

$$F = k\,x$$

where $k$ is the linear proportionality constant, called the *spring constant*. Use Mathcad's unit capabilities to determine the spring constants in N/m for the following springs:

a.  extended length, 12 cm; applied force, 800 N.
b.  extended length, 0.3 m; applied force, 1200 N.

   c.   extended length, 1.2 cm; applied force, 100 dynes.

   d.   extended length, 4 inches; applied force, 2000 $lb_f$.

*Note:* The preceding is a simplified version of Hooke's law that is applicable when the force is in the direction of motion. Sometimes you will see a minus sign in Hooke's law. It depends on whether the force being referred to is being applied to the spring or is within the spring, restraining the applied force.

## 2.4 SPECIFYING A SPRING CONSTANT

The backrest of a chair is to be spring loaded to allow the chair to recline slightly. The design specifications call for a deflection of no more than 2 inches when a 150-lb person leans 40% of his or her body weight on the backrest. (Assume that there are no lever arms between the backrest and the spring to account for in this problem.)

   a.   Use Newtons law (described in Problem 2.1) to determine the force applied to the backrest when a 150-lb person leans 40% of his or her body weight against it.

   b.   Determine the constant required for the spring.

   c.   If a 200-lb person puts 70% of his or her body weight on the backrest, what spring extension would be expected? (Assume that the applied force is still within the allowable limits for the spring.)

## 2.5 SIMPLE HARMONIC OSCILLATOR

50 gm

If a 50-gram mass is suspended on a spring and the spring is stretched slightly and released, the system will oscillate. The period, $T$, and natural frequency, $f_n$, of this simple harmonic oscillator can be determined using the formulas:

$$T = \frac{2\pi}{\sqrt{k/m}}$$

$$f_n = \frac{1}{T}$$

where $k$ is the spring constant and $m$ is the suspended mass. (This equation assumes that the spring has negligible mass.)

   a.   If the spring constant is 100 N/m, determine the period of oscillation of the spring.

   b.   What spring constant should be specified to obtain a period of one second?

## 2.6  DETERMINING THE CURRENT IN A CIRCUIT

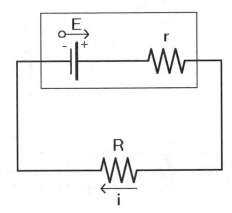

A real battery has an internal resistance, often shown by combining a cell symbol and a resistor symbol, as illustrated in the preceding figure. If a 9-volt battery has an internal resistance, $r$, of 15 ohms and is in a circuit with a 90-ohm resistor, what current would flow in the circuit?

*Note:* When resistors are connected in series, the combined resistance is simply the sum of the individual resistance values.

## 2.7  RESISTORS IN PARALLEL

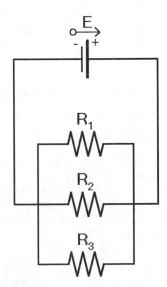

When multiple resistors are connected in parallel (see preceding diagram), the equivalent resistance of the collection of resistors can be computed as

$$\frac{1}{R_{eq}} = \sum_{i=1}^{N} \frac{1}{R_i}$$

where N is the number of resistors connected in parallel:

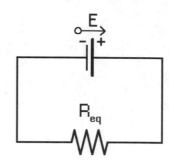

Compute the equivalent resistance in the circuit, and determine the current that would flow through the equivalent resistor.

**Data:**                         E = 9 volts.

$R_1$ = 20 ohms.

$R_2$ = 30 ohms.

$R_3$ = 40 ohms.

## 2.8  REDUCING $CO_2$ EMISSIONS

The Kyoto Accords call for the U.S. to reduce emissions of $CO_2$ by 7% below 1990 levels. Those reductions will almost certainly have to come from all three sectors mentioned in the Applications box, Global Warming example: residential and commercial, industrial, and transportation, since the emissions from each sector are of the same magnitude. This problem demonstrates how significant a reduction would be required if only one sector was used to accomplish the entire task. If the targeted reduction in $CO_2$ emissions came entirely from the transportation sector (cars, buses, trains, planes), what percentage reduction in $CO_2$ emissions would be required to achieve the target? Use the data presented in the Applications box to solve this problem.

## 2.9  AVERAGE FLUID VELOCITY

When a fluid is flowing in a pipe, the rate and direction at which the fluid moves—the fluid velocity—is not the same everywhere in the pipe. The fluid near the wall moves more slowly than the fluid near the center of the pipe, and things that cause the flow field to bend, such as obstructions and bends in the piping, cause some parts of the flow to move faster and in different directions than other parts of the flow. For many calculations, the details of the flow pattern are not important and an *average fluid velocity* can be used in design calculations. The average velocity, $V_{avg}$, can be determined by measuring the volumetric flow rate, Q, and dividing that by the cross-sectional area of the pipe, $A_{flow}$:

$$V_{avg} = \frac{Q}{A_{flow}}$$

a.   If 1000 gallons per minute (gpm) of water are flowing through a 4-inch (inside diameter) pipe, what is the average velocity of the water in the pipe?

b.   If the flow passes through a contraction into a section of 2-inch pipe, what is the average velocity in the smaller pipe?

c.   A common rule of thumb for trying to keep pumping costs low is to design for an average fluid velocity of about 3 ft/sec. What pipe diameter is required to obtain this average velocity with a volumetric flow rate of 1000 gpm?

*Note:* You may need to take a square root in part c. You can either use an exponent of 0.5 or use Mathcad's square root operator, √, which is available by pressing [ \ ] (backslash).

### 2.10  DESIGNING AN IRRIGATION SYSTEM

In arid areas, one cannot rely on periodic rains to water crops, so many farmers depend on irrigation systems. Center-pivot irrigation systems are a type of system that is commonly used. These systems have a $1/4$-mile-long water pipe on wheels that rotates (pivots) around the water source. The result is an irrigated circle with a diameter of $1/2$ mile, centered on the source. From an airplane, you can easily see where center-pivot systems are in use.

In the past, one large pulsating sprinkler was used for each wheeled section (120 feet) of pipe, and the sprinkler head was placed high to try to get wide coverage. In an attempt to utilize the water better, these systems have been radically reengineered. The large pulse sprinkler heads have been replaced by a series of small water spray nozzles 20 feet apart, and these have been placed much lower, just above crop level, to reduce the impact of wind on the water distribution pattern.

a.   How many acres of cropland would be irrigated using the center-pivot system just described?

b.   An acre-inch of water is the volume of water needed to cover an acre of ground with water to a depth of one inch (assuming no ground infiltration). How many acre-inches of water are required to provide one inch (depth) of water to the field? How many gallons is that?

c.   If the system makes a complete rotation every 40 hours, at what rate (gallons per minute) must water be pumped into the system?

An important feature of these irrigation systems is their ability to distribute water evenly. We'll return to this problem in Chapter 6 to see what is required to get a uniform water distribution.

# 3

# Mathcad Functions

## OPTICS

The use of *optics* can be dated back at least to the time when someone noticed that putting a curved piece of metal behind a lamp could concentrate the light. Or perhaps it goes back to the time when someone noticed that the campfire felt warmer if it was built next to a large rock. In any case, while the use of optics might be nearly as old as humanity itself, it is also a field that has seen major changes in the past 20 years. And these changes are affecting society in a variety of ways:

- Fiber-optic communication systems are now widely used and will become even more commonplace in the future.

- Lasers have moved from laboratory bench tops to supermarket checkout scanners and CD players.

- Traffic signs are much more visible at night now that they incorporate microreflective optical beads.

As these optical systems continue to develop, they will require the skills of engineers from many disciplines. Fiber-optic communication systems alone will make use of the following scientists and engineers:

## OBJECTIVES

*After reading this chapter, you should be able to:*

- To learn to use Mathcad's built-in functions, including:
  - trigonometric functions
  - logarithmic functions
  - advanced math functions
  - functions to read and write data files
- To learn to write your own functions.

- Material scientists to select and manipulate glass properties.
- Chemical engineers to design glass-processing facilities.
- Mechanical engineers to develop equipment designs for fiber production, cladding, wrapping, handling, and installation.
- Civil engineers to design the support structures for transmission lines.
- Electrical engineers to develop data transfer techniques.
- Computer scientists to design systems to encode and decode the transmissions.

Optics is a field that has been studied for centuries, but still has room for growth and continues to change the way we live. Any field that uses technology in society is a field in which engineers will be working.

## 3.1 MATHCAD FUNCTIONS

In a programming language, the term *function* is used to mean a piece of the program dedicated to a particular calculation. A function accepts input from a list of *parameters*, performs calculations, and then returns a value or a set of values. Functions are used whenever you want to:

- Perform the same calculations multiple times using different input values.
- Reuse the function in another program without retyping it.
- Make a complex program easier to comprehend.

Mathcad's functions work the same way and serve the same purposes. They receive input from a parameter list, perform a calculation, and return a value or a set of values. Mathcad's functions are useful when you need to perform the same calculation multiple times. You can also cut and paste a function from one worksheet to another.

### PROFESSIONAL SUCCESS

*When do you use a calculator to solve a problem, and when should you use a computer?*

These three questions will help you make this decision:

1.  Is the calculation long and involved?
2.  Will you need to perform the same calculation numerous times?

3.  Do you need to document the results for the future, either to give them to someone else or for you own reference?

A "yes" answer to any of these questions suggests that you consider using a computer. Moreover, a "yes" to the second question suggests that you may want to write a reusable function to solve the problem.

Mathcad provides a wide assortment of built-in functions. While most Mathcad functions *can* accept arrays as input, some Mathcad functions *require* data arrays as input. For example, the mean( ) function needs a column of data values in order to compute the average value of the data set. The functions that take arrays as input will be discussed in later chapters, after we describe how Mathcad handles matrices. In this chapter, we will only present functions that can take single-valued (scalar) inputs.

The following are the commonly used scalar functions:

- Elementary math functions and operators.
- Trigonometric functions.
- Advanced math functions.
- String functions.
- File-handling functions.

## 3.2 ELEMENTARY MATH FUNCTIONS AND OPERATORS

Many of the functions available in programming languages are implemented as operators in Mathcad. For example, to take the square root of four in FORTRAN, you would use `SQRT(4)`. The `SQRT( )` is FORTRAN's square root function. In Mathcad, the square root symbol is an operator available on the Arithmetic Palette, and shows up in a Mathcad worksheet just as you would write it on paper. Here are a couple of examples of Mathcad's square root function:

$$\sqrt{4} = 2$$

$$\sqrt{\frac{4 - \pi}{2}} = 0.655$$

Notice that the square root symbol changes size as necessary as you enter your equation.

### *Common Math Operators*

The following table presents some common mathematical operators in Mathcad:

| OPERATOR | MATHEMATICAL OPERATION | SOURCE PALETTE | ALTERNATE KEYSTROKE |
|---|---|---|---|
| Square Root | $\sqrt{}$ | Arithmetic Palette | [ \ ] (backslash) |
| $n^{\text{th}}$ Root | $\sqrt[n]{}$ | Arithmetic Palette | [ Ctrl–\ ] |
| Absolute Value | $|x|$ | Arithmetic Palette | [ \| ] (vertical bar) |
| Factorial | $x!$ | Arithmetic Palette | [ ! ] |
| Summation | $\Sigma x$ | Calculus Palette | [ Shift–4 ] |
| Product | $\Pi x$ | Calculus Palette | [ Shift–3 ] |

Many additional mathematical operations are available as built-in functions. Some of these elementary math functions are the logarithm and exponentiation functions and the round-off and truncation functions.

*Note:* Mathcad's help files include descriptions of every built-in function, including information about the requirements on the arguments or parameters. Excerpts from the Mathcad help files are shown in text boxes.[1]

### Logarithm and Exponentiation Functions

The following box shows Mathcad's logarithm and exponentiation functions:

| | | |
|---|---|---|
| `exp(z)` | The number $e$ raised to the power $z$. | **Arguments:** |
| `log(z)` | Base 10 log of $z$. | • $z$ must be a scalar (real, complex, or imaginary). |
| `ln(z)` | Natural log (base $e$) of $z$. | • $z$ must be dimensionless. |
| | | • For log and ln functions, $z$ cannot be zero. |

But `e` is also a predefined variable in Mathcad, so the following two calculations are equivalent:

$$\exp(3) = 20.086$$
$$e^3 = 20.086$$

If you know or can guess a function name and want to see the help information on the function in order to find out what arguments are required, type the function name on the worksheet and, while the edit lines are still around the function name, press the [F1] key. If Mathcad recognizes the function name you entered, it will display help information on that function. For example, if you type `log` and press [F1], the information shown in the preceding text box will be displayed.

If you don't know the function name, use the Help menu and search the Mathcad index for your subject. For example, you can access the index list from the Help menu by clicking Help / Mathcad Help / Index. A search box will appear. When you type the word "function" you will receive a lot of information about Mathcad's functions.

**PRACTICE!**

Try out Mathcad's operators and functions. First try these obvious examples:

a. $\sqrt{4}$

b. $\sqrt[3]{8}$

c. $|-7|$ (This is the absolute value operator from the Arithmetic Palette.)

d. $3!$

e. $\log(100)$

Then try these less obvious examples and check the results with a calculator:

a. $20!$

b. $\ln(-2)$

c. $\exp(-0.4)$

---

[1] The Mathcad help file text is reprinted here with permission of Mathsoft, Inc.

### *Using QuickPlots to Visualize Functions*

Mathcad has a feature called *QuickPlot* that produces the graph of a function. For example, to obtain a visual display of the natural log function, you should follow these steps:

1.   First, create a graph by either selecting X-Y Graph from the Graph Palette or pressing [Shift-2].
2.   Enter `ln(x)` in the *y*-axis placeholder. (The `x` can be any unused variable, but you need to use the same variable in step 3.)
3.   Enter `x` in the *x*-axis placeholder.

The result will look like this:

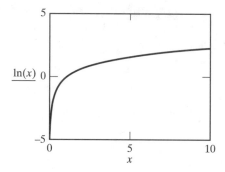

Mathcad shows what the function looks like over an arbitrary range of x values. The default range is −10 to +10, but the natural logarithm is not defined for negative numbers, so Mathcad used only positive numbers for this function. If you want to see the plot over a different range, just click on the *x*-axis and change the plot limits.

## 3.3   TRIGONOMETRIC FUNCTIONS

Mathcad's trigonometric functions work with angles in radians, but `deg` is a predefined unit so that you can display your calculated results in degrees. There is also a predefined unit `rad`. You probably won't need to use it, since Mathcad assumes radians if the unit is not included, but you can include the `rad` unit label to make your worksheet easier to read. For example, you might have

$$\text{angle} := 2 \cdot \pi$$
$$\text{angle} = 6.283$$
$$\text{angle} = 6.283 \circ \text{rad}$$
$$\text{angle} = 360 \circ \text{deg}$$

Mathcad's basic trigonometric functions are displayed in the following box:

| | | |
|---|---|---|
| `sin(z)` | `cos(z)` | **Arguments:** |
| `tan(z)` | `cot(z)` | • $z$ must be in radians. |
| `sec(z)` | `csc(z)` | • $z$ must be a scalar (real, complex, or imaginary). |
| | | • $z$ must be dimensionless. |

### Standard Trigonometric Functions

Mathcad's trigonometric functions require angles in radians, but as the examples that follow illustrate, you can work with either degrees or radians in Mathcad. To understand how this works, remember how Mathcad handles units: When you enter a value with units, Mathcad converts to its base units and stores the value. Then it performs the calculation using base units and displays the result:

$$\sin(30 \cdot \deg) = 0.5$$
$$\cos(\pi) = -1$$

When $\sin(30 \cdot \deg) =$ was entered in the preceding example, Mathcad converted the units that were entered (degrees) to base units (radians) and stored the value. Then the sine was computed using the stored value in base units, and the result was displayed. In the second example, no units were entered with the $\pi$, so Mathcad used the default unit, radians, and computed the result.

**Remember:** You can work with degrees with Mathcad's trigonometric functions, but you must include the deg unit abbreviation on each angle. When you do so, Mathcad automatically converts to radians before performing the calculation.

*Validate your functions and worksheets as you develop them.*

If you are "pretty sure" that the tangent of an angle is equal to the sine of the angle divided by the cosine of the angle, test the tan( ) function before building it into your worksheet. Learning to devise useful tests is a valuable skill. In this case, you could test the relationship between the functions like this:

$$\tan(30 \cdot \deg) = 0.577$$
$$\frac{\sin(30 \cdot \deg)}{\cos(30 \cdot \deg)} = 0.577$$

It only takes a second to test, and building a number of "pretty sure" items into a worksheet will quickly lead to a result with low confidence.

### Inverse Trigonometric Functions

The following box shows Mathcad's inverse trigonometric functions:

```
asin(z)
acos(z)
atan(z)
```

Arguments:

- $z$ must be a scalar.
- $z$ must be dimensionless.

Values returned are angles in radians between 0 and $2\pi$. Values returned are from the principal branch of these functions.

The angles returned by these functions will be in radians. You can display the result in degrees by including the deg unit abbreviation with the result. You can also include the rad unit abbreviation; doing so won't change the displayed angle, but it might help someone else understand your results. For example, you might have

$$\operatorname{asin}(0.5) = 0.524$$
$$\operatorname{asin}(0.5) = 30 \circ \deg$$
$$\operatorname{asin}(0.5) = 0.524 \circ \operatorname{rad}$$

## APPLICATIONS: RESOLVING FORCES

If one person pulls on a rope connected to a hook imbedded in a floor with a force of 400 N and another person pulls on the same hook with a force of 200 N, what is the total force on the hook?

*Answer: Can't tell—there's not enough information.*

What's missing in the statement is some indication of the direction of the applied forces, as force is a vector. If two people are pulling in the same direction, then the combined force is 600 N. But if they are pulling in different directions, it's a little tougher to determine the net force on the hook. To help find the answer, we often *resolve* the forces into horizontal and vertical components:

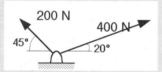

One person pulls to the right on a rope connected to a hook imbedded in a floor with a force of 400 N at an angle of 20° from horizontal. Another person pulls to the left on the same hook with a force of 200 N at an angle of 45° from horizontal. What is the net force on the hook?

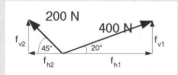

Since both people are pulling up, their vertical contributions add. But since one is pulling left and the other right, they are (in part) counteracting each other's efforts. To quantify this distribution of forces, we can calculate the horizontal and vertical components of the force being applied by each person. Mathcad's trigonometric functions are helpful for these calculations.

The 400-N force from person 1 resolves into a vertical component $f_{v1}$ and a horizontal component $f_{h1}$. The magnitudes of these force components can be calculated as follows:

$$f_{v1} := 400 \cdot \sin(20 \cdot \deg) \qquad\qquad f_{v1} = 136.808 \circ N$$
$$f_{h1} := 400 \cdot N \cdot \cos(20 \cdot \deg) \qquad\qquad f_{h1} = 375.877 \circ N$$

Similarly, the 200-N force from person 2 can be resolved into the following component forces:

$$f_{v2} := 200 \cdot N \cdot \sin(45 \cdot \deg) \qquad\qquad f_{v2} = 141.421 \circ N$$
$$f_{h2} := 200 \cdot N \cdot \cos(45 \cdot \deg) \qquad\qquad f_{h2} = 141.421 \circ N$$

Actually, force component $f_{h2}$ would usually be written as $f_{h2} = -141.421$ N, since it is pointed in the −x direction. If all angles had been measured from the same position (usually the 3-o'clock angle is called 0°), the angle on the 200−N force would have been at 135° and the signs would have taken care of themselves:

$$f_{h2} := 200 \cdot N \cdot \cos(135 \cdot \deg) \qquad f_{h2} = -141.421 \circ N$$

Once the force components have been computed, the net force in the horizontal and vertical directions can be determined. (Force $f_{h2}$ has a negative value in this calculation.) We obtain

$$f_{v\_net} := f_{v1} + f_{v2} \qquad\qquad f_{v\_net} = 278.229 \circ N$$
$$f_{h\_net} := f_{h1} + f_{h2} \qquad\qquad f_{h\_net} = 234.456 \circ N$$

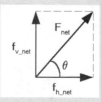

The net horizontal and vertical components can be recombined to find a combined net force on the hook, $F_{net}$, and angle, $\theta$:

$$F_{net} := \sqrt{f_{h\_net}^2 + f_{v\_net}^2}$$

$$\theta := atan\left(\frac{f_{v\_net}}{f_{h\_net}}\right)$$

$$F_{net} = 363.842 \circ N$$

$$\theta = 49.88 \cdot deg$$

*Note:* In this text horizontal and vertical force components are named with lowercase letters, while forces at arbitrary angles are given uppercase names.

### *Hyperbolic Trigonometric Functions*

Mathcad's hyperbolic trigonometric functions are as follows:

```
sinh(z)   cosh(z)
tanh(z)   csch(z)
sech(z)   coth(z)
```

Arguments:

- $z$ must be in radians.
- $z$ must be a scalar.
- $z$ must be dimensionless.

### *Inverse Hyperbolic Trigonometric Functions*

The following box shows the inverse hyperbolic trigonometric functions in Mathcad:

```
asinh(z)
acosh(z)
atanh(z)
```

Arguments:

- $z$ must be a scalar.
- $z$ must be dimensionless.

Values returned are from the principal branch of these functions.

The angles returned by the inverse hyperbolic trigonometric functions will be in radians, but you can put deg in the units placeholder to convert the displayed units.

**PRACTICE!**

Try out these Mathcad trigonometric functions:

**a.** $\sin(\pi/4)$

**b.** $\sin(90 \cdot deg)$

**c.** $\cos(180 \cdot deg)$

**d.** $asin(0)$

**e.** $acos(2 \cdot \pi)$

Try QuickPlots of these functions over the indicated ranges:

**a.** $\sin(x)$   $-\pi \leq x \leq \pi$

**b.** $\tan(x)$   $-\pi/2 \leq x \leq \pi/2$

**c.** $\sinh(x)$   $-10 \leq x \leq 10$

## 3.4 ADVANCED MATH FUNCTIONS

### *Round-Off and Truncation Functions*

Mathcad provides two functions that determine the nearest integer value. The `floor(x)` function returns the largest integer that is less than or equal to x, while the `ceil(x)` function returns the smallest integer that is greater than or equal to x. To remove the decimal places following a value, use the `floor( )` function. For example, to find the greatest integer less than or equal to $\pi$, either of the following will work:

$$\text{floor}(3.1416) = 3$$
$$\text{floor}(\pi) = 3$$

The second example used Mathcad's predefined variable for $\pi$.

If you want the values after the decimal point, i.e., the mantissa, use the `mod( )` function, which performs *modulo division*, returning the remainder after the division calculation:

| | |
|---|---|
| `mod(x,y)` | This function returns the remainder on dividing $x$ by $y$. The result has the same sign as $x$. |

Arguments:

- $x$ and $y$ should both be real scalars.
- $y$ must be nonzero.

Using the example of $\pi$ again we have

$$\text{mod}(3.1416, 3) = 0.1416$$
$$\text{mod}(\pi, 3) = 0.1416$$

Notice that the `mod( )` function will return the trailing decimal places only when the y argument is the integer less than or equal to x. You can create a user-written function that will always return the trailing decimal places using `mod( )` and `floor( )` together like this:

$$\text{trail}(x) := \text{mod}(x, \text{floor}(x))$$
$$\text{trail}(3.1416) = 0.1416$$
$$\text{trail}(\pi) = 0.1416$$

But the new `trail( )` function doesn't work correctly when x is negative, because it tries to divide −3.1416 by −4, which does not yield the trailing digits. An improved version uses Mathcad's absolute value operator, which is available on the Arithmetic Palette. For example,

$$\text{trail}(x) := \text{mod}(x, \text{floor}(|x|))$$
$$\text{trail}(3.1416) = 0.1416$$
$$\text{trail}(-3.1416) = -0.1416$$

The result has the same sign as the x value, which might be useful. If not, another absolute value operator around the entire right-hand side would force a positive result:

$$\text{trail}(x) := |\text{mod}(x, \text{floor}(|x|))|$$
$$\text{trail}(3.1416) = 0.1416$$
$$\text{trail}(-3.1416) = 0.1416$$

**PRACTICE!**

You can also compute the mantissa by subtracting `floor(x)` from `x`, but this approach also has trouble with negative numbers. For example,

$$\text{mantissa}(x) := x - \text{floor}(x)$$
$$\text{mantissa}(3.1416) = 0.1416|$$
$$\text{mantissa}(-3.1416) = 0.8584$$

Modify the `mantissa( )` function shown here so that it returns the correct mantissa when `x` is negative.

Mathcad provides an `if( )` function for making logical decisions, as well as functions for handling discontinuous systems and generating random numbers.

### The if( ) Function

Rules for the `if( )` function in Mathcad are as follows:

| `if(cond, Tval, Fval)` | This function returns one of two values, depending on the value of a logical condition. | `(i < 2)`<br>`(x < 1) * (x > 0)` for an "and" gate<br>`(x > 1) + (x < 0)` for an "or" gate |
|---|---|---|
| **Arguments:** | | • `Tval` is the value returned when `cond` is true. |
| • `cond` is usually an expression involving a logical operator. For example, you can use: | | • `Fval` is the value returned when `cond` is false. |

The returned "value" can be a simple scalar value, a computed value, or even a text string. For example, the `if( )` function can be used to determine whether water would be a liquid or a solid by checking the temperature of the water

$$\text{state}(\text{Temp}) := \text{if}(\text{Temp} > 0, \text{"liquid"}, \text{"solid"})$$
$$\text{state}(25) = \text{"liquid"}$$
$$\text{state}(-3) = \text{"solid"}$$

Or the `Tval` and `Fval` "values" can be formulas. Thus, we can create an absolute value function using `if( )` and changing the sign on `x` if `x < 0`:

$$\text{abs}(x) := \text{if}(x \geq 0, x, -x)$$
$$\text{abs}(12) = 12$$
$$\text{abs}(-6) = 6$$

**PRACTICE!**

Write an expression that returns a value of 1 if the volume in a tank is greater than or equal to 5000 gallons and a value of 0 otherwise. An expression like this might be used to control a valve on the flow into the tank, shutting the valve when the tank is full. Test your expression in Mathcad.

### Discontinuous Functions

Mathcad supports the following discontinuous functions:

| KRONECKER DELTA | HEAVISIDE STEP FUNCTION |
|---|---|
| $\delta(m,n)$   This function returns 1 if m = n and returns 0 otherwise. | $\phi(x)$   This returns 0 if $x$ is negative and returns 1 otherwise. |
| Arguments: | Arguments: |
| • Both $m$ and $n$ must be integers without units. | • $x$ must be a real scalar. |

### Random-Number-Generating Function

rnd(x)     Returns a random number (not an integer) between 0 and $x$.

A set of random numbers generated by rnd(x) will have a uniform distribution. Mathcad provides a number of other random-number-generating functions that produce sets of numbers with various distributions. For example, the rnorm(m, $\mu$, $\sigma$) function produces a vector of m values that are normally distributed about the value $\mu$ with a standard deviation $\sigma$.

## 3.5 STRING FUNCTIONS

Because text boxes can be used anywhere on a worksheet, the need for string-handling functions is greatly reduced in Mathcad. Still, if you need them, Mathcad does provide the typical functions for manipulating text strings. The following functions operate on text strings:

| | |
|---|---|
| concat(S1,S2) | Concatenates string S2 to the end of string S1. Returns a string. |
| strlen(S) | Determines the number of characters in the string S. Returns an integer. |
| substr(S,n,m) | Extracts a substring of S starting with the character in position n and having at most m characters. The arguments m and n must be integers. |
| search(S,SubS,x) | Finds the starting position of the substring SubS in S, beginning from position x in S. |
| str2num(S) | Converts a string of numbers S into a constant. |
| num2str(x) | Converts the number x into a string. |

The following example illustrates the use of the search( ) function to find the word Mathcad in the string called MyString. The position of the M in Mathcad is returned by the function. Since Mathcad says the first character of the string (the T in This) is in position zero, the M in Mathcad is in position 10 (the 11th character of the string).

MyString := "This is a Mathcad example."

pos := search(MyString, "Mathcad", 0)

pos = 10

$$\text{pos} := \text{search}(\text{MyString, "Mathcad", 0})$$
$$\text{pos} = -1$$

The last two lines illustrate that Mathcad differentiates between uppercase and lower-case letters. That is, Mathcad is *case sensitive*. The `search( )` function returns a −1 when the search string is not found.

## 3.6 FILE-HANDLING FUNCTIONS

Mathcad can read and write data to ASCII text files. The following functions are provided to accomplish this:

| | |
|---|---|
| `READ("file")` | Reads a single value from a data file. |
| `WRITE("file")` | Writes a single value to a data file. |
| `APPEND("file")` | Appends a single value to an existing data file. |
| `READPRN("file")` | Reads an array of values from a data file. |
| `WRITEPRN("file")` | Writes an array of values to a data file. |
| `APPENDPRN("file")` | Appends an array of values to an existing data file. |

The `file` is a text string containing either a file name (which should be in Mathcad's default directory) or a complete path name (preferred). The files created with these commands can be used to move data between Mathcad, spreadsheets, word processors, and graphing programs—but in many instances you can also cut and paste the data between programs by using the Windows clipboard, which is generally quicker.

By using the expression `WRITE("A:\testFile.txt"):=x`, the file `testFile.txt` is created on drive A:, and the current value of x is written to the file. Attempting to use the `WRITE( )` function a second time to save y to the same file would cause the value of x to be lost—`WRITE( )` only puts a single value in a file, as the following code shows:

```
x := 7
WRITE("A:\testFile.txt") := x
y := 12
WRITE("A:\testFile.txt") := y
READ("A:\testFile.txt") = 12
```

To prevent this, use `WRITE( )` for the first value written to the file and then use `APPEND( )` for additional values:

```
x := 7
WRITE("A:\testFile.txt") := x
y := 12
APPEND("A:\testFile.txt") := y
READPRN("A:\testFile.txt") = [ 7 12 ]
```

Note that `READPRN( )` was used in the second example. This is because the `READ( )` function reads only a single value, whereas testFile.txt contains two values. `READPRN( )` can read the entire file, not just the first value.

Mathcad provides a handy alternative to the file reading and writing functions called a *"file read or write component."* When you insert a component into a worksheet, the Component Wizard dialog is displayed that asks a series of questions, and then performs some task. For example, to read values from a text file called A:\testFile.txt you would do the following:

1.  Start the Component Wizard using the menu commands Insert/Component. This causes the Component Wizard dialog to be displayed.

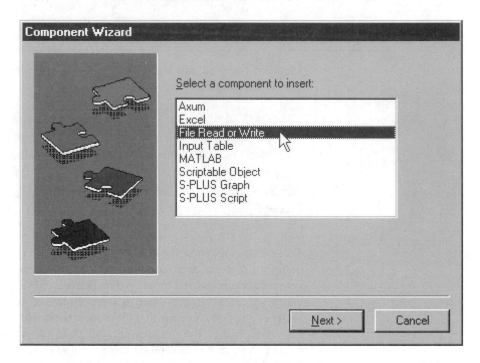

2.  Select the File Read or Write component from the list, and press Next >.

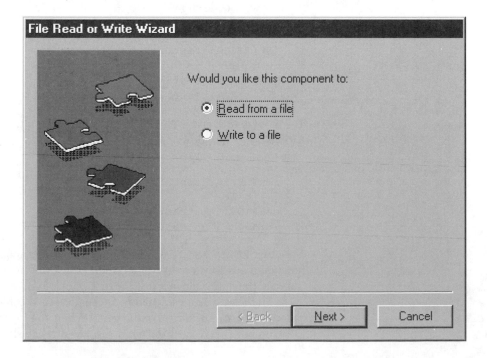

3. Select Read from a file, then press Next>.

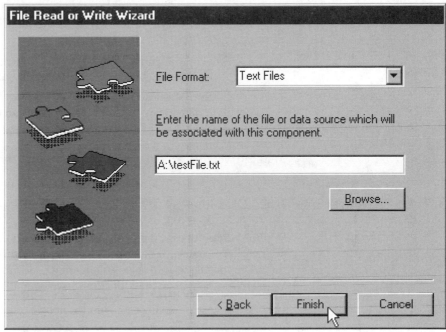

4. Select the File Format from the drop-down list. A text file has been used in this example. But Mathcad also knows how to work with several other formats, such as spreadsheets and graphing programs.

5. Enter the name of the file containing the data. Then click on the Finish button and Mathcad will place a picture of a disk (an icon), representing the File Read component, on your worksheet.

$$\blacksquare :=$$

$$\boxed{\blacksquare}$$
$$\text{A:\textbackslash testFile.txt}$$

6. Put a variable name in that placeholder next to the icon. The data in the file will be assigned to the variable. For example, the variable `Mydata` could be used.

$$\text{Mydata} :=$$

$$\boxed{\blacksquare}$$
$$\text{A:\textbackslash testFile.txt}$$

Once you fill in the placeholder, Mathcad will read the values from the file (if possible) and assign them to the variable `Mydata`. In this example, `Mydata` would have two values:

$$\text{Mydata} :=$$

$$\boxed{\blacksquare}$$
$$\text{A:\textbackslash testFile.txt}$$

$$\text{Mydata} = \begin{bmatrix} 7 \\ 12 \end{bmatrix}$$

The procedure for sending an array of values to a text file is essentially the same:

1. Start the Component Wizard using the menu commands Insert/Component.
2. Select the File Read or Write component from the list, and press Next >.
3. Select Write to a file, then press Next>.
4. Select the file format you want to Mathcad to use from the drop-down list.
5. Enter the name of the file that will receive the data and click on the Finish button. Mathcad will then place an icon representing the File Write component on your worksheet. There will be an empty placeholder below the icon.
6. Put the array name in the placeholder below the icon.

Mathcad will then send the values in the array to the file.

## 3.7 USER-WRITTEN FUNCTIONS

When Mathcad does not provide a built-in function, you can always write your own. The ability to use Mathcad's functions inside your own function definitions greatly increases the power of Mathcad to solve engineering problems and makes writing functions much simpler. Several user-written functions have been utilized in this chapter, including:

$$\text{trail}(x) := |\bmod(x, \text{floor}(|x|))|$$
$$\text{mantissa}(x) := x - \text{floor}(x)$$
$$\text{state}(\text{Temp}) := \text{if}(\text{Temp} > 0, \text{``liquid''}, \text{``solid''})$$
$$\text{abs}(x) := \text{if}(x \geq 0, x, -x)$$

Each of these user-written functions has a name (e.g., `trail`), a parameter list, and a mathematical expression of some sort on the right side. In these examples only a single argument was used in each parameter list, but multiple arguments are allowed and are very common. For example, a function to calculate the surface area of a cylinder could be written as

$$A_{cyl}(r, L) := 2 \cdot \pi \cdot r^2 + 2 \cdot \pi \cdot r \cdot L$$

Once the function has been defined, it can be used multiple times in the worksheet. In the following example, the function is employed four times, illustrating how functions can be used with and without units and with both values and variables:

$$A_{cyl}(7, 21) = 1.232 \cdot 10^3$$
$$A_{cyl}(7 \cdot cm, 21 \cdot cm) = 0.123 \cdot m^2$$
$$A_{cyl}(7 \cdot cm, 21 \cdot cm) = 1.232 \cdot 10^3 \circ cm^2$$
$$R := 7 \cdot cm \qquad L := 21 \cdot cm$$
$$A_{cyl}(R, L) = 1.232 \cdot 10^3 \circ cm^2$$

Recall that the $A_{cyl}$ function was defined using $r$ and $L$ for arguments. In a function definition, the arguments are dummy variables. That is, they show what argument is used in which location in the calculation, but neither $r$ nor $L$ needs to have defined values when the function is declared. They are just placeholders. When the function is used, the values in the $r$ and $L$ placeholders are put into the appropriate spots in the equation, and the computed area is returned.

In a function, you can use arguments with or without units, and the arguments can be values or defined variables. In the last calculation, $R$ and $L$ were used for radius and length, respectively. This choice of variable names is reasonable, but entirely irrelevant to Mathcad. Variables like Q and Z would work equally well, but they would make the worksheet harder to understand. For example, we might have

$$Q := 7 \cdot cm$$

$$Z := 21 \cdot cm$$

$$A_{cyl}(Q, Z) = 1.232 \cdot 10^3 \, {}^\circ cm^2$$

**PRACTICE!**

Define a function for computing the volume of a rectangular box, given the height, width, and length of the box. Then use the function to compute the volumes of several boxes:

**a.** H = 1, W = 1, L = 1

**b.** H = 1, W = 1, L = 10

**c.** H = 1 cm, W = 1 cm, L = 10 cm

**d.** H = 1 cm, W = 1 m, L = 10 ft

## APPLICATIONS:   FIBER OPTICS

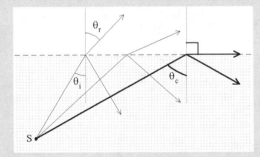

According to the *law of refraction*, the angle of incidence, $\theta_i$, is related to the angle of refraction, $\theta_r$, by the *index of refraction n,* for the two materials through which light passes. That is,

$$n_1 \sin(\theta_1) = n_2 \sin(\theta_2)$$

For light in a glass fiber ($n_1 \approx 1.5$) reflecting and refracting at the air ($n_2 \approx 1$) interface with an angle of incidence of 20°, what is the angle of refraction?

To solve this problem, we will use Mathcad's sin( ) and asin( ) functions and the built-in unit deg.

$$\theta_r := asin\left(\frac{1.5 \cdot \sin(20 \cdot deg)}{1}\right)$$

$$\theta_r = 30.866 \circ deg$$

When the angle of reflection is 90°, the angle of incidence is called the *critical angle*. For the fiber-optic material in air, what is the critical angle?

The critical angle is

$$\theta_c := asin\left(\frac{1 \cdot \sin(90 \cdot deg)}{1.5}\right)$$

$$\theta_c = 41.81 \circ deg$$

*Note:* The '1' in the first equation is there just to show how the index of refraction of air enters into the equation. It could be left out with no impact on the result.

The critical angle is important because, if you keep the angle of incidence greater than the critical angle, you get total internal reflection—there is no refracted ray, and thus no light is lost because of refraction. This is extremely important if the fiber-optic is to be used for transmitting signals, since refracted light shortens the transmission distance.

### Fiber Cladding

If the medium outside the fiber is something other than air, the critical angle changes. For example, if the fiber is in water ($n_2 \approx 1.33$), the critical angle is higher:

$$\theta_c := \operatorname{asin}\left(\frac{1.33 \cdot \sin(90 \cdot deg)}{1.5}\right)$$

$$\theta_c = 62.457 \circ deg$$

By increasing the refractive index of the material on the outside of the fiber, the angle of incidence can be closer to perpendicular to the wall of the fiber and still have total internal reflection. What happens if the material outside the fiber has a refractive index greater than 1.5? *Answer:* You get total internal reflection for *any* angle of incidence. To ensure that this is the case, fiber-optics are often coated with a second layer of glass with a slightly higher refractive index. This is called *cladding* the fibers.

## Summary

In this chapter, you learned that a function is a reusable equation that accepts arguments, uses the argument values in a calculation, and returns the result(s). Once a function has been defined in a worksheet, it can be used multiple times in that worksheet. You have learned to write your own functions and to use Mathcad's built-in functions in the following areas.

**MATHCAD SUMMARY**

**LOGARITHM AND EXPONENTION:**

| | |
|---|---|
| exp(x) | Raises e to the power x. |
| ln(x) | Returns the natural logarithm of x. |
| log(x) | Returns the base-10 logarithm of x. |

**TRIGONOMETRIC FUNCTIONS:** The units on the angle a in these functions must be radians. If you want to work in degrees, replace a by a · deg, where deg is a predefined unit for degrees:

| | |
|---|---|
| sin(a) | Returns the sine of a. |
| cos(a) | Returns the cosine of a. |
| tan(a) | Returns the tangent of a. |
| sec(a) | Returns the secant of a. |
| csc(a) | Returns the cosecant of a. |
| cot(a) | Returns the cotangent of a. |

**INVERSE TRIGONOMETRIC FUNCTIONS:** These functions take a value between −1 and 1 and return the angle in radians. You can display the result in degrees by using deg.

| | |
|---|---|
| asin(x) | Arcsine—returns the angle that has a sine value equal to x. |
| acos(x) | Arccosine—returns the angle that has a cosine value equal to x. |
| atan(x) | Arctangent—returns the angle that has a tangent value equal to x. |

**HYPERBOLIC TRIGONOMETRIC FUNCTIONS:**

| | |
|---|---|
| sinh(a) | cosh(a) |
| tanh(a) | csch(a) |
| sech(a) | coth(a) |

**INVERSE HYPERBOLIC TRIGONOMETRIC FUNCTIONS:**

`asinh(x)`

`acosh(x)`

`atanh(x)`

**ROUND-OFF AND TRUNCATION FUNCTIONS:**

| | |
|---|---|
| `floor(x)` | Returns the largest integer that is less than or equal to `x`. |
| `ceil(x)` | Returns the smallest integer that is greater than or equal to `x`. |
| `mod(x,y)` | Returns the remainder after dividing `x` by `y`. |

**ADVANCED MATH FUNCTIONS:**

| | |
|---|---|
| `if(cond, Tval, Fval)` | Returns `Tval` or `Fval`, depending on the value of a logical condition `cond`. |
| $\delta$`(m,n)` | Kronecker delta—returns 1 if `m = n` and returns 0 otherwise. |
| $\phi$`(x)` | Heaviside step function—returns 0 if `x` is negative and returns 1 otherwise. |
| `rnd(x)` | Returns a random number (not an integer) between 0 and `x`. |

**STRING FUNCTIONS:**

| | |
|---|---|
| `concat(S1,S2)` | Concatenates string `S2` to the end of string `S1`. Returns a string. |
| `strlen(S)` | Determines the number of characters in the string `S`. Returns an integer. |
| `substr(S,n,m)` | Extracts a substring of `S` starting with the character in position `n` and having at most `m` characters. The arguments `m` and `n` must be integers. |
| `search(S,SubS,x)` | Finds the starting position of the substring `SubS` in `S`, beginning from position `x` in `S`. |
| `str2num(S)` | Converts a string of numbers `S` into a constant. |
| `num2str(x)` | Converts the number `x` into a string. |

**FILE FUNCTIONS:**

| | |
|---|---|
| `READ("file")` | Reads a single value from a data file. |
| `WRITE("file")` | Writes a single value to a data file. |
| `APPEND("file")` | Appends a single value to an existing data file. |
| `READPRN("file")` | Reads an array of values from a data file. |
| `WRITEPRN("file")` | Writes an array of values to a data file. |
| `APPENDPRN("file")` | Appends an array of values to an existing data file. |

# Problems

### 3.1 USING THE ANGLE OF REFRACTION TO MEASURE THE INDEX OF REFRACTION

A laser in air ($n_2 \approx 1$) is aimed at the surface of a liquid with an angle of incidence of 45°. A photodetector is moved through the liquid until the beam is located at an angle of refraction of 32°. What is the index of refraction of the liquid?

### 3.2 MEASURING HEIGHTS

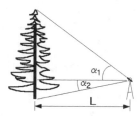

A surveyor's *transit* is a telescope-like device mounted on a protractor that allows the surveyor to sight distant points and then read the angle of the scope off the scale. With a transit, it is possible to get accurate measurements of large objects.

In this problem, a transit is being used to measure the height of a tree. The transit is set up 80 feet from the base of the tree ($L = 80$ ft), and the sights are set on the top of the tree. The angle reads 43.53° from the horizontal. Then the sights are set at the base of the tree, and the second angle is found to be 3.58°. Given this information, how tall is the tree?

### 3.3 RELATIONSHIPS BETWEEN TRIGONOMETRIC FUNCTIONS

Devise a test to demonstrate the validity of the following common trigonometric formulas. What values of $A$ and $B$ should be used to thoroughly test these functions?

a. $\sin(A + B) = \sin(A) \cdot \cos(B) + \cos(A) \cdot \sin(B)$
b. $\sin(2 \cdot A) = 2 \cdot \sin(A) \cdot \cos(A)$
c. $\sin^2(A) = \frac{1}{2} - \frac{1}{2} \cdot \cos(2 \cdot A)$

*Note:* In Mathcad, $\sin^2(A)$ should be entered as `sin(A)²`. This causes `sin(A)` to be evaluated first and that result to be squared.

### 3.4 LADDER SAFETY

Ladders are frequently used tools, but are also the source of many injuries. Improperly positioning a ladder is a common cause of falls.

Ladders are supposed to be set against walls at an angle such that the base of the ladder stands away from the wall 1 foot for every 4 feet of working length of the ladder. So the base of a 12-foot ladder with the top resting against a wall (as shown in the foregoing figure) should be 3 feet away from the wall. At this angle, most people can stand up straight on a rung and reach out and easily grab another rung with their hands. The 1-in-4 rule is for comfort and for safety—and it is written into OSHA regulations (OSHA Standards, 29.b.5.i).

a.    What is the angle θ between the floor and the ladder if the 1-in-4 rule is used?

b.    If the 1-in-4 rule is used, at what height does the top of a 12-foot ladder touch the wall?

## 3.5 VAPOR PRESSURE

Knowing the vapor pressure is important in designing equipment that will or might contain boiling or highly volatile liquids. When the pressure in a vessel is at or below the liquid's vapor pressure, the liquid will boil. If you are designing a boiler, then designing it to operate at the liquid's vapor pressure is a pretty good idea. But if you are designing a waste solvent storage facility, you want the pressure to be significantly higher than the liquid's vapor pressure. In either case, you need to be able to calculate the liquid's vapor pressure.

Antoine's equation is a common way to calculate vapor pressures for common liquids. It requires three coefficients that are unique to each liquid. If the coefficients are available, Antoine's equation[2] is easy to use. The equation says

$$\log(p_{vapor}) = A - \frac{B}{T + C}$$

where

| | |
|---|---|
| $p_{vapor}$ | is the vapor pressure of the liquid in mm Hg, |
| T | is the liquid temperature in °C, and |
| A,B,C | are coefficients for the particular liquid (found in tables). |

In using Antoine's equation, keep the following important considerations in mind

1.    Antoine's equation is a *dimensional equation;* that is, specific units must be used to get correct results.

2.    The log( ) function is not supposed to be used on a value with units, but that's the way Antoine's equation was written. Mathcad, however, will not allow you to take the logarithm of a value with units, so you must work without units while using Antoine's equation.

3.    There are numerous forms of Antoine's equation, each requiring specific units. The coefficients are always designed to go along with a particular version of the equation. You cannot use Antoine coefficients from one text in a version of Antoine's equation taken from a different text.

**Test Antoine's Equation**

Water boils at 100°C at 1 atm pressure. So the vapor pressure of water at 100°C should be 1 atm, or 760 mm Hg. Check this using Antoine's equation.

For water:    A = 7.96671    B = 1668.21    C = 228.0

**Use Antoine's Equation**

a.    The chemistry lab stores acetone at a typical room temperature of 25°C (77°F) with no problems. What would happen if, on a hot summer day, the air-conditioning failed and a storage cabinet in the sun reached 50°C (122°F)? Would the stored acetone boil?

---

[2] This version of Antoine's equation is from *Elementary Principles of Chemical Processes* by R. M. Felder and R. W. Rousseau, 1st ed., Wiley, New York (1978).

b. At what temperature would the acetone boil at a pressure of 1 atm?

For acetone:  A = 7.02447   B = 1161.0   C = 224

### 3.6 CALCULATING THE VOLUME AND MASS OF A SUBSTANCE IN A STORAGE TANK

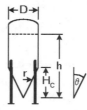

Vertical tanks with conical base sections are commonly used for storing solid materials such as grain, gravel, salt, catalyst particles, etc. The sloping sides help prevent plugging as the material is withdrawn.

If the height of solid in the tank is less than the height of the conical section, $H_c$, then the volume is computed by using the formula for the volume of a cone:

$$V = \frac{1}{3}\pi r^2 h$$

But if the tank is filled to a depth greater than $H_c$, then the volume is the sum of the filled conical section, $V_{cone}$, and a cylindrical section, $V_{cyl}$, of height $h = H_c$:

$$V = V_{cone} + V_{cyl}$$

$$V_{cone} = \frac{1}{3}\pi R^2 H_C$$

Here, R = D/2.

The radius of the tank depends on h if $h < H_c$, but has a value of R when $h \geq H_c$. The if( ) function can be used to return the correct value of r for any h:

$$r(h) := if(h < H_c, h \cdot \tan(\theta), R)$$

where $\theta$ is the angle of the sloping walls. (Variables H, R and $\theta$ must be defined before using this function.)

When working with solids, you often want to know the mass as well as the volume. The mass can be determined from the volume using the *apparent density*, $\rho_A$, which is the mass of a known volume of the granular material (including the air in between the particles) divided by the known volume. Since the air between the particles is much less dense than the solid particles themselves, the apparent density of a granular solid is typically much smaller than the true density of any individual particle.

a. Use Mathcad's if( ) function to create a function that will return the volume of solids for any height.

b. Use the function from part a to determine the volume and mass of stored material ($\rho_A$ = 20 lb/ft³) in a tank (D = 12 ft, $\theta$ = 30°) when the tank is filled to a depth h = 21 ft.

*(See related problem in Chapter 5.)*

### 3.7 FORCE COMPONENTS AND TENSION IN WIRES (BRIDGE, PART B)

A 150-kg mass is suspended by wires from two hooks. The lengths of the wires have been adjusted so that the wires are each 50° from horizontal. Assume that the mass of the wires is negligible.

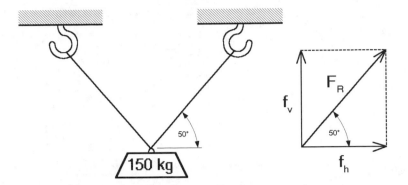

a. Since two hooks support the mass equally, the vertical component of force exerted by either hook will be equal to the force resulting from 75 kg being acted on by gravity. Calculate this vertical component of force, $f_v$, on the right hook. Express your result in newtons.

b. Compute the horizontal component of force, $f_h$, by using the result obtained in problem a. and trigonometry.

c. Determine the force exerted on the mass in the direction of the wire $F_R$ (equal to the tension in the wire).

d. If you moved the hooks farther apart to reduce the angle from 50° to 30°, would the tension in the wires increase or decrease? Why?

Related bridge problems: 2.2, 3.7, 3.8, 3.9, 3.10.

### 3.8  MULTIPLE LOADS (BRIDGE, PART C)

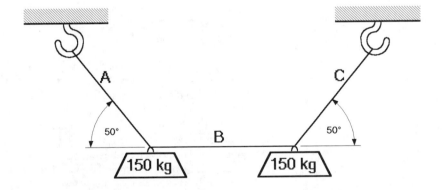

If two 150-kg masses are suspended on a wire, such that the section between the loads (wire $B$) is horizontal, then wire $B$ is under tension, but is doing no lifting. The entire weight of the 150-kg mass on the right is being held up by the vertical component of the force in wire $C$. In the same way, the mass on the left is being supported entirely by the vertical component of the force in wire $A$.

Calculate:

a. the vertical force component in wires $A$ and $C$.

b. the horizontal force component in each wire.

c. the tension in wire $A$.

Related bridge problems: 2.2, 3.7, 3.8, 3.9, 3.10.

### 3.9 TENSION AND ANGLES (BRIDGE, PART D)

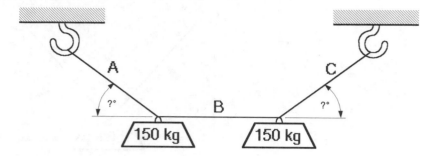

If the hooks are pulled farther apart, the tension in wire $B$ will change, and the angle of wires $A$ and $C$ with respect to the horizontal will also change.

    If the hooks are pulled apart until the tension in wire $B$ is 2000 N, determine:

a.  the angle between the horizontal and wire $C$.

b.  the tension in wire $C$.

How does the angle in part a change if the tension in wire $B$ is increased to 3000 N?
Related bridge problems: 2.2, 3.7, 3.8, 3.9, 3.10.

### 3.10 DESIGNING A SUSPENSION BRIDGE (BRIDGE, PART E)

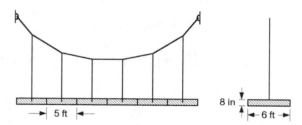

After fighting some particularly snarled traffic to get from their apartment to the pizza place across the street, some engineers decided that they should build a suspension bridge from one side of the street to the other. On the back side of a napkin, they sketched out the initial design shown in the accompanying figure. The plan calls for a single cable to be hung between the buildings, with one support wire to each deck section. The deck is to be 6 feet wide to allow pedestrian traffic on either side of the support wires. The bridge will be 30 feet long and made up of six 5-foot sections. The engineers want their design to be environmentally friendly, so the design calls for the decking to be made of a material constructed of used tires, with a density of 88 lb/ft³.

    *Note:* To help keep things straight, we use the term "wire" for the vertical wires connected to the deck sections and the term "cable" for the main suspension between the buildings.

a.  What is the mass of each deck section?

b.  What force is a deck section imparting to its suspension wire?

The engineers had quite a discussion about how much tension to impose on the bridge. One wanted to minimize the stress on the buildings by keeping the tension low, but others thought that would produce a "droopy" bridge. They finally decided that the tension in the center (horizontal) section would be five times the force that any deck section put on its suspension wire.

c.  What is the horizontal component of force in any of the cable sections?

At this point, the waiter walked up and made a comment that upset all of their plans. The result was a lively discussion that went on into the night, but no follow-through on the original design.

d.  Calculate all the forces and angles in the main cable segments.

*Hint:* Since the center segment of the cable has only a horizontal force component and you can calculate the tension in that segment, start in the center and work your way towards the outside. Also, since the bridge is symmetrical, you only need to solve for the angles and forces in one half of the bridge.

## SO WHAT DID THE WAITER SAY?

*"As soon as someone stands on that bridge, the deck will tip sideways and dump the person off."*

The engineers spent the rest of the evening designing solutions to this problem. Do you have any ideas?

Related bridge problems: 2.2, 3.7, 3.8, 3.9, 3.10.

# 4

# Working with Matrices

## TOTAL RECYCLE

NASA's Mission to Mars projects have focused attention on the idea of recovering and reusing oxygen, water, and essential nutrients on extended human excursions into space. Because the quantities of these materials that can be carried along are quite limited, the idea is to recycle everything. This is called *total recycle*. It is a great idea and an enormous engineering challenge.

The goal for NASA's Advanced Life Support Program[1] is to completely recycle water, oxygen, and food products—but not energy. Energy will be used to fuel the recycling systems. To date, water and oxygen recycle systems have been tested for up to 91 days.[2] A long-term test of a complete recycle system for food products is still many years away.

One of the many challenges of designing a total recycle system is handling the accumulation of chemicals generated at minute levels over long periods of time. For example, traces of copper (from pipes or cooling systems) are not a serious problem, but if the copper should somehow accumulate in the water system, the concentration could increase. The microbes used to degrade organic

## OBJECTIVES

*After reading this chapter, you should be able to:*

- To learn how to work with matrices in Mathcad, including:
  - Mathcad's definitions of "array", "matrix", and "vector".
  - Creating a matrix
  - Filling a matrix with values.
- To learn to perform basic mathematical operations on matrices, including:
  - Addition and subtraction
  - Matrix multiplication
  - Element-by-element multiplication
  - Transposition
  - Inversion
  - Finding the determinant of a matrix
- To learn to use Mathcad's built-in functions to manipulate matrices.

---

[1] Check NASA's Web site for more information on the processing steps required to implement the recycle systems: <http://pet.jsc.nasa.gov/alssee>.

[2] The Lunar–Mars Life Support Test Project Phase III (90-Day Human Test) was completed in December 1997.

wastes and the plants used to consume $CO_2$ and generate $O_2$ are both sensitive to copper. The loss of either of these systems would be catastrophic to the Mars mission. Special designs for handling trace contaminants and long-term testing is necessary to be sure that the total-recycle systems will work for extended missions into space.

Bringing total-recycle concepts into practice is not limited to the Mission to Mars. Just as individuals and communities are becoming increasingly involved in recycling activities, companies are also working to reduce the generation of waste products by recycling and reusing materials. There is a simultaneous push towards substituting less hazardous materials wherever possible. The separation processes required to effectively recycle materials and the equipment changes needed to allow the use of less hazardous materials will provide engineering opportunities for many years to come.

As with NASA's system, as our manufacturing facilities move towards total recycle, we may see more energy being used to fuel the separation systems that allow the materials to be recycled. In a time when there are concerns over the use of fossil fuels and global warming, using increasing amounts of energy to reduce wastes is problematic. The search for low-energy processes that simultaneously reduce waste products will be a tremendous challenge for the next generation of engineers and scientists.

## 4.1 MATHCAD'S MATRIX DEFINITIONS

A *matrix* is a collection of numbers that are related in some way. We commonly use matrices to hold data sets. For example, if you recorded the temperature of the concrete in a structure over time as the concrete set, the time and temperature values form a data set of related numbers. This data set would be stored in a computer as a matrix.

Common usage in mathematics calls a single column or row of values a *vector*. If the temperature and time values were stored separately, we would have both a time vector and a temperature vector. A *matrix* is a collection of one or more vectors. That is, a matrix containing a single row or column would also be a vector. On the other hand, a matrix containing three rows and two columns would be called a $3 \times 2$ matrix, not a vector. (But you could say the matrix is made up of three row vectors or two column vectors.) So every vector is a matrix, but only single-row or single-column matrices are called vectors.

Mathcad modifies these definitions slightly by adding the term *array*. In Mathcad, a vector has only one row or one column, and a matrix always has at least two rows or two columns. That is, there is no overlap in Mathcad's definitions of vectors and matrices. Mathcad uses the term *array* to mean a collection of related values that could be either a vector or a matrix. Mathcad uses the new term to indicate what type of parameter must be sent to functions that operate on vectors and matrices. For example, you can send either a vector or a matrix to the `rows(A)` function, so Mathcad's help files show an A as the function's parameter to indicate that either a vector or a matrix is acceptable.

> **DEFINITIONS USED IN MATHCAD HELP FILES**
> A Array argument—either a matrix or a vector.
> M Matrix argument—an array with two or more rows or columns.
> v Vector argument—an array containing a single row or column.

The `length(v)` function requires a vector and will not accept multiple rows or columns. Mathcad indicates this vector-only restriction in its help files by showing a v as the length function's parameter. The determinant operator, $|M|$, requires a square matrix and will not work on a vector. To show that a matrix is required, Mathcad's help files display an M as the operator's parameter.

### Array Origin

By default, Mathcad calls the first element in a vector the element zero. For a two-dimensional matrix, the *array origin* is 0,0 by default. If you would rather have Mathcad start counting elements at another value, you can change the default using the ORIGIN function. The following example illustrates how changing the origin from 0,0 to 1,1 changes the row and column numbering of the array elements.

$$\text{MyArray} := \begin{bmatrix} 12 & 15 & 17 \\ 23 & 25 & 29 \end{bmatrix}$$

$$\text{MyArray}_{0,0} = 12 \qquad\qquad \text{MyArray}_{0,1} = 15$$

$$\text{ORIGIN} := 1$$

$$\text{MyArray} = \begin{bmatrix} 12 & 15 & 17 \\ 23 & 25 & 29 \end{bmatrix}$$

$$\text{MyArray}_{1,1} = 12 \qquad\qquad \text{MyArray}_{1,2} = 15$$

Notice that the arrays look the same, but that the array origin has been changed to 1,1 after the ORIGIN statement, so the top-left element is now element 1,1 and not 0,0. You can also change the array origin for the entire worksheet. Use the Math menu, as Math/Options, and set the new value for the Array Origin on the options dialog box. The origins for all arrays on the worksheet will be changed.

### Maximum Array Size

There are two constraints on array sizes in Mathcad:

- If you enter the arrays from the keyboard, arrays may have no more than 100 elements. You can type in multiple arrays and join them to work around this limitation.
- The total number of elements in all arrays is dependent on the amount of memory on your computer, but will always be less than $8 \times 10^6$.

## 4.2  INITIALIZING AN ARRAY

Before an array can be used, it must be filled with values, or initialized. There are a number of methods for initializing an array in Mathcad. You can

- Type in the values from the keyboard.
- Read the values from a text file.
- Compute the values using a function or a range variable.
- Copy and paste the values from another Windows program.

Each of these options will be discussed in turn.

### *Typing Values into an Array*

You can enter a value into a particular element of an array using a standard Mathcad definition. For example, typing [G][ [ ] [3][ , ][2][ : ][6][4] puts the value 64 in the element at position 3,2 in the G matrix. If the G matrix has not been previously defined, then Mathcad will create a matrix large enough to a have an element at position 3,2, and it will fill the undefined elements with zeroes. In the following example, notice that the array origin is 0,0, so the 64 in element 3,2 is in the fourth row, and third column:

$$G_{3,2} := 64$$

$$G = \begin{bmatrix} 0 & 0 & 0 \\ 0 & 0 & 0 \\ 0 & 0 & 0 \\ 0 & 0 & 64 \end{bmatrix}$$

Filling a matrix by defining the contents of each element would be extremely slow. Fortunately, Mathcad has provided a better way. Rather than defining each element individually, Mathcad allows you to define an entire array at one time by first creating an array of placeholders and then filling in the placeholders by typing values from the keyboard. Begin by choosing a variable name for the matrix. We will use G again and create the left side of a definition by using [G][ : ]:

$$G := \blacksquare$$

To create the array, select (click on) the placeholder on the right side of the definition, and bring up the Insert Matrix dialog box by: (a) choosing Matrix from the Insert menu, (b) choosing Matrix from the Matrix Palette, or (c) using the keyboard shortcut [Ctrl-M]. The following figure shows what the dialog box looks like:

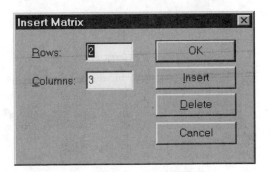

Enter the number of rows and columns you want in the G matrix:

Then click the OK button to insert the matrix of placeholders, and close the dialog box. (The Insert button creates the array of placeholders and leaves the dialog box open, which is useful if you are defining several arrays.) The matrix of placeholders looks like this:

$$G := \begin{bmatrix} \blacksquare & \blacksquare & \blacksquare \\ \blacksquare & \blacksquare & \blacksquare \\ \blacksquare & \blacksquare & \blacksquare \\ \blacksquare & \blacksquare & \blacksquare \end{bmatrix}$$

To complete the definition of array G, simply click on a placeholder and enter an element value. You can move to another placeholder either by using the mouse or by pressing [Tab] after each entry. The resulting matrix might look like this:

$$G := \begin{bmatrix} 1 & 1 & 1 \\ 2 & 4 & 8 \\ 3 & 9 & 27 \\ 4 & 16 & 64 \end{bmatrix}$$

**PRACTICE!**

Use the Insert Matrix dialog to create the following matrices:

$$t := (2 \quad 4 \quad 6 \quad 8 \quad 10)$$

$$W := \begin{bmatrix} 1 & 2 & 3 & 4 \\ 3 & 1 & 5 & 7 \end{bmatrix}$$

$$Y := \begin{bmatrix} 1 \cdot \sec & 2 \cdot \min & 3 \cdot hr \\ 4 \cdot \min & 5 \cdot \min & 6 \cdot \min \end{bmatrix}$$

### Reading Values from a Text File

Text, or ASCII, files are commonly used to move data between programs. For example, a recording instrument or data acquisition program might collect concentration data over time and save it to a disk as a text file. You can import the text file into Mathcad as a matrix for further analysis by using the READPRN( ) function.

*Note:* The PRN in READPRN( ) comes from an old file name extension. A .prn file was an ASCII text file that was usually sent to a printer back in the days when printers printed simple text files. Nowadays, the .prn extension is only one of several file name extensions used for text files.

A data file on a disk can be read and assigned to a Mathcad array variable by building the read operation into the matrix definition, like this:

$$C := \text{READPRN}(\text{"A:MyData.txt"})$$

$$C =$$

|   | 0  | 1    |
|---|----|------|
| 0 | 0  | 50   |
| 1 | 10 | 48.2 |
| 2 | 20 | 46.5 |
| 3 | 30 | 44.8 |
| 4 | 40 | 43.2 |
| 5 | 50 | 41.6 |
| 6 | 60 | 40.1 |
| 7 | 70 | 38.7 |
| 8 | 80 | 37.3 |
| 9 | 90 | 35.9 |

The text string sent to the READPRN( ) function tells Mathcad to read the MyData.txt file found on drive A:. This data file contains 25 rows, only part of which are displayed in the worksheet. (When only part of a matrix is displayed, Mathcad adds a shaded border at the top and on the left side of the matrix, showing which rows and columns are displayed.) To see the values that are not displayed, you would click on the portion of the C matrix that is displayed, and scroll bars would appear. You could then scroll the matrix to see the remaining values. The scroll bars will appear only when a matrix has been selected (by clicking on the displayed portion of the matrix) and when the matrix is too large to display in its entirety.

*Note:* If you want to write the values in array C into a text file, you assign the array to the WRITEPRN( ) function:

```
WRITEPRN("A:MyData.txt") : = C
```

### Units on Matrix Elements

If all of the elements of an array have the same units, you can multiply the entire array by the units. If not, each element can have its own units. These two time vector definitions are functionally equivalent:

$$\text{time} := \begin{bmatrix} 0 \\ 10 \\ 20 \\ 30 \end{bmatrix} \cdot \text{min}$$

and

$$\text{time} := \begin{bmatrix} 0 \cdot \text{min} \\ 10 \cdot \text{min} \\ 20 \cdot \text{min} \\ 0.5 \cdot \text{hr} \end{bmatrix}$$

### Computing Array Element Values Using Range Variables

Mathcad provides an unusual type of variable that takes on a whole series, or *range,* of values. These are called *range variables* and can often be used with arrays to identify particular elements of an array. For example, the first of the preceding `time` vectors could have been created using a range variable. The range variable needs to take the values 0, 1, 2, and 3, as it will be used to indicate each element of the `time` vector in turn. The range variable can have any name, but `i` and `j` are commonly used, since range variables are commonly used as index variables. The range variable is defined as [ i ][ : ][0][ ; ][3], or

$$i := 0 .. 3$$

Note that you indicate the range by pressing [ ; ] (semicolon), but Mathcad displays a series of dots (called an "ellipsis"). The range variable we've defined has four values, and anytime you use this variable in an equation, the equation will be evaluated four times, once with `i` = 0, once with `i` = 1, etc. Range variables can be very handy, but they do take a little getting used to.

Once the range variable has been defined, the elements of the `time` vector can be calculated using the range variable, like this:

$$time_i := (i \cdot 10) \cdot min$$

$$time = \begin{bmatrix} 0 \\ 10 \\ 20 \\ 30 \end{bmatrix} \cdot min$$

The range variable has been used as an index subscript (left-square-bracket subscript) on the left side of the definition, to indicate which element of the `time` vector is being computed, and is also used on the right side as part of the calculation itself. As the value of the range variable changes from 0 to 3, the computed element values change from 0 to 30 minutes.

**PRACTICE!**

What will the matrix `M` look like when defined by the following expressions:

**a.** `i := 0..4`
   `M_i := 2·i`

**b.** `i := 0..4`
   `j := 0..3`
   `M_{i,j} := (3 + 2·i - j)·ft`

### An Example of a Two-Dimensional Array

In the following equations range variables `r` and `c` and matrix, are defined to indicate the row and column of the element of `S` being computed, and the value of the element depends on the values of `r` and `c`:

$$r := 0 .. 4 \qquad c := 0 .. 2$$
$$S_{r,c} := r^2 + c^2$$

$$S = \begin{bmatrix} 0 & 1 & 4 \\ 1 & 2 & 5 \\ 4 & 5 & 8 \\ 9 & 10 & 13 \\ 16 & 17 & 20 \end{bmatrix}$$

### Computing Array Element Values Using the Matrix( ) Function

Mathcad's `matrix()` function allows you to fill an array with computed values without explicitly declaring range variables. Effectively, Mathcad declares the range variables based on the information you send to the `matrix()` function. The `matrix(r,c,f)` function creates a matrix with `r` rows and `c` columns in which the value of the i,j$^{th}$ element is computed using the function `f()`. This function must be a function of two variables and must be declared before calling the `matrix()` function. The function `f(i,j)` is evaluated repeatedly to fill the matrix, with i ranging from 0 to `r - 1`, and j ranging from 0 to `c - 1`.

The `S` matrix could be created using the `matrix()` function as follows:

$$\text{myFunc(r,c)} := r^2 + c^2$$

$$S := \text{matrix}(5, 3, \text{myFunc})$$

$$S = \begin{bmatrix} 0 & 1 & 4 \\ 1 & 2 & 5 \\ 4 & 5 & 8 \\ 9 & 10 & 13 \\ 16 & 17 & 20 \end{bmatrix}$$

**PRACTICE!**

What would the matrix returned by `matrix(4,4,f)` look like, if `f(r,c)` was defined as:

**a.** `f(r,c):= 2 + r + c`

**b.** `f(r,c):= 0.5·r + c²`

The following matrix was created using the `matrix( )` function:

$$M := \text{matrix}(3, 5, f)$$

$$M = \begin{bmatrix} 0 & 3 & 6 & 9 & 12 \\ 1 & 4 & 7 & 10 & 13 \\ 2 & 5 & 8 & 11 & 14 \end{bmatrix}$$

What did `f(r,c)` look like?

### Copying and Pasting Arrays from Other Windows Programs

A very convenient way to move values from another program into Mathcad is to copy the values in the other program (e.g., a spreadsheet) and then paste them into an array definition in Mathcad. If the values already exist in another Windows program, this can save a lot of typing.

In the next example, two columns of values are displayed in an Excel spreadsheet. The values shown in column B are computed by raising the values in column A to the third power. (You do not need to convert the spreadsheet formulas to values before moving the data to Mathcad.)

| B1 | ▼ | = | =A1^3 | |
|---|---|---|---|---|
| | A | B | C | D |
| **1** | 1 | 1 | | |
| 2 | 2 | 8 | | |
| 3 | 3 | 27 | | |
| 4 | 4 | 64 | | |
| 5 | 5 | 125 | | |
| 6 | | | | |

To create a 5 × 2 array in Mathcad containing these values, select the 10 values in cells A1..B5, and copy them to the Windows clipboard (using the spreadsheet's menu commands Edit/Copy, for example). Then begin an array definition in Mathcad:

$$C := \blacksquare$$

Click on the placeholder and paste the contents of the clipboard into the placeholder by using Mathcad's Edit/Paste menu commands.

The values displayed in the spreadsheet are now a Mathcad array:

$$C := \begin{bmatrix} 1 & 1 \\ 2 & 8 \\ 3 & 27 \\ 4 & 64 \\ 5 & 125 \end{bmatrix}$$

*Note:* The formulas used in the spreadsheet did not come across to Mathcad; just the displayed values were pasted.

---

**PROFESSIONAL SUCCESS**

*Let your software do the work.*

Retyping data, equations, and results into a report is tedious and tends to introduce errors. The past few generations of software products have had the ability to exchange data, and the capabilities of the products are improving with every new version. Mathcad can share information with other math packages, such as Excel and Matlab (data), and word processors, such as Microsoft Word (values, equations, graphs).[*] If you find yourself frequently reentering the same information into multiple software packages, you might want to see if there's a better way.

[*]Microsoft Word and Excel are products of the Microsoft Corporation, Redmond, WA. Matlab is produced by The Mathworks, Inc., Natick, MA.

---

### Creating an Identity Matrix

An *identity matrix* is a square matrix filled with ones along the diagonal and zeroes everywhere else. Mathcad's identity( ) function creates identity matrices. Since the number of rows is always equal to the number of columns in an identity matrix, you need to specify just one or the other, so the identity( ) function takes only a single parameter indicating the number of rows. Here's an example of the use of the `identity( )` function to create a 5 × 5 identity matrix called `ID`:

$$ID := \text{identity}(5)$$

$$ID = \begin{bmatrix} 1 & 0 & 0 & 0 & 0 \\ 0 & 1 & 0 & 0 & 0 \\ 0 & 0 & 1 & 0 & 0 \\ 0 & 0 & 0 & 1 & 0 \\ 0 & 0 & 0 & 0 & 1 \end{bmatrix}$$

## 4.3  MODIFYING AN ARRAY

Suppose you have just entered a large array from the keyboard and notice that you accidentally left out one row. You don't have to start all over again; you can insert a row or column into an existing array. You can also delete one or more rows or columns. In addition, Mathcad allows you to join arrays either side to side [`augment( )`] or one on top of the other [`stack( )`]. Finally, Mathcad lets you assign portions of an array to a new variable by using the `submatrix( )` function.

### Inserting a Row or Column into an Existing Array

Suppose that you have just entered a massive array by hand and discovered you left out a row. Don't worry; all is not lost. Mathcad will allow you to insert one or more rows into an existing array. Mathcad inserts the row after the currently selected row, so click on the row immediately above where you want the new row to be inserted. For example, to insert a new row just after the row containing 3, 9, and 27, click on the 3, 9, or 27 to indicate where the new row should be placed:

$$G := \begin{bmatrix} 1 & 1 & 1 \\ 2 & 4 & 8 \\ 3 & 9 & 27 \\ 4 & 16 & 64 \end{bmatrix}$$

Then bring up the Insert Matrix dialog box by pressing [Ctrl-M]. Indicate the number of rows to be added (and zero columns!), and then press the Insert or OK button:

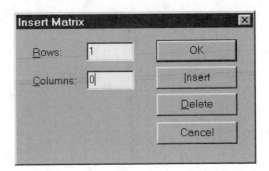

A row of placeholders is inserted into the matrix:

$$G := \begin{bmatrix} 1 & 1 & 1 \\ 2 & 4 & 18 \\ 3 & 9 & 27 \\ \blacksquare & \blacksquare & \blacksquare \\ 4 & 16 & 64 \end{bmatrix}$$

Click on the placeholders to enter values.

For example, to add two columns at the right side of the original G matrix;

1. Click on any element in the third column. Mathcad will insert the new columns to the right of the column you select:

$$G := \begin{bmatrix} 1 & 1 & 1| \\ 2 & 4 & 8 \\ 3 & 9 & 27 \\ 4 & 16 & 64 \end{bmatrix}$$

2. Bring up the Insert Matrix dialog box by pressing [Ctrl-M]. Indicate the number of columns to be added (and zero rows), and then press the Insert button:

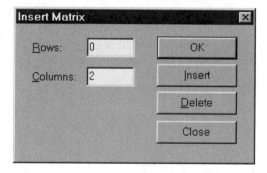

The result will be

$$G := \begin{bmatrix} 1 & 1 & 1 & \blacksquare\blacksquare \\ 2 & 4 & 8 & \blacksquare\blacksquare \\ 3 & 9 & 27 & \blacksquare\blacksquare \\ 4 & 16 & 64 & \blacksquare\blacksquare \end{bmatrix}$$

To add rows at the top of the array or columns at the left, select the entire array, rather than a single element, before inserting rows or columns:

$$G := \begin{bmatrix} 1 & 1 & 1 \\ 2 & 4 & 8 \\ 3 & 9 & 27 \\ 4 & 16 & 64 \end{bmatrix}$$

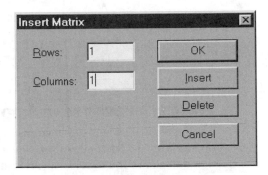

The matrix should now look like this:

$$G := \begin{bmatrix} | & | & | & | \\ | & 1 & 1 & 1 \\ | & 2 & 4 & 8 \\ | & 3 & 9 & 27 \\ | & 4 & 16 & 64 \end{bmatrix}$$

The preceding example illustrates that Mathcad will allow the addition of both rows and columns in a single operation.

### Deleting Rows and Columns

The procedure for deleting rows and columns is similar to that used to insert columns. To delete one or more rows, select an element in the first row or column to be deleted. If you want to delete three rows, the rows will include the row containing the selected element and the two rows immediately below it. Similarly, to delete two columns, select an element in the leftmost column to be removed. The deleted columns will include the column containing the selected element and the column to the right of it. For example, to delete the middle two rows of the original G array:

1. Select an element in the second row of the array:

$$G := \begin{bmatrix} 1 & 1 & 1 \\ 2 & 4 & 8 \\ 3 & 9 & 27 \\ 4 & 16 & 64 \end{bmatrix}$$

2. Bring up the Insert Matrix dialog box. Set the number of rows to be deleted to 2 and the number of columns to 0. Click the Delete button on the dialog box:

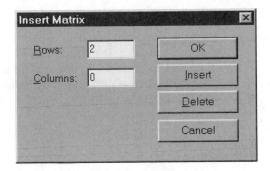

The middle two rows of the G matrix have been deleted:

$$G := \begin{bmatrix} 1 & 1 & 1 \\ 4 & 16 & 64 \end{bmatrix}$$

### Selecting a Portion of an Array

There are times when you need just a portion of an array. Mathcad provides a column operator [Ctrl-^] that allows you to select a single column and a submatrix( ) function that allows you to select an arbitrary subsection of an array.

### Selecting a Single Column

Mathcad's *column operator* allows you to take a single column (vector) of a multicolumn array and assign that column to a new variable. The column operator is available on the Matrix Palette or by pressing [Ctrl-6]. To see how the column operator is used, consider the time and concentration data that were read from the MyData.txt file:

$$C := \text{READPRN (“A:\textbackslash MyData.txt”)}$$

|   | 0 | 1 |
|---|---|---|
| 0 | 0 | 50 |
| 1 | 10 | 48.2 |
| 2 | 20 | 46.5 |
| 3 | 30 | 44.8 |
| 4 | 40 | 43.2 |
| 5 | 50 | 41.6 |
| 6 | 60 | 40.1 |
| 7 | 70 | 38.7 |
| 8 | 80 | 37.3 |
| 9 | 90 | 35.9 |

C =

The first column actually contains time information in minutes, and the second column contains concentration data in units of mg/L. Because the units on the columns are different, we can't just multiply the entire array by a set of units. But if we separate the time and concentration vectors, then we can put units on each vector.

We can use the column operator to extract the left column (column 0) and assign the values to a new variable, called time. We can build in units at the same time:

$$time := C^{<0>} \cdot min$$

|   | 0 |
|---|---|
| 0 | 0 |
| 1 | 10 |
| 2 | 20 |
| 3 | 30 |
| 4 | 40 |
| 5 | 50 |
| 6 | 60 |
| 7 | 70 |
| 8 | 80 |
| 9 | 90 |

$$time = \begin{array}{} \end{array} \cdot min$$

Similarly, we can pull out the concentration data and assign it to a new variable, `conc`:

$$conc := C^{<1>} \cdot \frac{mg}{L}$$

|   | 0 |
|---|---|
| 0 | 50 |
| 1 | 48.2 |
| 2 | 46.5 |
| 3 | 44.8 |
| 4 | 43.2 |
| 5 | 41.6 |
| 6 | 40.1 |
| 7 | 38.7 |
| 8 | 37.3 |
| 9 | 35.9 |

$$conc = \begin{array}{} \end{array} \cdot \frac{mg}{L}$$

This is an easy way to get units on values read in from text files. The column operator is also useful in getting vectors ready for plotting, since Mathcad allows you to plot one vector against another by simply entering the vector names in the placeholders on the $x$- and $y$-axes of an $x$–$y$ plot.

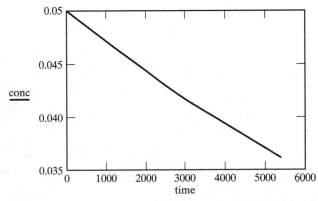

The values on the axes may surprise you, but remember that Mathcad always displays graphs in base units, so the concentrations are in kg/m³, and the times are in seconds.

*Note:* You can "trick" Mathcad into displaying values in the other units by dividing the vector names (on the axes) by the desired units. The resulting graph appears to display the correct values (but the axis labels can be quite misleading):

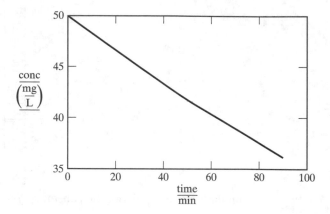

**PRACTICE!**

Create a $5 \times 5$ identity matrix using

```
ID := identity(5)
```

Then, use the column operator to pull out the center column of matrix ID. (column number 2) What would change when you used the column operator to extract the column number 2 if the identity matrix were created like this:

```
ORIGIN := 1
ID := identity(5)
```

### Selecting a Single Row

Mathcad does not provide a mechanism for selecting a single row, but you can get the job done by turning the array sideways (i.e., transposing the array) and selecting a column using the column operator. Going back to the G matrix that we used before, suppose we want to select the third row and assign it to a new variable, R3. We have

$$G := \begin{bmatrix} 1 & 1 & 1 \\ 2 & 4 & 8 \\ 3 & 9 & 27 \\ 4 & 16 & 64 \end{bmatrix}$$

We need to turn the G array around by using the transpose operator from the Matrix Palette:

$$G_{tr} := G^T$$

$$G_{tr} = \begin{bmatrix} 1 & 2 & 3 & 4 \\ 1 & 4 & 9 & 16 \\ 1 & 8 & 27 & 64 \end{bmatrix}$$

Then we can select what is now the third column (Mathcad's column number 2, since it starts counting at zero) by using the column operator:

$$R3_{tr} := G_{tr}{}^{<2>}$$

$$R3_{tr} = \begin{bmatrix} 3 \\ 9 \\ 27 \end{bmatrix}$$

Finally, we turn the result back into a row vector by transposing the $R3_{tr}$ vector:

$$R3 := R3_{tr}{}^T$$
$$R3 = [3 \ 9 \ 27]$$

This multistep operation can be carried out in a single command, thereby eliminating some variables:

$$R3 := [(G^T)^{<2>}]^T$$
$$R3 = [3 \ 9 \ 27]$$

If you need to extract a row frequently, you might want to create a function that operates like a "row operator":

$$row\_operator(A,r) := (A^T)^{<r>T}$$

This function can then be used to extract the third row of the G matrix:

$$R3 := row\_operator(G,2)$$
$$R3 = [3 \ 9 \ 27]$$

### Choosing a Subset of an Array

An alternative to all of the transposing that was done in the preceding example is Mathcad's submatrix($A, r_{start}, r_{stop}, c_{start}, c_{stop}$) function. This function takes a number of parameters and allows you to specify exactly which part of a matrix to extract. The first parameter, A, is the name of the array from which the submatrix is to be taken. The starting and stopping row and column numbers must be integers. Remember that, by default, Mathcad calls the top-left element, $A_{0,0}$. If you wanted to start with that element, then $r_{start}$ and $c_{start}$ would both be zero, not one.

To choose the third row of the G matrix, the submatrix( ) function could be used with the following arguments:

$$R3 := Submatrix(G, 2, 2, 0, 2)$$

These arguments tell the submatrix( ) function to start with the G array, rows 2 through 2 (using Mathcad's way of counting rows) and columns 0 through 2:

$$R3 := submatrix(G,2,2,0,2)$$
$$R3 = [3 \ 9 \ 27]$$

The submatrix( ) function can also return portions of an array that are not complete rows or columns. For example, the function could be used to extract the four elements in the top-left corner of the G matrix:

$$TL4 := submatrix(G,0,1,0,1)$$

$$TL4 = \begin{bmatrix} 1 & 1 \\ 2 & 4 \end{bmatrix}$$

### Combining Two Arrays

Mathcad provides two functions for combining arrays: `augment( )` and `stack( )`. Whereas the `stack( )` function stacks the matrices, `augment( )` connects them side by side. Here are a couple of simple examples:

$$A := \begin{bmatrix} 1 & 2 & 3 \\ 2 & 3 & 4 \\ 3 & 4 & 5 \end{bmatrix} \qquad B := \begin{bmatrix} 7 & 8 & 9 \\ 8 & 9 & 10 \\ 9 & 10 & 11 \end{bmatrix}$$

$$\text{Aug} := \text{augment}(A,B)$$

$$\text{Aug} := \begin{bmatrix} 1 & 2 & 3 & 7 & 8 & 9 \\ 2 & 3 & 4 & 8 & 9 & 10 \\ 3 & 4 & 5 & 9 & 10 & 11 \end{bmatrix}$$

$$\text{Stk} := \text{stack}(A,B)$$

$$\text{Stk} = \begin{bmatrix} 1 & 2 & 3 \\ 2 & 3 & 4 \\ 3 & 4 & 5 \\ 7 & 8 & 9 \\ 8 & 9 & 10 \\ 9 & 10 & 11 \end{bmatrix}$$

**PRACTICE!**

In what order would you use the `stack( )` and `augment( )` functions to create the following matrix from the matrices A and B in the previous section?

$$T = \begin{bmatrix} 1 & 2 & 3 & 1 & 2 & 3 \\ 2 & 3 & 4 & 2 & 3 & 4 \\ 3 & 4 & 5 & 3 & 4 & 5 \\ 7 & 8 & 9 & 1 & 2 & 3 \\ 8 & 9 & 10 & 2 & 3 & 4 \\ 9 & 10 & 11 & 3 & 4 & 5 \end{bmatrix}$$

How would the `submatrix( )` function be used to extract the matrix

$$T_{sub} = \begin{bmatrix} 5 & 3 & 4 \\ 9 & 1 & 2 \\ 10 & 2 & 3 \\ 11 & 3 & 4 \end{bmatrix}$$

from the T matrix?

## 4.4 ARRAY OPERATIONS

Array operations such as addition and multiplication require that certain conditions be met and that certain procedures be followed. For each of the standard array operations that follow the requirements and the procedures are listed.

### Array Addition and Subtraction

**Requirement:** The arrays to be added or subtracted must be the same size.
**Procedure:** Element-by-element addition.

Array addition and subtraction in Mathcad are handled just like scalar addition and subtraction:

$$A := \begin{bmatrix} 1 & 2 & 3 \\ 2 & 3 & 4 \\ 3 & 4 & 5 \end{bmatrix} \qquad B := \begin{bmatrix} 7 & 8 & 9 \\ 8 & 9 & 10 \\ 9 & 10 & 11 \end{bmatrix}$$

$$Sum := A + B$$

$$Sum = \begin{bmatrix} 8 & 10 & 12 \\ 10 & 12 & 14 \\ 12 & 14 & 16 \end{bmatrix}$$

$$Dif := Sum - B$$

$$Dif = \begin{bmatrix} 1 & 2 & 3 \\ 2 & 3 & 4 \\ 3 & 4 & 5 \end{bmatrix}$$

*Note:* Array subtraction is not a standard array operation; you usually have to multiply by $-1$ and then add. Array subtraction, however, is defined in Mathcad.

### Matrix Multiplication

**Requirement:** The inside dimensions of the arrays to be multiplied must be equal. The outside dimensions determine the size of the product matrix. Thus, we might have

$$D_{2\times3} \times E_{3\times2} \qquad \text{inner dimensions are equal (3)}$$
$$\text{product dimensions will be } 2 \times 2$$

**Procedure:** Working across the columns of the first array and down the rows of the second array, multiply elements and add the results. Mathematically, matrix multiplication is summarized as

$$Prod_{0,0} = [(1 \times 10) + (2 + 12) + (3 \times 14)] = 76$$
$$Prod_{0,1} = [(1 \times 11) + (2 \times 13) + (3 \times 15)] = 82$$
$$Prod_{1,0} = [(4 \times 10) + (5 \times 12) + (6 \times 14)] = 184$$
$$Prod_{1,1} = [(4 \times 11) + (5 \times 13) + (6 \times 15)] = 199$$

$$D := \begin{bmatrix} 1 & 2 & 3 \\ 4 & 5 & 6 \end{bmatrix} \qquad E := \begin{bmatrix} 10 & 11 \\ 12 & 13 \\ 14 & 15 \end{bmatrix}$$

$$Prod := D \cdot E$$

$$Prod = \begin{bmatrix} 76 & 82 \\ 184 & 199 \end{bmatrix}$$

**PRACTICE!**

> The order in which the matrices are multiplied makes a difference. What is the result of the following matrix multiplication?
>
> $$\text{Prod}_2 := \text{E} \cdot \text{D}$$

### Element-by-Element Multiplication

Sometimes you don't want true matrix multiplication, but rather, you want each element of the first matrix multiplied by the corresponding element of the second matrix. Element-by-element multiplication is available in Mathcad by means of the *vectorize* operator on the Matrix Palette.

**Requirement:** The arrays must be the same size for element-by-element multiplication.

**Procedure:** Multiply each individual element of the first matrix by the corresponding element of the second matrix:

$$A := \begin{bmatrix} 1 & 2 & 3 \\ 2 & 3 & 4 \\ 3 & 4 & 5 \end{bmatrix} \qquad B := \begin{bmatrix} 7 & 8 & 9 \\ 8 & 9 & 10 \\ 9 & 10 & 11 \end{bmatrix}$$

$$\text{ElemMult} = \overrightarrow{(A \cdot B)}$$

$$\text{ElemMult} = \begin{bmatrix} 7 & 16 & 27 \\ 16 & 27 & 40 \\ 27 & 40 & 55 \end{bmatrix}$$

**PRACTICE!**

> Compare the results of the following matrix multiplications:
>
> $$A \cdot B$$
>
> $$\overrightarrow{(A \cdot B)}$$

### Transposition

**Requirement:** Any array can be transposed.

**Procedure:** Interchange row and column elements, $\text{Trans}_{j,i} = \text{C}_{i,j}$:

$$C := \begin{bmatrix} 1 & 1 \\ 2 & 8 \\ 3 & 27 \\ 4 & 64 \\ 5 & 125 \end{bmatrix}$$

$$\text{Trans} := C^T$$

$$\text{Trans} = \begin{bmatrix} 1 & 2 & 3 & 4 & 5 \\ 1 & 8 & 27 & 64 & 125 \end{bmatrix}$$

### Inversion

When you invert a scalar, you divide 1 by the scalar, and the result is a value that, when multiplied by the original value, yields 1 as a product. Similarly, when you multiply an inverted matrix by the original matrix, you obtain an identity matrix as a result.

**Requirement:** Only square matrices can be inverted, and the matrix must be nonsingular.

**Procedure:** The procedure for inverting a matrix is quite involved. You first augment the matrix with an identity matrix and then use row operations by multiplying by scale factors and then adding and subtracting rows to convert the original matrix into an identity matrix. The same row operations will transform the original identity matrix into the inverse matrix. (For more details, see any text on matrix mathematics.) Suffice it to say that for large matrices the inversion process requires many calculations, and there can be significant round-off error associated with the process. How big is a "large" matrix? That depends on how accurate you want your solutions to be, but when matrices get above about 20 × 20, you should start trying to find solution methods that avoid inversion.

Inverting a matrix in Mathcad is easy; you simply raise the matrix to the −1 power:

$$F := \begin{bmatrix} 2 & 3 & 5 \\ 7 & 2 & 4 \\ 8 & 11 & 6 \end{bmatrix}$$

$$F^{-1} = \begin{bmatrix} -0.1517 & 0.1754 & 0.0095 \\ -0.0474 & -0.1327 & 0.128 \\ 0.2891 & 0.0095 & -0.0806 \end{bmatrix}$$

If Mathcad cannot invert the matrix, it will tell you the matrix is singular.

*Note:* A system of linear equations can be written in matrix form, consisting of a coefficient matrix, an unknown vector, and a right-hand-side vector:

$$[C][x] = [r]$$

One common solution method requires that the coefficient matrix be inverted and multiplied by the right-hand-side vector to calculate the values of the unknowns:

$$[x] = [C]^{-1}[r]$$

If the coefficient matrix is singular that is, it cannot be inverted, then there is no unique solution to the original set of equations. If there is a solution to the equations, you should be able to invert the coefficient matrix.

## APPLICATION: REMOVAL OF $CO_2$ FROM A GAS STREAM

Solutions of various ethanolamines (e.g., monoethanolamine (MEA), diethanolamine (DEA)) or potassium carbonate in water are commonly used to remove $CO_2$ from gas streams. The solution contacts the gas stream in a tall tower. The liquid flows down while the gas flows up, and the tower is designed to provide good contact between the liquid and the gas.

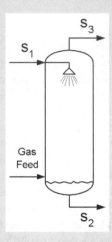

100 moles of a gas stream containing 10% $CO_2$ and 90% other combustion products (OCP) is fed at the bottom of the tower, and a solution (SOLN) containing 2% $CO_2$ and 98% MEA is fed at the top ($s_1$). The exiting streams are analyzed and found to contain the following products:

liquid out ($s_2$):   12% $CO_2$   1% OCP   87% SOLN
gas out ($s_3$):   1% $CO_2$   99% OCP

How many moles are in each of the unknown streams $s_1$, $s_2$, and $s_3$?

### Solution

This problem can be solved by writing material balances. The material balance for $CO_2$, for example, simply states that the $CO_2$ going into the process (10% of the 100 moles of gas in and 2% of the liquid in) must come out again (1% of the gas out and 12% of the liquid out). In mathematical terms, we have

$CO_2$ Balance:   $10 + 0.02 \cdot s_1$
$= 0.12 \cdot s_2 + 0.01 \cdot s_3$

The idea that the $CO_2$ entering the tower must leave again is true if the process operates at steady state ($CO_2$ is not accumulating in the tower) and if there is no chemical reaction involving $CO_2$ taking place in the tower.

Similar balances can be written for OCP and SOLN:

OCP Balance:   $90 = 0.01 \cdot s_2 + 0.99 \cdot s_3$
SOLN Balance:   $0.98 \cdot s_1 = 0.87 \cdot s_2$

To solve for the moles in $s_1$, $s_2$, and $s_3$, we first collect all the terms involving an 's' on one side and all the constants on the other:

$$0.02 \cdot s_1 \ -0.12 \cdot s_2 \ -0.01 \cdot s_3 = -90$$
$$-0.01 \cdot s_2 \ -0.99 \cdot s_3 = -90$$
$$0.98 \cdot s_1 \ -0.87 \cdot s_2 \qquad = 0$$

This set of equations can be written in matrix form as a coefficient matrix C and a right-hand-side vector r. Using Mathcad, we define the matrices as follows:

$$C := \begin{bmatrix} 0.02 & -0.12 & -0.01 \\ 0 & -0.01 & -0.99 \\ 0.98 & -0.87 & 0 \end{bmatrix} \qquad r := \begin{bmatrix} -10 \\ -90 \\ 0 \end{bmatrix}$$

We solve for the s vector (the numbers of moles in the unknown streams) by inverting the C matrix and multiplying the result with the r vector:

$$C_{inv} := C^{-1} \qquad C_{inv} = \begin{bmatrix} -8.691 & 0.088 & 1.198 \\ -9.79 & 0.099 & 0.2 \\ 0.099 & -1.011 & -2.018 \cdot 10^{-3} \end{bmatrix}$$

$$s := C_{inv} \cdot r \qquad s = \begin{bmatrix} 79 \\ 89 \\ 90 \end{bmatrix}$$

Stream $s_1$ contains 79 moles (77.4 moles SOLN, 1.6 moles $CO_2$), stream $s_2$ contains 89 moles, and stream $s_3$ contains 90 moles.

*Note:* This is a way to get $CO_2$ out of a combustion gas, but it doesn't get it out of the environment. The $CO_2$ is still present. It has simply been moved from one stream to another. Still, a process like this might be used as part of a solution to the global warming problem. By heating up the MEA solution, the $CO_2$ comes out of solution. This process is a way to obtain concentrated $CO_2$, which might then be used for another purpose. For example, it could be used by growing plants or perhaps turned into ethanol and used as a fuel to replace fossil fuels.

### *Determinant*

The *determinant* is a scalar value that can be computed from a square matrix. The process for computing a determinant is fairly straightforward, but tedious for matrices larger than $3 \times 3$. Fortunately, Mathcad will compute determinants automatically. The determinant operator is found on the Matrix Palette.

For a $1 \times 1$ matrix (a single value), the determinant of the matrix is simply the value in the matrix. Vertical bars are used to indicate the determinant. For example,

$$|4| = 4$$

For a $2 \times 2$ matrix, the determinant is computed by multiplying diagonal elements and subtracting the results:

$$A := \begin{bmatrix} A_{00} & A_{01} \\ A_{10} & A_{11} \end{bmatrix}$$

$$D = |A| = A_{00} \cdot A_{11} - A_{10} \cdot A_{01}$$

For larger matrices, the determinants are found by breaking down the matrix into smaller units called cofactors, calculating the determinants for each cofactor, and summing the results. The general equation for computing a determinant is

$$D = A_{i0} + C_{i0} + A_{i1}C_{i1} + \ldots + A_{i(n-1)}C_{i(n-1)} \qquad i = 0 \ldots (n-1)$$

where the *C*'s are the cofactors. For a $3 \times 3$ matrix, the cofactors are computed as follows:

- The cofactor for element $A_{00}$ is computed from the shaded terms in the following matrix and is $C_{00} = +(A_{11} \cdot A_{22} - A_{21} \cdot A_{12})$. *Note the plus sign before this cofactor.*

$$\begin{matrix} \boxed{A_{00}} & A_{01} & A_{02} \\ A_{10} & A_{11} & A_{12} \\ A_{20} & A_{21} & A_{22} \end{matrix}$$

- For element $A_{10}$, the cofactor is $C_{10} = -(A_{01} \cdot A_{22} - A_{21} \cdot A_{02})$. *Note the minus sign before this cofactor.*

$$\begin{matrix} A_{00} & A_{01} & A_{02} \\ \boxed{A_{10}} & A_{11} & A_{12} \\ A_{20} & A_{21} & A_{22} \end{matrix}$$

- For element $A_{20}$, the cofactor is $C_{20} = +(A_{01} \cdot A_{12} - A_{11} \cdot A_{02})$. *Note the plus sign before this cofactor.*

$$
\begin{matrix}
A_{00} & A_{01} & A_{02} \\
A_{10} & A_{11} & A_{12} \\
\boxed{A_{20}} & A_{21} & A_{22}
\end{matrix}
$$

- The sign in front of the cofactor equation alternates between plus and minus, depending on the position of the cofactor in the matrix, with $C_{00}$ (the top-left element) always taking the plus sign:

$$
\begin{matrix}
\boxed{+} & - & + \\
- & + & - \\
+ & - & +
\end{matrix}
$$

With numbers, the process looks like this:

$$
F := \begin{bmatrix} 2 & 3 & 5 \\ 7 & 2 & 4 \\ 8 & 11 & 6 \end{bmatrix}
$$

$$C_{0,0} := 2 \cdot 6 - 11 \cdot 4 \qquad\qquad C_{0,0} = -32$$

$$C_{1,0} := -(3 \cdot 6 - 11 \cdot 5) \qquad\quad C_{1,0} = 37$$

$$C_{2,0} := 3 \cdot 4 - 2 \cdot 5 \qquad\qquad C_{2,0} = 2$$

$$D := F_{0,0} \cdot C_{0,0} + F_{1,0} \cdot C_{1,0} + F_{2,0} \cdot C_{2,0} \qquad D = 211$$

Or, using the determinant operator from the Matrix Palette, we obtain

$$|F| = 211$$

*Note:* In the preceding example, the determinant was computed using cofactors for elements in the left column. Actually, you can use cofactors for the elements in any column or row to compute the determinant.

### How Is the Determinant Used?

The determinant shows up in a number of engineering calculations, but one of the most straightforward applications is using a determinant to find out whether a system of simultaneous linear equations has a unique solution. If the determinant of the coefficient matrix is nonzero, then the system has a unique solution. For example, we could have checked whether the coefficient matrix in the last Application example could be solved by calculating its determinant:

$$
C := \begin{bmatrix} 0.02 & -0.12 & -0.01 \\ 0 & -0.01 & -0.99 \\ 0.98 & -0.87 & 0 \end{bmatrix} \qquad |C| = 0.099
$$

Because the determinant is nonzero, there should be a solution, and there is.

*Note:* The calculation of determinants suffers from the same problem encountered with matrix inversion: For a large matrix, the number of calculations required leads to round-off errors on digital computers.

## PRACTICE!

Each of the following two systems of equations has no unique solution. Verify this statement by calculating the determinant of the coefficient matrix.

**a.** The second and third equations are identical:

$$2 \cdot x_1 + 3 \cdot x_2 + 1 \cdot x_3 = 12$$
$$1 \cdot x_1 + 4 \cdot x_2 + 7 \cdot x_3 = 16$$
$$1 \cdot x_1 + 4 \cdot x_2 + 7 \cdot x_3 = 16$$

**b.** The third equation is the sum of the first and second equations:

$$2 \cdot x_1 + 3 \cdot x_2 + 1 \cdot x_3 = 12$$
$$1 \cdot x_1 + 4 \cdot x_2 + 7 \cdot x_3 = 16$$
$$3 \cdot x_1 + 7 \cdot x_2 + 8 \cdot x_3 = 28$$

The following two systems of equations might have solutions. Use the determinant to find out for sure whether they do.

**a.**

$$2 \cdot x_1 + 3 \cdot x_2 + 1 \cdot x_3 = 12$$
$$1 \cdot x_1 + 4 \cdot x_2 + 7 \cdot x_3 = 16$$
$$4 \cdot x_1 + 1 \cdot x_2 + 3 \cdot x_3 = 9$$

**b.**

$$2 \cdot x_1 + 3 \cdot x_2 + 1 \cdot x_3 = 12$$
$$1 \cdot x_1 + 4 \cdot x_2 + 7 \cdot x_3 = 16$$
$$7 \cdot x_1 + 18 \cdot x_2 + 23 \cdot x_3 = 48$$

## 4.5 ARRAY FUNCTIONS

Several functions are sometimes useful when working with arrays. The `min(A)` and `max(A)` functions find the minimum and maximum values in the array specified as the function's parameter:

$$C := \begin{bmatrix} 1 & 1 \\ 2 & 8 \\ 3 & 27 \\ 4 & 64 \\ 5 & 125 \end{bmatrix} \qquad \begin{aligned} \max(C) &= 125 \\ \min(C) &= 1 \end{aligned}$$

$$a := \begin{bmatrix} 3 \\ 2 \\ 7 \\ 4 \end{bmatrix} \qquad \begin{aligned} \max(a) &= 7 \\ \min(a) &= 2 \end{aligned}$$

Four additional functions return information on the size of an array or a vector. The `cols(A)` function returns the number of columns in array A, while the `rows(A)` function returns the number of rows in A. For vectors, there is a `length(v)` function that returns the number of elements in the vector and a `last(v)` function that returns the index of the last element of the vector. For example,

$$C := \begin{bmatrix} 1 & 1 \\ 2 & 8 \\ 3 & 27 \\ 4 & 64 \\ 5 & 125 \end{bmatrix} \qquad \begin{array}{l} \text{rows(C)} = 5 \\ \text{cols(C)} = 2 \end{array}$$

$$a := \begin{bmatrix} 3 \\ 2 \\ 7 \\ 4 \end{bmatrix} \qquad \begin{array}{r} \text{rows(a)} = 4 \\ \text{cols(a)} = 1 \\ \text{length(a)} = 4 \\ \text{last(a)} = 3 \qquad a_3 = 4 \end{array}$$

Note that the `rows(A)` and `cols(A)` functions work with either matrices or vectors, but the `length(v)` and `last(v)` functions operate only on vectors. The value returned by `last(v)` will be one less than that returned by `length(v)` as long as the matrix ORIGIN is zero.

### Sorting

There are three functions for sorting vectors and arrays in Mathcad. The `sort(v)` function arranges the elements of a vector in increasing order. You can combine the `sort(v)` function with the `reverse(v)` function to get the elements of a vector arranged in decreasing order:

$$a_1 := \text{sort}(a)$$

$$a_1 = \begin{bmatrix} 2 \\ 3 \\ 4 \\ 7 \end{bmatrix}$$

$$a_2 := \text{reverse}(a_1)$$

$$a_2 = \begin{bmatrix} 7 \\ 4 \\ 3 \\ 2 \end{bmatrix}$$

Note that the `reverse(v)` function is not a sorting function: It doesn't perform a sort, but just reverses the order of the elements in a vector.

There are two sorting functions for arrays: `csort(A,n)` and `rsort(A,n)`. The `csort(A,n)` function arranges the rows of array A such that the elements in column n will be in increasing order. To sort array H on the left column, use the command `csort(H,0)`, as shown here:

$$H := \begin{bmatrix} 7 & 9 & 2 \\ 4 & 8 & 1 \\ 8 & 2 & 0 \\ 3 & 7 & 4 \end{bmatrix}$$

$$H_1 := \text{csort}(H, 0) \qquad H_1 = \begin{bmatrix} 3 & 7 & 4 \\ 4 & 8 & 1 \\ 7 & 9 & 2 \\ 8 & 2 & 0 \end{bmatrix}$$

To sort array H on the rightmost column, use the command `csort(H,2)`:

$$H_2 := \text{csort}(H, 2) \qquad H_2 = \begin{bmatrix} 8 & 2 & 0 \\ 4 & 8 & 1 \\ 7 & 9 & 2 \\ 3 & 7 & 4 \end{bmatrix}$$

To rearrange the columns so that the elements in the top row are in increasing order, use the `rsort(A, 0)` command:

$$H_3 := \text{rsort}(H, 0) \qquad H_3 = \begin{bmatrix} 2 & 7 & 9 \\ 1 & 4 & 8 \\ 0 & 8 & 2 \\ 4 & 3 & 7 \end{bmatrix}$$

## APPLICATIONS: TOTAL RECYCLE

One of the many tests performed during NASA's Lunar–Mars Life Support Test Project III (LMLSTP III) was the cultivation of wheat to consume $CO_2$, produce $O_2$, and contribute to the food requirements of the crew. The gas flows between the crew's cabin and the plant growth center pass through two concentrators, one for oxygen and the other for carbon dioxide:

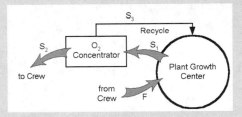

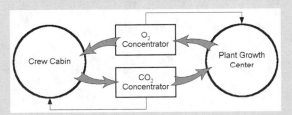

Let us take a look at how Mathcad's matrix-handling features can help us determine the flow rates through the plant growth center and the $O_2$ concentrator. In the following figure, the unknown streams have been labeled $S_1$ through $S_3$:

The feed to the plant growth center, F, will be treated as a known commodity. NASA's Web site[3] states that the concentration of $CO_2$ in stream F is 85 to 95% pure $CO_2$. (We'll assume 85% on a molar basis.) The amount of $CO_2$ entering the plant growth center must be equal to the amount of $CO_2$ being generated by the crew. The LMLSTP III had a crew of four, and a typical rate of $CO_2$ production for a resting person is 200 ml/min.[4] With the understanding that the crew is working, not resting, we'll assume a $CO_2$ generation rate of 1000 ml/min. This is the rate at which $CO_2$ enters the plant growth center, and it is 85% of F. The

---

[3] <http://pet.jsc.nasa.gov/alssee>.
[4] This value is from the "standard man data" in *Biomedical Applications of Heat and Mass Transfer*, by R. C. Seagrave, Iowa State University Press, Ames, Iowa (1971).

remainder of F is assumed to contain $O_2$ and $N_2$ in the ratio commonly found in air: 21:79 (21 moles of $O_2$ for every 79 moles of $N_2$). With these (numerous) assumptions, the contents of stream F can be summarized as follows:

F **Contains:** 0.0444 moles (per minute)

mole fractions:   0.8500 or 85 mole % $CO_2$
0.0313 or 3.13 mole % $O_2$
0.1187 or 11.87 mole % $N_2$

From other statements in the NASA Web site, and a good healthy assumption about how the $O_2$ concentrator works, the compositions of the other streams are expected to be something like the following:

| MOLE FRACTION | $S_1$ | $S_2$ | $S_3$ |
|---|---|---|---|
| $CO_2$ | 0.00079 | 0 | 0.00080 |
| $O_2$ | 0.20983 | 0.85000 | 0.20665 |
| $N_2$ | 0.78938 | 0.15000 | 0.79255 |

With these compositions, we can write material balances to find the molar flow rates in streams $S_1$ through $S_3$.

Since $CO_2$ is being consumed and $O_2$ is being produced in the growth center, the simplest balance we can write is on $N_2$ (no reaction term is needed):

$N_2$ balance around the plant growth center:

$N_2$ in F + $N_2$ in $S_3$ = $N_2$ in $S_1$
$0.1187 \cdot 0.0444$ mole + $0.79255 \cdot S_3$ = $0.78938 \cdot S_1$

There is no reaction in the $O_2$ concentrator, so simple material balances could be written on any component. However, the very small amounts of $CO_2$ and the very small change in $CO_2$ composition across the $O_2$ concentrator make a $CO_2$ balance a poor choice, because these low-precision values can turn into large errors. So we write $O_2$ and $N_2$ balances around the concentrator:

$O_2$ balance around the $O_2$ concentrator:

$O_2$ in $S_1$ = $O_2$ in $S_3$ − $O_2$ in $S_2$
$0.20983 \cdot S_1$ = $0.20665 \cdot S_3$ − $0.85 \cdot S_2$

$N_2$ balance around the $O_2$ concentrator:

$N_2$ in $S_1$ = $N_2$ in $S_3$ − $N_2$ in $S_2$
$0.78938 \cdot S_1$ = $0.79255 \cdot S_3$ − $0.15 \cdot S_2$

In matrix form, the coefficient matrix and right-hand-side vector for these three equations look like this:

$$F := 0.0444 \cdot mole$$

$$C := \begin{bmatrix} 0.78938 & -0.15 & -0.79255 \\ -0.78938 & 0 & 0.79255 \\ 0.20983 & -0.85 & -0.20665 \end{bmatrix}$$

$$r := \begin{bmatrix} 0 \\ -0.1187 \cdot F \\ 0 \end{bmatrix} \cdot mol$$

The coefficient matrix C can then be inverted and multiplied by the right-hand-side vector r to find the flow rates in the three unknown streams:

$$C^{-1} = \begin{bmatrix} -1.414 \cdot 10^3 & -1.349 \cdot 10^3 & 249.591 \\ -6.667 & -6.667 & 0 \\ -1.409 \cdot 10^3 & -1.343 \cdot 10^3 & 248.593 \end{bmatrix}$$

$$S := C^{-1} \cdot r \qquad S = \begin{bmatrix} 7.111 \\ 0.035 \\ 7.076 \end{bmatrix} \cdot mol$$

So the flow rates are $S_1$ = 7.111 moles (per minute), $S_2$ = 0.035 moles, and $S_3$ = 7.076 moles.

## SUMMARY

In this chapter, we learned about how to work with matrices in Mathcad. Matrix values can be entered from the keyboard, computed from equations, read from data files, or copied from other programs. Once a matrix exists, there are a variety of ways it can be modified and manipulated to insert or delete rows or columns or choose a portion of a matrix and assign it to another variable.

The standard array operations were described, including addition, multiplication, transposition, and inversion. The way Mathcad handles these operations is summarized in the following two lists:

**MATHCAD SUMMARY**

**MATRIX FUNDAMENTALS:**

| | |
|---|---|
| `ORIGIN` | Changes the starting value of the first array element (0 by default). |
| `[Ctrl-M]` | Opens the matrix dialog to create a matrix and to insert or delete rows or columns. |
| `Matrix(r,c,f)` | Creates a matrix with r rows and c columns using function f. Function f is user defined and must be a function of two variables. |
| `Identity(c)` | Creates an identity matrix with c rows and columns. |
| `[Ctrl-6]` | Selects a single column of a matrix. |
| `Submatrix(A,`$r_{start}$`,` $r_{stop}$`,`$c_{start}$`,`$c_{stop}$`)` | Extracts a portion of matrix A. |
| `Augment(`$A_1$`,` $A_2$`)` | Combines arrays $A_1$ and $A_2$ side by side |
| `Stack(`$A_1$`,` $A_2$`)` | Stacks array $A_1$ on top of $A_2$. |
| `READPRN(path)` | Reads array values from a text file. |
| `WRITEPRN(path)` | Writes array values to a text file. |

**MATRIX OPERATIONS:**

| | |
|---|---|
| `+` | Addition of matrices. |
| `[Shift-8]` | Matrix multiplication. |
| $\rightarrow$ | Vectorize (from the Matrix Palette)—used when you want element-by-element multiplication instead of matrix multiplication. |
| `T` | Transpose (from the Matrix Palette). |
| `[Shift-6]` | Invert Matrix. |
| `|M|` | Determinant (from the Matrix Palette). |
| `sort(v)` | Sorts vector v into ascending order. |
| `reverse(v)` | Reverses the order of vector v—this operation is used after `sort(v)` to get a vector sorted into descending order. |
| `csort(A,n)` | Sorts array A so that the values in column n are in ascending order. |
| `rsort(A,n)` | Sorts array A so that the values in row n are in ascending order. |

# Problems

### 4.1  SIMULTANEOUS EQUATIONS

The following arrays represent coefficient matrices and right-hand-side vectors for sets of simultaneous linear equations written in matrix form

$$[C][x] = [r].$$

Calculate the determinant of these coefficient matrices to see whether each set of simultaneous equations can be solved, and if so, solve for the solution vector [x].

$$C = \begin{bmatrix} 3 & 1 & 5 \\ 2 & 3 & -1 \\ -1 & 4 & 0 \end{bmatrix} \qquad r = \begin{bmatrix} 20 \\ 5 \\ 7 \end{bmatrix}$$

$$C = \begin{bmatrix} 4 & 2 & 1 \\ 2 & 3 & 0 \\ 0 & 4 & -1 \end{bmatrix} \qquad r = \begin{bmatrix} 18 \\ 6 \\ -2 \end{bmatrix}$$

$$C = \begin{bmatrix} 7 & 3 & 1 \\ 2 & -5 & 6 \\ 1 & 5 & 1 \end{bmatrix} \qquad r = \begin{bmatrix} 108 \\ -62 \\ 56 \end{bmatrix}$$

$$C = \begin{bmatrix} 4 & 2 & 1 & 0 \\ 2 & 3 & 0 & 1 \\ 0 & 4 & -1 & 3 \\ 2 & 1 & 4 & 2 \end{bmatrix} \qquad r = \begin{bmatrix} 13 \\ 8 \\ 4 \\ 19 \end{bmatrix}$$

## 4.2 SIMULTANEOUS EQUATIONS II

Write the following sets of simultaneous equations in matrix form, and solve (if possible):

a.
$$3x_1 + 1x_2 + 5x_3 = 20$$
$$2x_1 + 3x_2 - 1x_3 = 5$$
$$-1x_1 + 4x_2 \qquad = 7$$

b.
$$6x_1 + 2x_2 + 8x_3 = 14$$
$$x_1 + 3x_2 + 4x_3 = 5$$
$$5x_1 + 6x_2 + 2x_3 = 7$$

c.
$$4y_1 + 2y_2 + 1y_3 + 5y_4 = 52.9$$
$$3y_1 + y_2 + 4y_3 + 7y_4 = 74.2$$
$$2y_1 + 3y_2 + y_3 + 6y_4 = 58.3$$
$$3y_1 + y_2 + y_3 + 3y_4 = 34.2$$

## 4.3 MATERIAL BALANCES ON A GAS ABSORBER

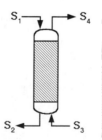

The following equations are material balances for $CO_2$, $SO_2$, and $N_2$ around the gas absorber shown in the accompanying figure. Stream $S_1$ is known to contain 99 mole % MEA and 1 mole % $CO_2$. The flow rate in $S_1$ is 100 moles per minute.

| COMPONENT | $S_1$ | $S_2$ | $S_3$ | $S_4$ |
|---|---|---|---|---|
| $CO_2$ | 0.01000 | 0.07522 | 0.08000 | 0.00880 |
| $SO_2$ | 0 | 0.01651 | 0.02000 | 0.00220 |
| $N_2$ | 0 | 0 | 0.90000 | 0.98900 |
| MEA | 0.99000 | 0.90800 | 0 | 0 |

The compositions used in the material balances are tabulated as follows:

$CO_2$ Balance:   $CO_2$ in $S_1$ + $CO_2$ in $S_3$ = $CO_2$ in $S_2$ + $CO_2$ in $S_4$

     $1 \text{ mole} + 0.08000 \cdot S_3 = 0.07522 \cdot S_2 + 0.00880 \cdot S_4$

$SO_2$ Balance:   $SO_2$ in $S_1$ + $SO_2$ in $S_3$ = $SO_2$ in $S_2$ + $SO_2$ in $S_4$

     $0 + 0.02000 \cdot S_3 = 0.01651 \cdot S_2 + 0.00220 \cdot S_4$

$N_2$ Balance:   $N_2$ in $S_1$ + $N_2$ in $S_3$ = $N_2$ in $S_2$ + $N_2$ in $S_4$

     $0 + 0.90000 \cdot S_3 = 0 + 0.98900 \cdot S_4$

Solve the material balances for the unknown flow rates $S_2$ through $S_4$.

## 4.4 MATERIAL BALANCES ON AN EXTRACTOR

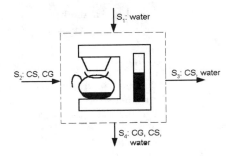

This problem focuses on a low-cost, high-performance chemical extraction unit: a drip coffee-maker. The ingredients are water, coffee solubles (CS), and coffee grounds (CG). Stream $S_1$ is water only, and the coffeemaker is designed to hold 1 liter. Stream $S_2$ is the dry coffee placed in the filter and contains 99% grounds and 1% soluble ingredients. The product coffee contains 0.4% CS and 99.6% water. Finally, the waste product ($S_3$) contains 80% CG, 19.6% water, and 0.4% CS. (All percentages are on a volume basis.)

 Write material balances on water, CS, and CG, then solve the material balances for the volumes $S_2$ through $S_4$.

## 4.5 FLASH DISTILLATION

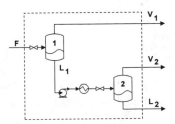

When a hot, pressurized liquid is pumped into a tank (flash unit) at a lower pressure, the liquid boils rapidly. This rapid boiling is called a *flash*. If the liquid contains a mixture of chemicals, the vapor and liquid leaving the flash unit will have different compositions, and the flash unit can be used as a separator. The physical principle involved is vapor–liquid equilibrium: The vapor and the liquid leaving the flash unit are in equilibrium. This allows the composition of the outlet streams to be determined from the operating temperature and pressure of the flash unit. Multiple flash units can be used together to separate multicomponent mixtures.

 A mixture of methanol, butanol, and ethylene glycol is fed to a flash unit operating at 165°C and 7 atm. The liquid from the first flash unit is recompressed, reheated, and sent to a second flash unit operating at 105°C and 1 atm. The compositions of the feed stream $F$ and the three product streams are listed in the following table:

| COMPONENT | MASS FRACTION IN STREAM | | | |
| --- | --- | --- | --- | --- |
| | FEED | $V_1$ | $V_2$ | $L_2$ |
| Methanol | 0.300 | 0.716 | 0.533 | 0.086 |
| Butanol | 0.400 | 0.268 | 0.443 | 0.388 |
| Ethylene Glycol | 0.300 | 0.016 | 0.024 | 0.526 |

The mixture is fed to the process at a rate of 10,000 kg/h. Write material balances for each chemical, and then solve for the mass flow rate of each product stream ($V_1$, $V_2$, $L_2$). A material balance is simply a mathematical statement that all of the methanol (for example) going into the process has to come out again. (This assumes steady state and no chemical reactions.) The methanol balance is as follows

methanol in the Feed = methanol in $V_1$ + methanol in $V_2$ + methanol in $L_2$

$$0.300 \cdot (10{,}000 \text{ kg/h}) = 0.716 \cdot V_1 + 0.533 \cdot V_2 + 0.086 \cdot L_2$$

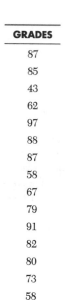

## 4.6  FINDING THE MEDIAN GRADE

It is common for instructors to report the average grade on an examination. An alternative way to let students know how their score compares with the rest of the class is to find the *median* score. If the scores are sorted, the median score is the value in the middle of the data set.

a.  Use the `sort( )` function to sort the 15 scores (elements 0 to 14) listed here, and then display the value of element 7 in the sorted array. Element 7 will hold the median score for the sorted grades.

b.  Check your result by using Mathcad's `median( )` function on the original vector of grades.

## 4.7  CURRENTS IN MULTILOOP CIRCUITS

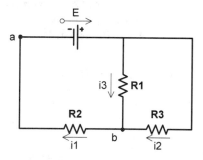

Multiloop circuits are analyzed using Kirchhoff's voltage law, described in Chapter 2, and Kirchhoff's current law, namely,

*At any junction in a circuit, the input current(s) must equal the output current(s).*

The latter is simply a statement of conservation of current: All of the electrons entering a junction have to leave again, at least at steady state.

Applying the current law at point *b* yields

$$i_3 + i_2 = i_1$$

Applying the voltage law to the left loop and the overall loop provides two more equations:

$$E - i_3 R_1 - i_1 R_2 = 0$$
$$E - i_2 R_3 - i_1 R_2 = 0$$

We thus have three equations in the unknowns: $i_1$, $i_2$, $i_3$.

Use the following resistance values, and solve the system of simultaneous equations to determine the current in each portion of the circuit:

$$E = 9 \text{ volts}$$
$$R_1 = 20 \text{ ohms}$$
$$R_2 = 30 \text{ ohms}$$
$$R_3 = 40 \text{ ohms}$$

### 4.8 THE WHEATSTONE BRIDGE

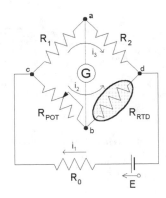

Resistance temperature devices (RTDs) are often used as temperature sensors. As the temperature of the device changes, its resistance changes. If you can determine an RTD's resistance, you can look on a table to find the temperature. A circuit known as a Wheatstone bridge can be used to measure unknown resistances. In the preceding figure, an RTD has been built into the bridge as the unknown resistance.

To use the Wheatstone bridge, the adjustable resistor $R_{POT}$ (called a potentiometer) is adjusted until the galvanometer $G$ shows that points a and b are at the same potential. Once the bridge has been adjusted so that no current is flowing through the galvanometer (because there is no different in potential between a and b), the reading on the potentiometer and the known resistances $R_1$ and $R_2$ can be used to compute the resistance of the RTD.

### How Does It Work?

Because resistors $R_1$ and $R_{POT}$ come together at point c, and we know the voltages at a and b are the same, there must be the same voltage drop across $R_1$ and $R_{POT}$ (not the same current), so

$$i_3 \cdot R_1 = i_2 \cdot R_{POT}$$

Similarly, because $R_2$ and $R_{RTD}$ are connected at point d, we can say that

$$i_3 \cdot R_2 = i_2 \cdot R_{RTD}$$

If you solve for $i_3$ in one equation and substitute into the other, you get

$$R_{RTD} = R_{POT} \frac{R_2}{R_1}$$

In this way, if you know $R_1$ and $R_2$ and have a reading on the potentiometer, you can calculate $R_{RTD}$.

a.  Given the following resistances, what is $R_{RTD}$? Assume that a 9-volt battery is used for E.

$$R_0 = 20 \text{ ohms}$$
$$R_1 = 10 \text{ ohms}$$
$$R_2 = 5 \text{ ohms}$$
$$R_{POT} \text{ adjusted to } 12.3 \text{ ohms}$$

b. Use Kirchoff's current law at either point c or d, and Kirchoff's voltage law to determine the $i_1$, $i_2$, and $i_3$.

## 4.9 STEADY-STATE CONDUCTION I

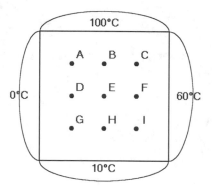

Steady-state conduction in two dimensions is described by Laplace's equation:

$$\frac{\partial^2 T}{\partial x^2} + \frac{\partial^2 T}{\partial y^2} = 0$$

The partial derivatives in Laplace's equation can be replaced by finite differences (see Chapter 7) to obtain approximate solutions giving the expected temperature at various points in the two-dimensional region:

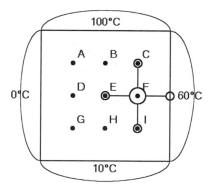

The difference equation is

$$\frac{T_{i-1,j} - 2T_{i,j} + T_{i+1,j}}{(\Delta x)^2} + \frac{T_{i,j-1} - 2T_{i,j} + T_{i,j+1}}{(\Delta y)^2} = 0$$

where $T_{i,j}$ is the temperature at a point $(i,j)$ in the conducting region, $T_{i-1,j}$ is the temperature at the point to the left to point $i,j$, etc. If $\Delta x$ and $\Delta y$ are equal, these two terms can be combined and the subscripts replaced by more descriptive terms:

$$T_{\text{left}} + T_{\text{above}} + T_{\text{right}} + T_{\text{below}} - 4T_{\text{center}} = 0$$

Using this equation at each of the nine points in the region shown generates nine equations in nine unknowns that can be solved simultaneously for the temperature at each point. For example, applying the equation at point F gives the equation

$$T_E + T_C + 60° + T_I - 4T_F = 0$$

Develop the system of nine equations, write them in matrix form, and determine the temperature at points A through I.

### 4.10 STEADY-STATE CONDUCTION II

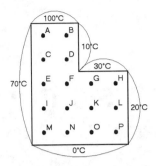

In the previous problem, Laplace's equation was applied to steady-state conduction in a square region. Actually, the equation can be applied to any region composed of rectangles or any shape that can be approximated with rectangles. Again, the final version of the equation presented in the last problem does require that the distance between the points be the same in the $x$ and $y$ directions.

Apply Laplace's equation to the following L-shaped region, and determine the temperatures at points $A$ through $P$.

# 5

# Data Analysis Functions

## RISK ANALYSIS

Each year you can read in the newspapers of earthquakes with terrible consequences in terms of lost lives and property. There have also been serious earthquakes in highly populated areas in California with, relatively speaking, considerably less damage. The difference is *risk analysis* and *risk management*. Because of the serious threat earthquakes pose in many parts of California, the State has spent a great deal of time and effort trying to learn what might happen in an earthquake (risk analysis) and has invested heavily in trying to minimize the consequences of a major earthquake (risk management).

Because engineers work on projects that can impact large numbers of people, safety and risk management is a standard practice. What happens if the device fails? If this power line fails, can we get power to the hospital from another direction? Can we use an inflatable bag to improve passenger safety in an automobile accident? But what about small children in automobiles with airbags? These questions are all related to risk analysis and management.

Understanding the potential risks associated with a process or product requires a thorough knowledge of the process or product, and the ability and willingness to con-

## SECTIONS

- 5.1 Graphing with Mathcad
- 5.2 Statistical Functions
- 5.3 Interpolation
- 5.4 Curve Fitting
- Summary

## OBJECTIVES

*After reading this chapter, you should be able to:*

- To learn how to create graphs in Mathcad, including:
  - Element-by-element graphing using range variables
  - Graphing one vector against another
  - QuickPlots of functions—letting Mathcad automatically evaluate a function over a range of values and plot the result
- To learn about Mathcad's built-in functions for statistical analysis.
- To use Mathcad's interpolation functions, including
  - Linear interpolation
  - Spline interpolation
- To learn to use linear regression fit curves to data.

sider what might possibly go wrong. What would happen if that pipe leaving that vessel of toxic material were to break? There's usually someone who will say, "It'll never happen. Pipes don't just break." While it's true that pipes don't spontaneously give way, they do corrode with time, and a 12-foot truck driving under an 11-foot pipe can remove a pipe instantly. The idea is that you have to be willing to think outside of normal operating procedure to perform a risk analysis.

It takes a lot of work to try to anticipate how a process or product might fail, and to quantify the outcome of a potential failure. If that pipe breaks, how far will the toxin/flame/explosion spread? There are models to help quantify risk, but they require good data on the products and processes involved. Getting the data into a form that the models can use requires a lot of analysis. That's why risk analysis is a good lead-in to a chapter on Mathcad's data analysis functions.

## 5.1 GRAPHING WITH MATHCAD

Engineers spend a lot of time analyzing data. By looking at data from a current design, you can learn what can be changed to make the device, system, or process work better. Mathcad's data analysis functions can provide a lot of help in understanding and evaluating data sets.

One of the most fundamental steps in analyzing data is visualizing the data, usually in the form of a graph. Mathcad provides a variety of graphing options.

### *Plotting Vector against Vector*

The easiest way to create a graph in Mathcad is to simply plot one vector against another. For example, a vector of temperature values can be plotted against a vector of time values. This method works well for many data analysis situations, because the data are often already available in vector form as in the following example:

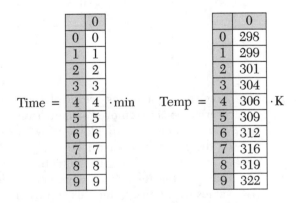

When you plot one vector against another vector, the vectors must each have the same number of elements. The preceding vectors each have 10 elements, so they can be plotted against each other. To create an x–y graph, use the Graph Palette and click on the X–Y Plot button, or use the keyboard shortcut [Shift-2]. The result is as follows:

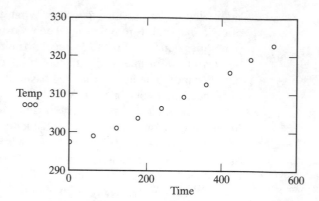

Note that the temperature values look fine, but the time values are not the same as those shown in the Time vector. Mathcad always plots values in its default (base) units. The base unit for temperature (in the default SI unit system) is kelvins, so the temperature values were unaffected. The time values were plotted as Mathcad saved them, in seconds. There is a trick that is sometimes used to get the right values to display on the graph: You can get the values in minutes by dividing the Time on the $x$–axis by minutes, as shown in the following figure:

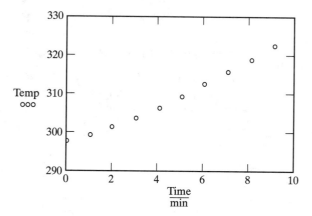

Now the right values are displayed, but the axis labels are hard to interpret. An alternative is to remove the units from the Time and Temp vectors and then plot the values. Then you can add your own axis labels to indicate the units. (Double-click on the graph to add axis labels.)

*Note:* Removing the units from the Temp values is not really necessary in this example, but it has been done here to demonstrate a general approach to graphing values with units. Using this approach, we obtain

$$Time_{plot} := \frac{Time}{min}$$

$$Temp_{plot} := \frac{Temp}{K}$$

The plotted result is

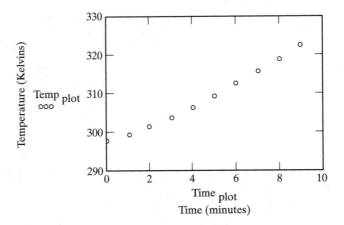

The process of removing the units and plotting only values is exactly what is being accomplished with the "trick" used to plot time on the previous graph. Hopefully, making the process more explicit and including units with the axis labels makes the graph easier to read.

### Element-by-Element Plotting

In older versions of Mathcad, the standard method for graphing was to plot one element of a vector against one element of another vector. This method is still available and can sometimes be convenient. To plot the temperature and time vectors element by element, we must define a range variable containing as many elements as each of the vectors. This is easily done using the last(v) function as follows:

$$i := 0 .. \text{last(Time)}$$

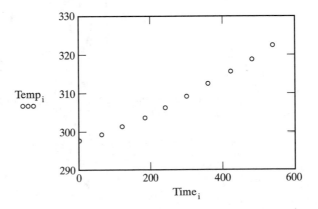

The index of the last element of the Time vector was 9, so the range variable, i, was defined over the range 0 to 9. The range indicator ("..", or ellipsis) is entered by using the [ ; ] (semicolon) key. The subscripts on the Temp and Time vectors are array index subscripts, entered by using the [ [ ] (left square bracket). While this plot looks the same as that created by plotting the vectors directly, the use of the range variable gives you a lot of control over how the elements are plotted. For example, you could change the order of the plotted elements by changing the subscript on the Temp vector. The graph will then look like this:

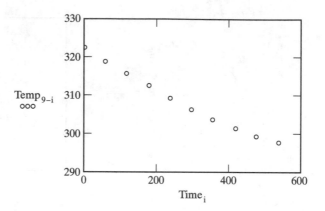

## QuickPlots

The final method for creating a graph using Mathcad is called a QuickPlot, which is used when you want to see what a function looks like. You proceed by creating an $x$–$y$ graph and then entering the function on the $y$-axis. Functions always have one or more parameters, such as the x in the function sin(x). Now, enter the parameter on the $x$-axis. By default, Mathcad will automatically evaluate the function for a range of parameter values, from −10 to +10. For sin(x), the results will look like this:

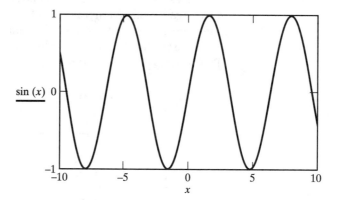

To plot a different range, simply click on the $x$-axis of the graph and change the displayed axis limits.

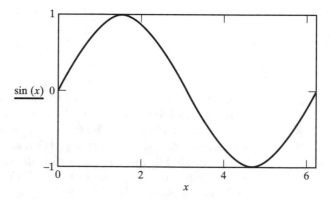

Here, the $x$–axis limits were changed to 0 and $2\pi$ to plot one complete sine wave.

**PRACTICE!**

**a.** Try QuickPlots of other common functions, like ln(x) and exp(x).

**b.** See what Quickplots of the following functions look like (the Φ is available on the Greek Palette, the absolute value operator on the Arithmetic Palette):

- if (sin(x) > 0, −sin(x), sin(x))
- $\Phi(|\mathrm{mod}(x,2)| -1)$—*this uses the Heaviside step function to generate a square wave*

### *Modifying Graphical Display Attributes*

You can change the appearance of a graph by double clicking anywhere on the graph. This will bring up the graph-formatting dialog box. From this dialog box, you can change the

- Axis characteristics (linear or logarithmic plots, for example, and whether or not grid lines are displayed)
- Trace (curve) characteristics, such as the symbol and line style
- Label text and position.

For example, we can use the formatting dialog box to show the curve by using a dashed line and adding grid lines and labels to the sine graph. The necessary changes to the dialog boxes are circled in the following figures:

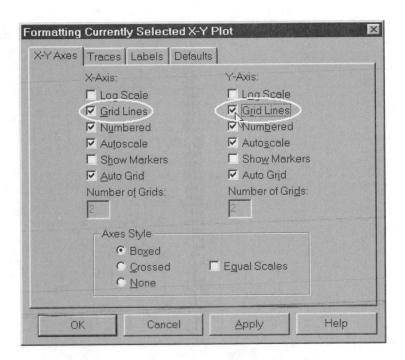

To change a graph's format, double click in the middle of the graph to open the formatting dialog box. Then turn on the grid lines by using the check boxes on the X–Y Axes panel. Next, switch to the Traces panel and choose a dashed line for trace 1. (There is only one trace, or curve, displayed on this graph.)

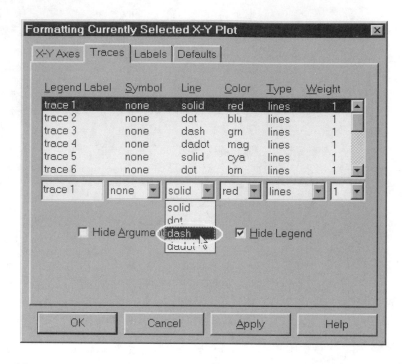

Finally, add a title and axis labels to the graph by using the Labels panel. The screen should look like this:

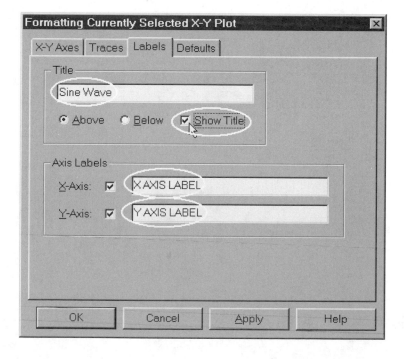

Then, click on the dialog's OK button to make the changes to the graph. The graph will look like this:

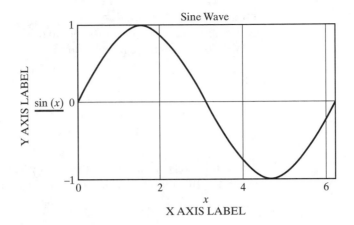

## 5.2  STATISTICAL FUNCTIONS

Mathcad provides several functions for commonly used statistical calculations, including `mean(A)`, `stdev(A)`, and `var(A)` to calculate, respectively, the mean, standard deviation, and variance of a population. As the following examples illustrate, these functions work with vectors or matrices, and they can handle units:

| APPLICATIONS: SAMPLES AND POPULATIONS |
| --- |

- The transparency of each windshield on an assembly line might be measured before the windshield is installed. Since every windshield is included in the data set, the data set is called a *population*.
- One out of every thousand windshields might be tested for impact strength (i.e., broken).

The results from the broken windshields are used to represent the impact strength of all the windshields. Since the data set does not include all of the windshields, it is called a *sample*. Any time you use a sample, you need to be careful to try to get a *representative* sample (usually a random sample).

$$C = \begin{bmatrix} 1 & 1 \\ 2 & 8 \\ 3 & 27 \\ 4 & 64 \\ 5 & 128 \end{bmatrix} \qquad a = \begin{bmatrix} 3 \\ 2 \\ 7 \\ 4 \end{bmatrix}$$

$C_{avg} := mean(C)$  $\qquad$  $C_{avg} = 24$

$a_{avg} := mean(a)$  $\qquad$  $a_{avg} = 4$

$Temp_{avg} := mean(Temp)$  $\qquad$  $Temp_{avg} = 308.733 \cdot K$

$Temp_{std} := stdev(Temp)$  $\qquad$  $Temp_{std} = 7.961 \cdot K$

$Temp_{var} := var(Temp)$  $\qquad$  $Temp_{var} = 63.377 \cdot K^2$

Mathcad's help files indicate that the functions for the standard deviation and variance of a sample are `Stdev(v)` and `Var(v)`, respectively. The uppercase `S` and `V` were used to differentiate the functions for populations and samples. However, these sample functions work only for vectors and do not handle units. An alternative is to compute the sample values from the population values:

$$\text{stdevS(A)} := \text{stdev(A)} \cdot \sqrt{\frac{\text{rows(A)} \cdot \text{cols(A)}}{\text{rows(A)} \cdot \text{cols(A)} - 1}}$$

$$\text{varS(A)} := \text{var(A)} \cdot \left(\frac{\text{rows(A)} \cdot \text{cols(A)}}{\text{rows(A)} \cdot \text{cols(A)} - 1}\right)$$

These functions are not in Mathcad, so you must include the definitions in your worksheet, but they do work with both vectors and matrices, and they can handle units:

$$\text{stdevS(Temp)} = 8.392 \cdot \text{K}$$
$$\text{varS(Temp)} = 70.418 \cdot \text{K}^2$$

**PRACTICE!**

The standard deviation lets you know how far a typical value is from the mean value of the data set. The data sets shown here have approximately the same mean value. Which has the greatest standard deviation? Use Mathcad's `stdev( )` function to check your result.

$$\text{Set}_1 = \begin{bmatrix} 2.5 \\ 2.5 \\ 2.5 \\ 2.5 \\ 2.5 \end{bmatrix} \qquad \text{Set}_2 = \begin{bmatrix} 2.2 \\ 2.6 \\ 2.6 \\ 2.5 \\ 2.4 \end{bmatrix} \qquad \text{Set}_3 = \begin{bmatrix} 1.6 \\ 1.6 \\ 2.8 \\ 2.1 \\ 3.8 \end{bmatrix}$$

## 5.3 INTERPOLATION

If you have a data set—for example, a set of temperature values at various times—and you want to predict a temperature at a new time, you could fit a function to the data and calculate the predicted temperature at the new time. Or you can interpolate between data set values. Mathcad provides a number of functions for linear interpolation and cubic spline interpolation. The linear interpolation function, `linterp(vx,vy,x_new)`, predicts a new $y$ value at the new $x$ value (specified in the function's argument list) by using a linear interpolation and by using the x values in the data set nearest to the new x value.

As an example, consider the temperature and time data presented in Chapter 4:

| Time = | | 0 | |
|---|---|---|---|
| | 0 | 0 | |
| | 1 | 1 | |
| | 2 | 2 | |
| | 3 | 3 | |
| | 4 | 4 | ·min |
| | 5 | 5 | |
| | 6 | 6 | |
| | 7 | 7 | |
| | 8 | 8 | |
| | 9 | 9 | |

| Temp = | | 0 | |
|---|---|---|---|
| | 0 | 298 | |
| | 1 | 299 | |
| | 2 | 301 | |
| | 3 | 304 | |
| | 4 | 306 | ·K |
| | 5 | 309 | |
| | 6 | 312 | |
| | 7 | 316 | |
| | 8 | 319 | |
| | 9 | 322 | |

The temperature vector includes temperatures at 2 and 3 minutes, but not at 2.3 minutes. We can use the `linterp( )` function to interpolate between the temperature values at 2 and 3 minutes to predict the temperature at 2.3 minutes:

$$\text{Temp}_{\text{interp}} := \text{linterp}(\text{Time, Temp, } 2.3 \cdot \text{min})$$
$$\text{Temp}_{\text{interp}} = 302.165 \cdot \text{K}$$

You can also use `linterp( )` to extrapolate beyond the limits of a data set, although extrapolation is always risky. The temperature data were collected from time 0 to 9 minutes. We can extrapolate to a time of 20 minutes by using `linterp( )`:

$$\text{Temp}_{\text{interp}} := \text{linterp}(\text{Time, Temp, } 20 \cdot \text{min})$$
$$\text{Temp}_{\text{interp}} = 360.398 \cdot \text{K}$$

Extrapolation will give you a result, but there is no guarantee that it is correct. Since the result is outside the range of the data set, the result is uncertain. For this data set, the heater might have been turned off after 9 minutes, and the temperatures might have started to decrease with time. Because the data set only includes temperatures between 0 and 9 minutes, we cannot know what happened at later times.

An alternative to linear interpolation is *cubic spline interpolation*. This technique puts a curve (a cubic polynomial) through every three adjacent data points, which results in a curve that passes through each data point with continuous first and second derivatives. Interpolation for values between points can be done using the cubic polynomial. To use cubic spline interpolation in Mathcad, you first need to fit the cubic polynomial to the data by using the `cspline(vx, vy)` function. This function returns a vector of second-derivative values, `vs`, that is then used in the interpolation, which is performed with the `interp(vs, vx, vy, x_new)` function:

$$\text{vs} := \text{cspline}(\text{Time, Temp})$$
$$\text{Temp}_{\text{interp}} := \text{interp}(\text{vs, Time, Temp, } 2.3 \cdot \text{min})$$
$$\text{Temp}_{\text{interp}} = 302.136 \cdot \text{K}$$

You can also extrapolate with the cubic spline, but this is risky. Because the cubic spline technique fits each group of three adjacent points with a cubic polynomial, it runs into trouble at each end of the data set, since the first and last points do not have another point on each side. Hence, the cubic spline method must do something special for these endpoints. Mathcad provides three methods for handling the endpoints:

- `cspline( )`—creates a spline curve that is cubic at the endpoints.
- `pspline( )`—creates a spline curve that is parabolic at the endpoints.
- `lspline( )`—creates a spline curve that is linear at the endpoints.

These spline functions will all yield the same interpolated results for interior points, but can give widely varying results if you extrapolate your data set:

$$\text{vs} := \text{cspline}(\text{Time, Temp}) \qquad \text{interp}(\text{vs, Time, Temp, } 20 \cdot \text{min}) = 365.401 \cdot \text{K}$$
$$\text{vs} := \text{pspline}(\text{Time, Temp}) \qquad \text{interp}(\text{vs, Time, Temp, } 20 \cdot \text{min}) = 368.65 \cdot \text{K}$$
$$\text{vs} := \text{lspline}(\text{Time, Temp}) \qquad \text{interp}(\text{vs, Time, Temp, } 20 \cdot \text{min}) = 325.525 \cdot \text{K}$$

**CAUTIONS**

1. Extrapolation (predicting values outside the range of the data set) should be avoided whenever possible. The temperatures used in the foregoing example were recorded for times ranging from 0 to 9 minutes. Predicting a temperature at 9.2 minutes is safer than predicting one at 90 or 900 minutes, but you

are still making an assumption that nothing changed between 9.0 and 9.2 minutes. (The researcher might have turned off the heater, and the temperatures might have started falling.)

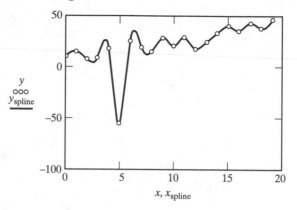

2.  Cubic spline fits to noisy data can produce some amazing results. In the accompanying graph, an outlier at $x = 5$ was included in the data set to demonstrate how this single bad point affects the spline curve for adjacent points as well. Interpolation using these curves is a very bad idea. Regression to find the "best fit" curve, then using the regression result to predict new values is a better idea for noisy data.

## Using a QuickPlot to Plot the Spline Curve

If you want to see what the spline curve looks like, Mathcad's QuickPlot feature will allow you to see the curve with little effort. Since a QuickPlot will evaluate a function multiple times over a range of values, simply let Mathcad evaluate the `interp( )` function many times and display the result. For the temperature/time data, this means calculating the second-derivative values by using `cspline( )` (or `pspline( )` or `lspline( )`) and then creating the Quickplot.

In the following figure, the `t` in the `interp( )` function and on the $x$-axis is a dummy variable. Mathcad evaluates the `interp( )` function for values of `t` between −10 and 10 (by default) and displays the result. We need to change the limits on the $x$-axis to coincide with the time values in the data set, 0 to 9 minutes. To change the axis limits, click on the $x$-axis and then edit the limit values.

$$vs := cspline(Time, Temp)$$

*Note:* The graph also demonstrates why it is not a good idea to extrapolate by using the `interp( )` function. The data set gives no evidence that the temperatures were very high before the experiment started (or negative times), but that is what the `cspline( )` fit predicts. The results obtained by using `lspline( )` would be very different. Check it out! The spline fit of the actual data set (not extrapolated) with the *x*-axis limits changed is shown.

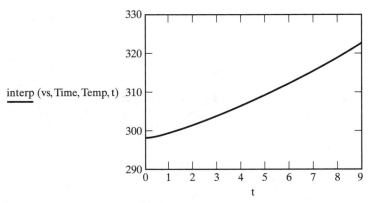

interp (vs, Time, Temp, t)

The curve looks well behaved in this range of times, typical of a spline fit to clean data.

**PRACTICE!**

The following "noisy" data were created by adding random numbers to the "clean" data set:

$$x = \begin{bmatrix} 0.0 \\ 0.5 \\ 1.0 \\ 1.5 \\ 2.0 \\ 2.5 \\ 3.0 \end{bmatrix} \qquad y_{clean} = \begin{bmatrix} 0.00 \\ 0.48 \\ 0.84 \\ 1.00 \\ 0.91 \\ 0.60 \\ 0.14 \end{bmatrix} \qquad y_{noisy} = \begin{bmatrix} 0.24 \\ 0.60 \\ 0.69 \\ 1.17 \\ 0.91 \\ 0.36 \\ 0.18 \end{bmatrix}$$

**a.** Compare the cubic spline fit of each data set by plotting the cubic spline interpolation for each data set.

**b.** Use the `interp( )` function to predict the *y*-value corresponding to x = 1.5 for each data set.

## 5.4 CURVE FITTING

### Simple Linear Regression

Mathcad provides a number of functions to fit curves to data and to use fitted curves to predict new values. One of the most common curve-fitting applications is *linear regression.* Simple linear regression is carried out in Mathcad by using two or three functions: `slope(vx,vy)`, `intercept(vx,vy)`, and `corr(vx,vy)`. These functions respectively return the *slope, intercept,* and *correlation coefficient* of the best fit straight line through the data represented by the x and y vectors. For example, for the time–temperature data of the preceding section,

$$b := \text{intercept (Time, Temp)} \qquad b = 296.369 \cdot K$$

$$m := \text{slope (Time, Temp)} \qquad m = 2.756 \cdot \frac{K}{\min}$$

The temperature values predicted by the model equation can be calculated from the slope and intercept values by using a range variable to keep track of the times. Then the quality of the fit can be determined by using the `corr( )` function:

$$i := 0 \mathrel{..} \text{last(Time)}$$

$$\text{Temp}_{\text{pred}_i} := b + m \cdot \text{Time}_1$$

$$R2 := \text{corr}(\text{Temp}, \text{Temp}_{\text{pred}})^2 \qquad R2 = 0.98904$$

Here, the correlation coefficient was squared to calculate the *coefficient of determination* (usually called the $R^2$ value) for the regression. An $R^2$ value of 1 implies that the regression line is a perfect fit to the data. The value 0.98904 suggests that the regression line is a pretty good fit to the data, but it is always a good idea to plot the original data together with the regression line. The result looks like this:

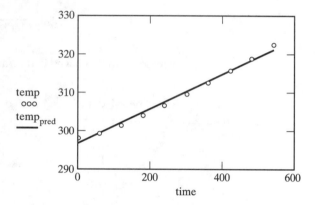

With this plot, we can clearly see that the actual curve of temperature versus time is not linear. This becomes quite apparent if you plot the *residuals:*

$$\text{Residual}_i := \text{Temp}_i - \text{Temp}_{\text{pred}_i}$$

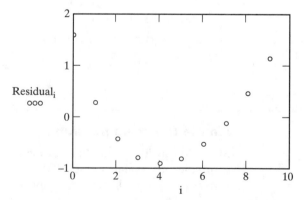

A residual plot should show randomly scattered points. Obvious trends in a residual plot, such as the "U" shape in the preceding plot, suggest that the equation used to fit the data was a poor choice. Here, it is saying that the linear equation is not a good choice for fitting this nonlinear data.

The foregoing example was included as a reminder that, while you can perform a simple (straight-line) linear regression on any data set, it is not always a good idea to do so. Nonlinear data require a more sophisticated curve-fitting approach.

**PRACTICE!**

Two sets of y values are shown. The noisy data were calculated from the clean data by adding random values. Try linear regression on these data sets. What is the impact of noisy data on the calculated slope, intercept, and $R^2$ value?

$$x = \begin{bmatrix} 0 \\ 1 \\ 2 \\ 3 \\ 4 \\ 5 \end{bmatrix} \qquad y_{\text{clean}} = \begin{bmatrix} 1 \\ 2 \\ 3 \\ 4 \\ 5 \\ 6 \end{bmatrix} \qquad y_{\text{noisy}} = \begin{bmatrix} 0.85 \\ 1.91 \\ 3.03 \\ 3.96 \\ 5.10 \\ 5.90 \end{bmatrix}$$

**PROFESSIONAL SUCCESS**

*Visualize your data and results.*

Numbers, such as the data set shown below, are a handy way to store information, but for most of us, a data set is hard to visualize.

| x | y | x | y |
|---|---|---|---|
| −1.0000 | −0.5478 | 0.1367 | 0.0004 |
| −0.9900 | −0.4252 | 0.1543 | 0.3042 |
| −0.9626 | −0.3277 | 0.2837 | 0.5407 |
| −0.9577 | −0.7865 | 0.4081 | 0.0122 |
| −0.9111 | −0.2327 | 0.4242 | 0.7593 |
| −0.8391 | −0.9654 | 0.5403 | 0.0304 |
| −0.7597 | −0.1030 | 0.6469 | 0.0565 |
| −0.7481 | −0.9997 | 0.6603 | 0.9821 |
| −0.6536 | −0.9791 | 0.7539 | 0.0999 |
| −0.5477 | −0.0319 | 0.8439 | 0.9617 |
| −0.5328 | −0.8888 | 0.9074 | 0.2277 |
| −0.4161 | −0.0130 | 0.9147 | 0.8781 |
| −0.2921 | −0.0043 | 0.9602 | 0.7795 |
| −0.2752 | −0.5260 | 0.9887 | 0.4184 |
| −0.1455 | −0.0005 | 0.9912 | 0.6536 |
| 0.0044 | 0.0088 | 1.0000 | 0.5403 |

A quick glance at the data at the left suggests that the y values get bigger as the x values get bigger. To try to describe there data, linear regression could be performed to calculate a slope and an intercept:

m := slope(x,y)      m = 0.653
b := intercept(x,y)      b = $1.211 \cdot 10^{-3}$
r2 := corr(x,y)$^2$      r2 = 0.667

But by graphing the data, it becomes clear that simple linear regression is not appropriate for this data set:

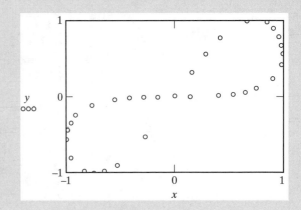

### Generalized Linear Regression

The `linfit(vx, vy, vf)` function performs a linear regression with an arbitrary linear model. For example, we might try to improve the fit of the regression line to the temperature–time data by using a second-order polynomial, such as

$$\text{Temp}_{\text{pred}} = b_0 + b_1 \text{ time} + b_2 \text{ time}^2$$

The `linfit( )` function will find the coefficients $b_0$, $b_1$, and $b_2$ that best fit the model to the data. However, the `linfit( )` function does not handle units, so we first remove the units from the `Time` and `Temp` vectors:

$$\text{time} := \frac{\text{Time}}{\text{min}} \qquad \text{temp} := \frac{\text{Temp}}{\text{K}}$$

Then we define the linear model. The second-order polynomial has three terms: a constant, a term with time raised to the first power, and a term with time raised to the second power. We define this functionality in the vector function `f( )` and then perform the regression by using the `linfit( )` function. The coefficients computed by `linfit( )` are stored in the vector b. For example, for the time–temperature data,

$$f(x) := \begin{bmatrix} 1 \\ x \\ x^2 \end{bmatrix}$$

$$b := \text{linfit(time, temp, f)}$$

$$b = \begin{bmatrix} 297.721 \\ 1.742 \\ 0.113 \end{bmatrix}$$

We can then use the coefficients with the second-order polynomial to compute predicted temperature values at each time:

$$\text{temp}_{\text{pred}_i} := b_0 + b_1 \cdot \text{time}_i + b_2 \cdot (\text{time}_i)^2$$

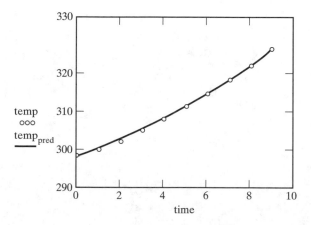

As the preceding graph shows, the second-order polynomial appears to do a much better job of fitting the data than the linear model does. We can quantify the "goodness of fit" using the `corr( )` function:

$$r2 := \text{corr}(\text{temp}, \text{temp}_{\text{pred}})^2$$
$$r2 = 0.99961$$

The $R^2$ value is closer to 1 than the $R^2$ we obtained by using simple slope–intercept linear regression, indicating that the polynomial is a better fit than the straight line obtained by using simple linear regression.

**PRACTICE!**

Look at the following data, and decide whether or not to include an intercept in the regression model:

$$x = \begin{bmatrix} 0.0 \\ 0.5 \\ 1.0 \\ 1.5 \\ 2.0 \\ 2.5 \\ 3.0 \end{bmatrix} \qquad y_{\text{clean}} = \begin{bmatrix} 0.00 \\ 0.48 \\ 0.84 \\ 1.00 \\ 0.91 \\ 0.60 \\ 0.14 \end{bmatrix}$$

*Note:* These are the same data used in the "Practice!" box for the spline fit (to save typing).

Now try using the following polynomial models to fit the data using the `linfit( )` function:

**a.** $y_p = b_0 + b_1 x + b_2 x^2$     or,     $y_p = b_0 x + b_1 x^2$

**b.** $y_p = b_0 + b_1 x + b_2 x^2 + b_3 x^3$     or,     $y_p = b_0 x + b_1 x^2 + b_2 x^3$

### Other Linear Models

The models used in the earlier examples, namely,

$$\text{temp}_{\text{pred}} = b + m \cdot \text{time}$$

and

$$\text{temp}_{\text{pred}} = b_0 + b_1 \cdot \text{time} + b_2 \cdot \text{time}^2$$

are both linear models (linear in the coefficients, not in `time`). Since `linfit( )` works with any linear model, you could try fitting equations such as

$$\text{temp}_{\text{pred}} = b_0 + b_1 \cdot \sinh(\text{time}) + b_2 \cdot \text{atan}(\text{time}^2)$$

or

$$\text{temp}_{\text{pred}} = b_0 \cdot \exp(\text{time}^{0.5}) + b_1 \cdot \ln(\text{time}^3)$$

These equations are linear in the coefficients (the b's) and are compatible with `linfit( )`. The `F(x)` function for each equation would look like this:

$$F(x) := \begin{bmatrix} 1 \\ \sinh(x) \\ \text{atan}(x) \end{bmatrix} \qquad F(x) := \begin{bmatrix} \exp(x^{0.5}) \\ x^3 \end{bmatrix}$$

There is no reason to suspect that either of these last two models would be a good fit to the temperature–time data. In general, you choose a linear model either from some theory that suggests a relationship between your variables or from looking at a plot of the data set.

## PRACTICE!

A plot of the data used in the spline fit and polynomial regression "Practice!" boxes has a shape something like half a sine wave. Try fitting the data with a linear model such as

**a.** $y_p = b_0 + b_1 \sin(x)$

**b.** $y_p = b_0 + b_1 \cos(x)$

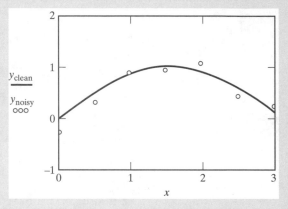

Do the following data suggest that the model should include an intercept?

$$
x = \begin{bmatrix} 0.0 \\ 0.5 \\ 1.0 \\ 1.5 \\ 2.0 \\ 2.5 \\ 3.0 \end{bmatrix}
\qquad
y_{\text{clean}} = \begin{bmatrix} 0.00 \\ 0.48 \\ 0.84 \\ 1.00 \\ 0.91 \\ 0.60 \\ 0.14 \end{bmatrix}
\qquad
y_{\text{noisy}} = \begin{bmatrix} -0.25 \\ 0.33 \\ 0.88 \\ 0.92 \\ 1.07 \\ 0.44 \\ 0.25 \end{bmatrix}
$$

## APPLICATIONS: FITTING PHYSICAL PROPERTY DATA

Silane is an interesting chemical that is being increasingly employed in the manufacture of silicon wafers and chips used in the electronics industry. It is highly flammable and, under the right conditions, will spontaneously ignite upon contact with air. The manufacturers of silane must take special precautions to minimize the risks associated with this gas.

**SILANE**

| VAPOR PRESSURE (Pa) | |
|---|---|
| $T_{MIN}$ (K) | 88.48 |
| $T_{MAX}$ (K) | 269.7 |

| TEMP | $P_{VAPOR}$ |
|---|---|
| 88.48 | 21 |
| 97.54 | 167 |
| 106.60 | 640 |
| 115.66 | 2227 |

| TEMP | $P_{VAPOR}$ |
|---|---|
| 124.72 | 6110 |
| 133.79 | 14144 |
| 142.85 | 30318 |
| 151.91 | 57430 |
| 160.97 | 100078 |
| 170.03 | 163913 |
| 179.09 | 254015 |
| 188.15 | 378009 |
| 197.21 | 541607 |
| 206.27 | 754829 |
| 215.33 | 1027536 |
| 224.40 | 1372259 |
| 233.46 | 1804187 |
| 242.52 | 2341104 |
| 251.58 | 3006269 |
| 260.64 | 3827011 |
| 269.70 | 4838992 |

Analyzing the risks associated with possible accidents is an important part of a chemical facility's safety program and a big part of some chemical engineers' jobs. There are computer programs to help perform risk analyses, but they require some knowledge of the chemical, physical, and biomedical properties of the chemicals involved. Risk analysis programs have been written to use standardized fitting equations, so if you add your own information, it must be in a standard form. The accompanying silane vapor pressure data were calculated by using the ChemCad Physical Properties Database.[1]

## Standard Fitting Equation for Vapor Pressure[2]

The standard equation for fitting a curve to vapor pressure $p^*$ is

$$\ln(p^*) = a + b/T + c\ln(T) + dT^e$$

You must specify $a$ and $b$; $a$, $b$ and $c$; or $a$, $b$, $c$, $d$, and $e$. If $e$ is used, the equation becomes nonlinear, and other techniques are used to estimate the value of $e$. For silane, the value of $e$ is expected to be 1.

To try fitting this data by using the first three terms ($a$, $b$ and $c$), we would use the `linfit( )` function with the `f( )` vector defined as

$$f(x) := \begin{bmatrix} 1 \\ \dfrac{1}{x} \\ \ln(x) \end{bmatrix}$$

The coefficients themselves would be computed by `linfit( )` by using the *vectorize* operator (from the Matrix Palette) on the natural logarithm function to take the log of each element of the $P_{vapor}$ vector:

$$\text{coeffs} := \text{linfit}(\text{Temp}, \overrightarrow{\ln(P_{vapor})}, f)$$

$$\text{coeffs} = \begin{bmatrix} 30.303 \\ -1.802 \cdot 10^3 \\ -1.494 \end{bmatrix}$$

Finally, we can plot the original data and the predicted vapor pressures by using the computed coefficients, just to make sure that the process worked and to verify that the last term is not required.

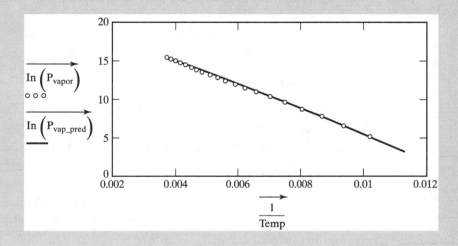

[1] ChemCad is a product of Chemstations, Inc., Houston, TX.
[2] *ChemCad User Guide*, version III, p. 11.64.

## SUMMARY

In this chapter, you learned to use Mathcad's built-in functions for data analysis. You learned to make *X–Y* graphs from data, to calculate statistical values from data, to interpolate between data set values, and to fit curves (linear models) to data. You also have learned about the risk associated with extrapolating data, especially with nonlinear methods like cubic splines.

## MATHCAD SUMMARY

### X-Y GRAPHS
#### VECTOR AGAINST VECTOR:

1. Select X-Y Plot from the Graph Palette.
2. Enter the name of your vector of independent values on the *x*-axis.
3. Enter the name of your vector of dependent values on the *y*-axis.

#### ELEMENT BY ELEMENT:

1. Declare a range variable starting at 0 and going to last($v$), where $v$ is one of your data set vectors.
2. Select X-Y Plot from the Graph Palette.
3. Enter the name of your vector of independent values on the *x*-axis—with an index subscript containing the range variable.
4. Enter the name of your vector of dependent values on the *y*-axis—with an index subscript containing the range variable.

#### QUICKPLOT:

1. Select X-Y Plot from the Graph Palette.
2. Enter your function name on the *y*–axis, with a dummy variable as an argument.
3. Enter the dummy variable on the *x*-axis.
4. Adjust the *x*-axis limits to change the displayed range.

#### STATISTICAL FUNCTIONS:

mean(A)    Returns the mean (arithmetic average) of the values in *A*.
stdev(A)   Returns the population standard deviation of the values in *A*.
var(A)     Returns the population variance of the values in *A*.

#### INTERPOLATION:

linterp(vx, vy, $x_{new}$)    Returns the *y* value corresponding to $x = x_{new}$, computed by using linear interpolation of the *x* and *y* data.

cspline(vx, vy)    Returns the vector of second derivatives that specify a spline curve that is cubic at the endpoints.

pspline(vx, vy)    Returns the vector of second derivatives that specify a spline curve that is parabolic at the endpoints.

| `lspline(vx,vy)` | Returns the vector of second derivatives that specify a spline curve that is linear at the endpoints. |
| `interp(vs,vx,vy,x`$_{new}$`)` | Uses the vector of second derivatives from any of the spline functions previously listed and returns the $y$ value corresponding to $x = x_{new}$, which is computed by using spline interpolation of the $x$ and $y$ data. |

**REGRESSION:**

| `slope (vx,vy)` | Returns the slope of the best fit (minimum total squared error) straight line through the data in $vx$ and $vy$. |
| `intercept(vx,vy)` | Returns the intercept of the best fit straight line through the data in $vx$ and $vy$. |
| `corr(vx,vy)` | Returns the coefficient of correlation (usually called $R$) of the best fit straight line through the data in $vx$ and $vy$. The coefficient of determination, $R^2$, can be computed from $R$ and is more commonly used. |
| `linfit(vx,vy,vf)` | Returns the coefficients that best fit the linear model described by $vf$ to the data in $vx$ and $vy$. The vector $vf$ is a vector of functions you provide that describes the linear model you want to use to fit to the data. |

# Problems

### 5.1  SIMPLE LINEAR REGRESSION

Plot each of the following three data sets to see whether a straight line through each set of points seems reasonable. If so, use the `slope( )` and `intercept( )` functions to calculate the regression coefficients for the set. (The same $x$ data have been used in each example to minimize typing.)

| x | y₁ | y₂ | y₃ |
|---|-----|------|-------|
| 0 | 2 | 0.4 | 10.2 |
| 1 | 5 | 3.6 | 4.2 |
| 2 | 8 | 10.0 | 12.6 |
| 3 | 11 | 9.5 | 11.7 |
| 4 | 14 | 12.0 | 28.5 |
| 5 | 17 | 17.1 | 42.3 |
| 6 | 20 | 20.4 | 73.6 |
| 7 | 23 | 21.7 | 112.1 |

### 5.2  CHOOSING A FITTING FUNCTION

Half the challenge of regression analysis is choosing the right fitting function. The purpose of this exercise is to demonstrate the general shape of some typical fitting functions and then to have you choose an appropriate function and fit a curve to some data.

### Typical Fitting Functions

Make QuickPlots of the following functions over the indicated range of the independent variable x:

| FUNCTION | COEFFICIENTS | RANGE |
|---|---|---|
| $a + bx$ | $a = 5$ | $0 < x < 10$ |
| | $b = 1$ | |
| $a + bx + cx^2$ | $a = 5$ | $0 < x < 10$ |
| | $b = 1$ | |
| | $c = 1$ | |
| $a + bx + cx^2 + dx^3$ | $a = -20$ | $0 < x < 10$ |
| | $b = 50$ | |
| | $c = -10$ | |
| | $d = 0.6$ | |
| $a + b \ln(x)$ | $a = 2$ | $0 < x < 1$ |
| | $b = 1$ | |
| $a + be^x$ | $a = 2$ | $0 < x < 3$ |
| | $b = 1$ | |
| $a + be^{-x}$ | $a = 2$ | $0 < x < 3$ |
| | $b = 1$ | |
| $a + b/x$ | $a = 1$ | $0 < x < 1$ |
| | $b = 1$ | |

| x | y |
|---|---|
| 0.4 | 38.9 |
| 0.9 | 19.8 |
| 1.4 | 14.2 |
| 1.9 | 10.8 |
| 2.4 | 9.8 |
| 2.9 | 7.3 |
| 3.4 | 7.5 |
| 3.9 | 4.6 |
| 4.4 | 6.6 |
| 4.9 | 6.5 |
| 5.4 | 5.3 |
| 5.9 | 5.0 |
| 6.4 | 3.3 |
| 6.9 | 5.3 |
| 7.4 | 4.9 |

### Selecting and Fitting a Function to Data

Now graph the data shown, and select an appropriate fitting function. Use `linfit( )` to regress the data with your selected function. Plot the original data and the values predicted by your fitting function on the same graph to visually verify the fit.

## 5.3 THERMOCOUPLE CALIBRATION

Thermocouples are made by joining two dissimilar metal wires. Contact between the two metals results in a small, but measurable, voltage drop across the junction. This voltage drop changes as the temperature of the junction changes; thus, the thermocouple can be used to measure temperature if you know the relationship between temperature and voltage. Equations for common types of thermocouples are available, or you can simply take a few data points and prepare a calibration curve. This is especially easy for thermocouples because, for small temperature ranges, the relationship between temperature and voltage is nearly linear.

| T (°C) | V (mV) |
|---|---|
| 10 | 0.397 |
| 20 | 0.796 |
| 30 | 1.204 |
| 40 | 1.612 |
| 50 | 2.023 |
| 60 | 2.436 |
| 70 | 2.851 |
| 80 | 3.267 |
| 90 | 3.662 |

a. Use the `slope( )` and `intercept( )` functions to find the coefficients of a straight line through the following data:

   *Note:* The thermocouple voltage changes because the temperature changes—that is, the voltage *depends* on the temperature. For regression, the independent variable (temperature) should always be on the x-axis, and the dependent variable (voltage) should be on the y-axis.

b. Calculate a predicted voltage at each temperature, and plot the original data and the predicted values together to make sure that your calibration curve actually fits the data.

## 5.4 ORIFICE METER CALIBRATION

| Q ft³/min | ΔP psi |
|-----------|--------|
| 3.9 | 0.13 |
| 7.9 | 0.52 |
| 11.8 | 1.18 |
| 15.7 | 2.09 |
| 19.6 | 3.27 |
| 23.6 | 4.71 |
| 27.5 | 6.41 |
| 31.4 | 8.37 |
| 35.3 | 10.59 |
| 39.3 | 13.08 |

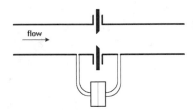

Orifice meters are commonly used to measure flow rates, but they are highly nonlinear devices. Because of this nonlinearity, special care must be taken when preparing calibration curves for these meters. The equation relating the flow rate Q, to the pressure drop across the orifice ΔP (the measured variable) is

$$Q = \frac{A_o C_o}{\sqrt{1 - \beta^4}} \sqrt{\frac{2 g_c \Delta P}{\rho}}$$

For purposes of creating a calibration curve, the details of the equation are unimportant (as long as the other terms stay constant). What is necessary is that we see the theoretical relationship between Q and ΔP, namely, that

$$Q \propto \sqrt{\Delta P}$$

Also, the pressure drop across the orifice plate depends on the flow rate, not the other way around. So $\sqrt{\Delta P}$ should be regressed as the dependent variable (y values) and the Q as the independent variable (x values).

| x | y |
|-------|-------|
| 0.000 | 0.000 |
| 0.022 | 0.066 |
| 0.046 | 0.133 |
| 0.071 | 0.201 |
| 0.098 | 0.269 |
| 0.126 | 0.335 |
| 0.156 | 0.399 |
| 0.189 | 0.461 |
| 0.224 | 0.519 |
| 0.261 | 0.574 |
| 0.302 | 0.626 |
| 0.346 | 0.674 |
| 0.393 | 0.720 |
| 0.445 | 0.762 |
| 0.502 | 0.802 |
| 0.565 | 0.839 |
| 0.634 | 0.874 |
| 0.710 | 0.907 |
| 0.796 | 0.939 |
| 0.891 | 0.970 |
| 1.000 | 1.000 |

a. Using the accompanying data, regress Q and $\sqrt{\Delta P}$ to create a calibration curve for this orifice meter.

b. Calculate and plot predicted values together with the original data to check your results.

*Note:* If you use the `slope( )` and `intercept( )` functions in this problem, you will need to use the *vectorize* operator as well, because taking the square root of an entire matrix is not defined. The vectorize operator tells Mathcad to perform the calculations (square root, for example) on each element of the matrix. The `slope( )` function might look like this:

$$m := \text{slope}(Q, \overrightarrow{\sqrt{\Delta P}})$$

## 5.5 VAPOR–LIQUID EQUILIBRIUM

When a liquid mixture is boiled, the vapor that leaves the vessel is enriched in the more volatile component of the mixture. The vapor and liquid in a boiling vessel are in equilibrium, and vapor–liquid equilibrium (VLE) data are available for many mixtures. The data are usually presented in tabular form, as in the accompanying table, which represents VLE data for mixtures of methanol and *n*-butanol boiling at 12 atm. From the VLE data, we see that if a 50:50 liquid mixture of the alcohols is boiled, the vapor will contain about 80% methanol.

VLE data are commonly used in designing distillation columns, but an equation relating vapor mass fraction to liquid mass fraction is a lot handier than tabulated values.

Use the `linfit( )` function and the tabulated VLE data to obtain an equation relating the mass fraction of methanol in the vapor (y) to the mass fraction of vapor in the

| SILANE | |
|---|---|
| Tmin (K) | 88.48 |
| Tmax (K) | 161.00 |

| TEMP | $C_P$ |
|---|---|
| 88.48 | 59874 |
| 92.11 | 60171 |
| 95.73 | 60676 |
| 99.36 | 60156 |
| 102.98 | 60358 |
| 106.61 | 60863 |
| 110.24 | 60604 |
| 113.86 | 60784 |
| 117.49 | 61037 |
| 121.11 | 61215 |
| 124.74 | 61026 |
| 128.37 | 61231 |
| 131.99 | 61289 |
| 135.62 | 61655 |
| 139.24 | 61160 |
| 142.87 | 61658 |
| 146.50 | 62038 |
| 150.12 | 62085 |
| 153.75 | 61864 |
| 157.37 | 61712 |
| 161.00 | 62368 |

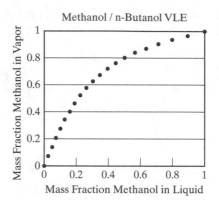

Methanol / n-Butanol VLE

liquid (x). Test different linear models (e.g., polynomials) to see which gives the best fit to the experimental data. For your best model, calculate predicted values using the coefficients returned by linfit( ), and plot the predicted values and the original data values on the same graph.

**Data:** The VLE data shown were generated from version 4.0 of ChemCad. The x column represents the mass fraction of methanol in the boiling mixture. (The mass fraction of *n*-butanol in the liquid is calculated as 1-x for any mixture.) The mass fraction of methanol in the vapor leaving the solution is shown in the y column.

### 5.6  FITTING PHYSICAL PROPERTY DATA

In the Applications example, experimental data on the vapor pressure of silane were fit to a standard equation. Try fitting a curve to data for silane's liquid heat capacity. The standard fitting equation for this property is

$$C_P = a + bT + cT^2 + dT^3 + eT^4$$

Not all coefficients need to be used (any order polynomial is acceptable).

**Data:** The data set for the liquid heat capacity (J/kmol K) of silane is shown at the right. Find the coefficients for the best fitting model for the data.

### 5.7  STATISTICS: COMPETING COLD REMEDIES

Two proposed cold remedies, CS1 (cough syrup) and CS2 (chicken soup), have been compared in a hospital study. The objective was to determine which treatment caused patients to recover more quickly. The duration of sickness was defined as the time (days) between when patients reported to the hospital requesting treatment and when they requested to leave the hospital. The results are tabulated as follows:

| CS1 | | CS2 | |
|---|---|---|---|
| PATIENT # | DURATION | PATIENT # | DURATION |
| 1 | 8.10 | 1 | 5.79 |
| 2 | 7.25 | 2 | 2.81 |
| 3 | 5.89 | 3 | 3.27 |
| 4 | 7.12 | 4 | 4.87 |
| 5 | 5.60 | 5 | 5.49 |
| 6 | 1.85 | 6 | 6.60 |
| 7 | 4.00 | 7 | 2.63 |
| 8 | 5.58 | 8 | 4.64 |

| | CS1 | | CS2 | |
|---|---|---|---|---|
| PATIENT # | DURATION | | PATIENT # | DURATION |
| 9 | 9.92 | | 9 | 6.96 |
| 10 | 4.25 | | 10 | 5.83 |

a. Determine the mean recovery time for each medication.

b. Which remedy caused the fastest recoveries?

### 5.8 STATISTICS: QUALITY CONTROL

A beverage bottling plant uses a sampling protocol for quality control. At random intervals, a bottle is pulled off the line and the volume is measured to make sure that the filling operation is working correctly. The company has several criteria it watches:

- Ideally, the company wants to put an average of 2.03 liters in each bottle. Since the plant must shut down whenever it is found that less than the labeled amount (on average) is being put in each bottle, setting the target amount higher than 2.0 liters reduces the number of times they have to shut down the process to recalibrate the equipment. If the average fill volume is less than 2.03 liters, but greater than 2.00 liters, the equipment will not be shut down immediately, but will be recalibrated the next time the equipment is down for any reason (cleaning, breakage, etc.)

- If the average fill volume exceeds 2.06 liters, the equipment must be shut down for recalibration to prevent bottles from overflowing.

- If the standard deviation exceeds 40 ml, the equipment must be shut down for recalibration. This is to eliminate customer complaints about incompletely filled bottles, as well as to prevent bottles from overflowing.

- Given the sample volumes (liters) in the accompanying table, should the equipment be shut down and recalibrated?

| | |
|---|---|
| 2.00 | 2.09 |
| 1.99 | 2.08 |
| 2.00 | 2.09 |
| 1.97 | 2.07 |
| 1.93 | 1.97 |
| 2.03 | 2.03 |
| 2.02 | 1.99 |
| 2.06 | 2.07 |
| 2.16 | 2.02 |
| 2.08 | 1.99 |

### 5.9 INTERPOLATION

Use linear interpolation with the thermocouple calibration data in Problem 5.3 to predict

a. the thermocouple voltage at a temperature of 85°C.

b. the temperature of the junction when the thermocouple voltage is 2.500 mV.

Use a cubic spline interpolation with the orifice meter calibration data in Problem 5.4 to predict

c. the flow rate corresponding to a pressure drop of 9.5 psi.

d. the pressure drop to be expected at a flow rate of 15 ft³/min.

### 5.10 RELATING HEIGHT TO MASS FOR A SOLIDS STORAGE TANK

Solids storage tanks are sometimes mounted on *load cells* (large scales, basically) so that the mass of solids in the tank is known, rather than the height of the solids. To make sure they do not overfill the tank, the operators might ask for a way to calculate the height of material in the tank, given the mass reading from the load cells.

| h (ft) | m (lb) |
|---|---|
| 0 | 0 |
| 2 | 56 |
| 4 | 447 |
| 6 | 1508 |
| 8 | 3574 |
| 10 | 6981 |
| 12 | 11470 |
| 14 | 16000 |
| 16 | 20520 |
| 18 | 25040 |
| 20 | 29570 |
| 22 | 34090 |
| 24 | 38620 |

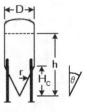

The values shown in the accompanying table relating height and mass in the tank were obtained using the results of Problem 3.2 and are the starting point for this problem. As in

Problem 3.2, the tank has a conical base section ($\theta$ = 30°) and a diameter of 12 feet. The apparent density of the solids in the tank is 20 lb/ft³.

Use a cubic spline to fit a curve to the mass (as `x`) and height (as `y`) data, and then use the `interp( )` function to predict the height of solids in the tank when the load cells indicate 3200 kg solids.

*Note:* The load cells actually measure the mass of the tank and the stored solids, but adjusting the display to read 0 kg before adding any solids effectively causes the load cells to display only the mass of the solids. This is called setting the *tare weight* for the load cells.

# 6

# Mathcad's Symbolic Math Capabilities

## COMPOSITE MATERIALS

The field of composite materials has already had an impact on most of us in the developed world. The sporting goods industry, for example, has found that the lighter and stronger composite materials allow sports enthusiasts to go faster and farther. Composites are common in modern aircraft for the same reasons. But the field of composite materials is just getting started.

Material scientists have long analyzed the behavior of materials under various stresses. Concrete, for example, is known to perform well under compression, but doesn't hold up under tension. Cables are designed for holding loads under tension, but do nothing under compression. (You can't push a rope!) The analytical skills of the materials scientists are still required to understand composite materials, but they now go a step further: It has become possible to talk about designing materials for specific purposes. If a part needs to perform better under tension, you might change the type of fibers used in the composite. If the part needs better resistance to compression, the type of matrix used to surround the fibers might be changed. For better bending performance, the bonding between the fibers and the matrix might be improved. But in order to design a better

## SECTIONS

- 6.1 Symbolic Math Using Mathcad
- 6.2 Solving an Equation Symbolically
- 6.3 Manipulating Equations
- 6.4 Polynomial Coefficients
- 6.5 Symbolic Matrix Math
- 6.6 Symbolic Integration
- 6.7 Symbolic Differentiation
- Summary

## OBJECTIVES

*After reading this chapter, you should be able to:*

- To learn to use Mathcad's symbolic math capabilities to:
  - Solve for a particular variable in an equation.
  - Manipulate mathematical expressions (e.g., substituting and factoring expressions, and expanding terms).
- To see how Mathcad can perform matrix operations symbolically.
- To learn to use symbolic math to integrate and differentiate functions.

composite material, you have to know how each element of the composite works, as well as how all the elements interact with each other. You also need to understand the chemical and physical natures of the elements of the composite, in addition to as the properties imparted to the elements and the final composite by the manufacturing processes. This is a field that will require the skills of a wide range of scientists and engineers working together.

In the past, composites have been used primarily to improve the structural performance of a system. The mechanical properties of composites are still an important research area, but these materials also have interesting potential for improving electrical, chemical, and thermal properties of systems. Some years back, there was talk of room-temperature superconductors that could revolutionize power distribution systems. The excitement in that area has died down, but the research continues. Strong bone replacements could be made of composites that are biologically inert to reduce the risk of rejection. Composite engines and furnaces could operate more efficiently at higher temperatures. Some success has already been seen in each of these areas, and the future for these materials appears to be especially bright.

## 6.1 SYMBOLIC MATH USING MATHCAD

Scientists and engineers commonly want a numerical value as the result of a calculation, and Mathcad's numerical math features provide this type of result. However, there are times when you need a result in terms of the mathematical symbols themselves, and you can use Mathcad's *symbolic math* capability for this type of calculation. A symbolic result may be required when:

- You want to know how Mathcad obtained a numerical result by seeing the equation solved symbolically.
- You want greater precision on a matrix inversion, so you have Mathcad invert the matrix symbolically, rather than numerically.
- You want to integrate a function symbolically, to use the result in another function.

Mathcad provides symbolic math functions in two locations: the *Symbolics menu* at the top of the window and the *Symbolic Keyword Palette*. Both locations provide access to essentially the same symbolic capabilities, with one important distinction: the Symbolic Keyword Palette uses the *live symbolic operator*, or → symbol. This is called a "live" operator because it will automatically recalculate the value of an expression whenever information to the left of or above the operator changes.

The results of calculations carried out using the Symbolics menu are not live. That is, once a symbolic operation has been performed using commands from the Symbolics menu, the result will not be automatically updated, even if the input data change. Thus, to update a result using the Symbolics menu, you must repeat the calculation.

The Symbolics menu is a bit more straightforward for solving for a particular variable and for factoring an expression. The Symbolic Keyword Palette is simpler for substitution. Both approaches will be demonstrated.

### Symbolics Menu

The Symbolics menu is on the menu bar at the top of the Mathcad window. One of the first considerations in using the symbolic commands is how you want the results to be displayed. You can set this feature by using the Evaluation Style dialog box from the Symbolics menu:

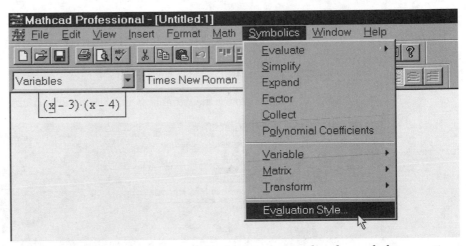

The Evaluation Style dialog box controls whether the results of a symbolic operation are presented to the right of the original expression or below the original expression. When results are placed below the original expression, the new equation regions can start running into existing regions. This can be avoided by having Mathcad insert blank lines before displaying the results. By default, Mathcad places the results below the original expression and adds blank lines for the results to avoid overwriting other equation regions:

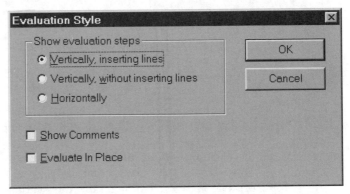

*Note:* If you select "Evaluate in Place", your original expression will be replaced by the computed result.

As an example of using the Symbolics menu we will find the solutions to the following equation:

$$(x - 3) \cdot (x - 4)$$

This equation has two obvious solutions ($x = 3$, $x = 4$), so it is easy to see whether Mathcad is finding the correct solutions.

---

**PROFESSIONAL SUCCESS**

*Keep test expressions as simple as possible.*

When you are choosing mathematical expressions to test the features of a software package or to validate your own functions, try to come up with a test that:

- Is just complex enough to demonstrate that the function is (or is not) working correctly.

- Has an obvious, or at least known, solution, so that it is readily apparent whether the test succeeded or failed.

Since we want to find the values of x that satisfy the equation, click on the equation and select either one of the x variables. Note that the symbolic equality, =, was used in the equation.

$$(x - 3) \cdot (x - 4) = 0$$

To solve for the variable x, use Symbolics/Variable/Solve:

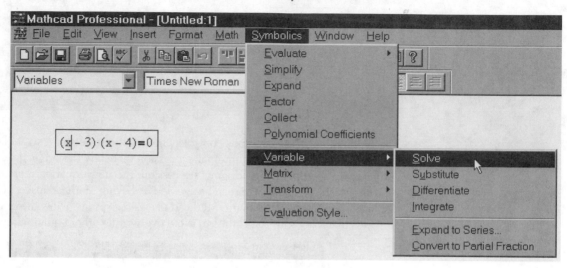

The solutions—the two values of x that satisfy the equation—are presented as a two-element vector:

$$(x - 3) \cdot (x - 4) = 0$$

$$\begin{bmatrix} 3 \\ 4 \end{bmatrix}$$

Symbolic operations are often performed on expressions, rather than complete equations. If you solve the expression $(x - 3) \cdot (x - 4)$ for x, Mathcad will set the expression to zero before finding the solutions. Thus, we would have

$$(x - 3) \cdot (x - 4)$$

$$\begin{bmatrix} 3 \\ 4 \end{bmatrix}$$

### Symbolic Keyword Palette

The Symbolic Keyword Palette is available from the Math Palette. Click on the button showing a mortarboard icon to open the Symbolic Keyword Palette. When opened, the Symbolic Keyword Palette looks like this:

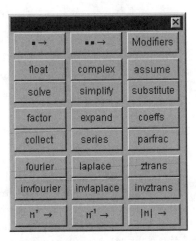

To use the features on this palette, first enter an expression, and then select the expression and click one of the buttons on the palette to perform a symbolic operation on the expression. From the preceding example, we know that the equation

$$(x - 3) \cdot (x - 4) = 0$$

has two solutions, x = 3 and x = 4. Mathcad can also find those solutions using the [solve] button on the Symbolic Keywords Palette.

## 6.2  SOLVING AN EQUATION SYMBOLICALLY

If you enter an incomplete equation, such as the left-hand side of the previous equation, Mathcad will set the expression equal to zero when the solve operation is performed. So, in Mathcad, finding the solution to this equation by using symbolic mathematics is usually carried out in the following manner. Enter the expression to be solved, and select the expression:

$$(x - 3) \cdot (x - 4)$$

Then click on the [solve] button on the Symbolic Keyword Palette:

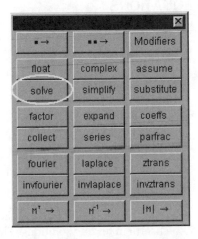

The word "solve" appears after the expression, with an empty placeholder. Mathcad wants to know which variable to solve for. Enter an *x* in the placeholder and then press [enter]:

$$(x - 3) \cdot (x - 4) \ \text{solve}, \ \blacksquare \ \rightarrow$$

Mathcad returns the result. In this case, since there are two solutions, the solutions are returned as a two-element vector:

$$(x - 3) \cdot (x - 4) \quad \text{solve}, x \rightarrow \begin{bmatrix} 3 \\ 4 \end{bmatrix}$$

*Note:* When using the Palette, you tell Mathcad which variable to solve for by typing the variable name into the placeholder. When using the Symbolics menu to solve for x, you tell Mathcad to solve for x by first selecting one of the x variables in the expression and then choosing "solve" from the menu.

If Mathcad cannot solve an expression symbolically, nothing will be displayed on the right side of the arrow operator, and the expression will be displayed in red to indicate that an error has occurred.

$$(x - 3) \cdot (x - 4) \quad \text{solve}, y \rightarrow$$

If you click on the expression, Mathcad will display an error message indicating that no solution was found

**PRACTICE!**

Use Mathcad to solve the following equations. (You can leave off the zero when entering the expressions into Mathcad.)

**a.** $(x - 1) \cdot (x + 1) = 0.$

**b.** $x^2 - 1 = 0.$

**c.** $(y - 2) \cdot (y + 3) = 0.$

**d.** $3z^2 - 2z + 8 = 0.$

**e.** $\dfrac{x + 4}{x^2 + 6x - 2} = 0.$

## 6.3 MANIPULATING EQUATIONS

A number of algebraic manipulations, such as factoring out a common variable, are frequently used when working with algebraic expressions, and Mathcad implements these through the Symbolic Palette. These routine manipulations include the following:

- *Expanding* a collection of variables (e.g., after factoring).
- *Factoring* a common variable out of a complex expression.
- *Substituting* one variable or expression for another variable.
- *Simplifying* a complex expression.
- *Collecting terms* on a designated variable.

A *partial fraction expansion* in which a complex expression is expanded into an equivalent set of multiplied fractions is a somewhat more complex operation, but one that can be useful in finding solutions. This procedure will not work on all fractional expressions, but can be very useful in certain circumstances.

Examples of each of the preceding manipulations follow.

### Expand

Expanding the expression $(x - 3) \cdot (x - 4)$ yields a polynomial in $x$. To expand an expression using the Symbolics menu, select the expression, and then choose Symbolics/ Expand.

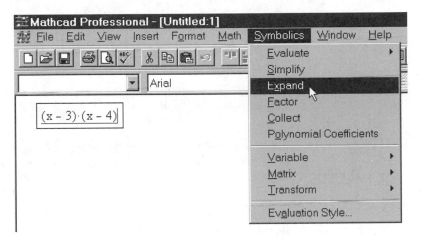

After expansion, the result is placed below the original expression:

$$(x - 3) \cdot (x - 4)$$

$$x^2 - 7 \cdot x + 12$$

Alternatively, select the expression, and the press the [expand] button on the Symbolic Keyword Palette. In the placeholder, tell Mathcad to expand on $x$:

$$(x - 3) \cdot (x - 4) \text{ expand, } x \rightarrow x^2 - 7 \cdot x + 12$$

### Factor

Factoring reverses the expand operation, pulling an $x$ out of the polynomial:

$$x^2 - 7 \cdot x + 12 \text{ factor, } x \rightarrow (x - 3) \cdot (x - 4)$$

Probably a more common usage of the factor operation is to pull a similar quantity out of a multiterm expression. For example, $2\pi r$ appears in both terms in the expression for the surface area of a cylinder. To factor this expression, select the terms to be factored (the entire expression in this case), and then use Symbolics/Factor. The result is placed below the original expression:

$$2 \cdot \pi \cdot r^2 + 2 \cdot \pi \cdot r \cdot L$$

$$2 \cdot r \cdot \pi \cdot (r + L)$$

You can also factor only a portion of an expression. For example, we could factor only the right-hand side of the following equation:

$$A_{cyl} = 2 \cdot \pi \cdot r^2 + 2 \cdot \pi \cdot r \cdot L$$

To factor only the right-hand side, select that side (shown above), and then use Symbolics/Factor:

$$A_{cyl} = 2 \cdot r \cdot \pi \cdot (r + L)$$

**PRACTICE!**

Try using the Symbolics menu to factor these expressions:

**a.** $6x^2 + 4x$.

**b.** $3xy + 4x - 2y$. (Select only part of this expression before factoring.)

### Substitute

The substitute operation replaces a variable by another expression. Substitution is a bit simpler using the Palette buttons, so that approach will be shown first.

**SUBSTITUTION USING THE SYMBOLIC PALETTE**

A simple replacement, such as replacing all the x's in an expression with y's, is easily carried out using the [substitute] button on the Symbolic Palette:

$$(x-3) \cdot (x-4) \text{ substitute, } x = y \rightarrow (y-3) \cdot (y-4)$$

But you can also replace a variable with a more complicated expression. For example, suppose you wanted to replace the x's with an exponential expression, such as $e^{-t/\tau}$. The [substitute] button can handle this; simply enter the complete exponential expression into the placeholder in the substitute command:

$$(x-3) \cdot (x-4) \text{ substitute, } x = e^{\frac{-t}{\tau}} \rightarrow \left(\exp\left(\frac{-t}{\tau}\right) - 3\right) \cdot \left(\exp\left(\frac{-t}{\tau}\right) - 4\right)$$

**SUBSTITUTION USING THE SYMBOLICS MENU**

If you want to use the Symbolics menu to carry out a substitution, there are two things to keep in mind:

1. The new expression (the expression that will be substituted into the existing expression) must be copied to the Windows clipboard before performing the substitution.

2. You must select the variable to be replaced before performing the substitution.

To repeat the last example, the $e^{-t/\tau}$ would be entered into the Mathcad worksheet, selected, and copied to the Windows clipboard using Edit/Copy.

$$e^{\frac{-t}{\tau}}$$

Then one of the x variables in $(x - 3) \cdot (x - 4)$ would be selected. (This will tell Mathcad to replace all of the xs in the expression with the contents of the Windows clipboard.) Finally, the substitution is performed using Symbolics/Variable/Substitute, and the results are placed below the original expression. The final Mathcad worksheet now looks like this (with the added comments):

$$e^{\frac{-t}{\tau}}$$            *entered on worksheet, then copied to Windows clipboard*

$$(x-3) \cdot (x-4)$$            *one x selected before substitution*

$$\left(\exp\left(\frac{-t}{\tau}\right) - 3\right) \cdot \left(\exp\left(\frac{-t}{\tau}\right) - 4\right)$$            *the result of the substitution*

### Simplify

According to the Mathcad help files, the Simplify menu command "performs arithmetic, cancels common factors, uses basic trigonometric and inverse function identities, and simplifies square roots and powers." If we try to simplify $(x - 3) \cdot (x - 4)$ using Symbolics/Simplify, the expression is returned unchanged: Mathcad thinks that $(x - 3) \cdot (x - 4)$ is as simple as this expression gets. In order to demonstrate the Simplify operation, we need to complicate the example a little. Consider this modification of the example:

$$(x - \sqrt{9}) \cdot (x - 2^2)$$

If we try to simplify this expression using Symbolics/Simplify, the original expression is returned:

$$(x - \sqrt{9}) \cdot (x - 2^2)$$
$$(x - 3) \cdot (x - 4)$$

The Simplify operation simplified the square root (selecting the positive root) and power. Perhaps a more significant use of the Simplify operation is obtaining a common denominator. For example, by selecting the entire expression

$$\frac{a}{(x - 3)} + \frac{b}{(x - 4)}$$

and then using the Symbolics/Simplify function, the terms will combine over a common denominator:

$$\frac{(a \cdot x - 4 \cdot a + b \cdot x - 3 \cdot b)}{((x - 3) \cdot (x - 4))}$$

You can also factor the numerator to see the process used to obtain the common denominator. First, you factor the a out of the first two terms in the numerator by selecting those two terms, i.e.,

$$\frac{(a \cdot x - 4 \cdot a + b \cdot x - 3 \cdot b)}{((x - 3) \cdot (x - 4))}$$

and using Symbolics/Factor. Then, choose the last two terms in the new numerator,

$$\frac{(a \cdot (x - 4) + b \cdot x - 3 \cdot b)}{((x - 3) \cdot (x - 4))}$$

and again use Symbolics/Factor. The final result is

$$\frac{(a \cdot (x - 4) + b \cdot (x - 3))}{((x - 3) \cdot (x - 4))}$$

**PRACTICE!**

Use the Symbolics menu to simplify these expressions:

a. $\dfrac{x}{x + 4} - \dfrac{12}{x + 2}$.

**b.** $\dfrac{1}{x} + \dfrac{x}{x-7} - \dfrac{x+6}{x^2}.$

**c.** $\sqrt{\dfrac{4x}{y^2}}.$

## Collect

The Collect operation is used to rewrite a set of summed terms as a polynomial in the selected variable (if it is possible to do so). For example, the Expand function, operating on the x in $(\mathtt{x} - 3) \cdot (\mathtt{x} - 4)$, returned a polynomial. So we know that that expression can be written as a polynomial in x. The Collect function should also return that polynomial, and in the following example, we observe that it does:

$$(x-3)\cdot(x-4)$$
$$x^2 - 7\cdot x + 12$$

What is the difference between the Collect and Expand operations if they both return a polynomial? The Expand operation evaluates all powers and products of sums in the selected expression. For the expression $(\mathtt{x} - 3)\cdot(\mathtt{x} - 4)$, the result was a polynomial, but this is not always true. The Collect operation attempts to return a polynomial in the selected variable. For example, using the Expand and Collect operations on the result of the common-denominator example yields very different results, as is shown in these examples:

$$\frac{(a\cdot x - 4\cdot a + b\cdot x - 3\cdot b)}{((x-3)+(x-4))} \text{ expand, } x \rightarrow \frac{1}{((x-3)\cdot(x-4))}\cdot a\cdot x -$$

$$\frac{4}{((x-3)\cdot(x-4))}\cdot a + \frac{1}{((x-3)\cdot(x-4))}\cdot b\cdot x - \frac{3}{((x-3)\cdot(x-4))}\cdot b$$

$$\frac{(a\cdot x - 4\cdot a + b\cdot x - 3\cdot b)}{((x-3)+(x-4))} \text{ collect, } x \rightarrow \frac{((a+b)\cdot x - 4\cdot a - 3\cdot b)}{((x-3)\cdot(x-4))}$$

## Partial Fractions Expansion

A partial fractions expansion on a variable is a method for expanding a complex expression into a sum of (hopefully) simpler expressions with denominators containing only linear and quadratic terms and no functions of the variable in the numerator. As a first example, a partial fractions expansion, based upon x, on

$$\frac{(a\cdot(x-4)+b\cdot(x-3))}{((x-3)\cdot(x-4))}$$

gives back the original function

$$\frac{a}{(x-3)} + \frac{b}{(x-4)}$$

This was accomplished by selecting an x (any of them) and then choosing Symbolics/Variable/Convert to Partial Fraction from the Symbolics menu.

A slightly more complex example is to take the ratio of two polynomials and expand it by using partial fractions. The process is the same as described in the preceding example: Select the variable upon which you want to expand (z in this example), and then choose Symbolics/Variable/Convert to Partial Fraction from the Symbolics menu. The result will look like this:

$$\frac{(9 \cdot z^2 - 40 \cdot z + 23)}{(z^3 - 7 \cdot z^2 + 7 \cdot z + 15)}$$

$$\frac{2}{(z-3)} + \frac{3}{(z+1)} + \frac{4}{(z-5)}$$

An expanded example involving two variables illustrates how the partial fraction expansion depends on the selected variable. The starting expression now involves both $z$ and $y$.

$$\frac{(7 \cdot z^3 + 19 \cdot z^2 - 43 \cdot z^2 \cdot y - 100 \cdot z \cdot y + 9 \cdot z - 33 \cdot y + 60 \cdot y^2 \cdot z + 105 \cdot y^2)}{(z^4 + 4 \cdot z^3 - 8 \cdot z^3 \cdot y - 32 \cdot z^2 \cdot y + 3 \cdot z^2 - 24 \cdot z \cdot y + 15 \cdot y^2 \cdot z^2 + 60 \cdot y^2 \cdot z + 45 \cdot y^2)}$$

A partial fraction expansion on $z$ requires that each denominator be linear or quadratic in $z$ and precludes any function of $z$ from every numerator. The result is

$$\frac{5}{(2 \cdot (z+3))} + \frac{3}{(2 \cdot (z+1))} - \frac{2}{(-z+5 \cdot y)} - \frac{1}{(-z+3 \cdot y)}$$

On the other hand, a partial fraction expansion on $y$ precludes functions of $y$ in the numerators, but allows functions of $z$. The result of a partial fractions expansion on $y$ is

$$\frac{(4 \cdot z + 7)}{(z^2 + 4 \cdot z + 3)} - \frac{2}{(-z+5 \cdot y)} - \frac{1}{(-z+3 \cdot y)}$$

## 6.4 POLYNOMIAL COEFFICIENTS

If you have an expression that can be written as a polynomial, Mathcad will return a vector containing the coefficients of the polynomial. This operation is available from the Symbolics menu using Symbolics/Polynomial Coefficients.

The coefficients of the polynomial $x^2 - 7x + 12$ are pretty obvious. If you select any $x$ in the expression,

$$x^2 - 7 \cdot x + 12$$

and then ask for the vector of polynomial coefficients as Symbolics/Polynomial Coefficients, the coefficients are returned as a vector.

$$x^2 - 7 \cdot x + 12$$

$$\begin{bmatrix} 12 \\ -7 \\ 1 \end{bmatrix}$$

*Note:* While Mathcad's symbolic math functions typically display the higher powers first (i.e., the $x^2$ before the $7x$), the first polynomial coefficient in the returned vector is the constant, 12.

When your expression is written as a polynomial, the coefficients are apparent. However Mathcad's symbolic processor can return the polynomial coefficients of expressions that are not displayed in standard polynomial form. For example, we know that $x^2 - 7x + 12$ is algebraically equivalent to $(x - 3) \cdot (x - 4)$. Using Symbolics/Polynomial Coefficients on $(x - 3) \cdot (x - 4)$ returns the same polynomial coefficients as in the standard form case:

$$(x-3)\cdot(x-4)$$

$$\begin{bmatrix} 12 \\ -7 \\ 1 \end{bmatrix}$$

## 6.5 SYMBOLIC MATRIX MATH

Mathcad provides symbolic matrix operations from either the Symbolics menu or the Symbolic Keywords Palette. These are very straightforward operations and only summarized in this section.

### *Tranpose*

To transpose a matrix, select the entire matrix and then choose Symbolics/Matrices/ Transpose. The original and transposed matrices are, respectively,

$$\begin{bmatrix} 1 & 1 \\ 2 & 8 \\ 3 & 27 \\ 4 & 64 \\ 5 & 125 \end{bmatrix}$$

and

$$\begin{bmatrix} 1 & 2 & 3 & 4 & 5 \\ 1 & 8 & 27 & 64 & 125 \end{bmatrix}$$

### *Inverse*

To invert a matrix symbolically, select the entire matrix and then choose Symbolics/ Matrices/Invert. The original and inverted matrices are, respectively,

$$\begin{bmatrix} 2 & 3 & 5 \\ 7 & 2 & 4 \\ 8 & 11 & 6 \end{bmatrix}$$

and

$$\begin{bmatrix} \dfrac{-32}{211} & \dfrac{37}{211} & \dfrac{2}{211} \\ \dfrac{-10}{211} & \dfrac{-28}{211} & \dfrac{27}{211} \\ \dfrac{61}{211} & \dfrac{2}{211} & \dfrac{-17}{211} \end{bmatrix}$$

If you want to see the inverted matrix represented as values rather than fractions, select the entire inverted matrix, then choose Symbolics/Evaluate/Floating Point, and, finally, enter the number of digits to display. Twenty digits is the default, but that is often excessive. Here, the result is displayed with a floating-point precision of 4 digits:

$$\begin{bmatrix} -.1517 & .1754 & .009479 \\ -.04739 & -.1327 & .128 \\ .2891 & .009479 & -.08057 \end{bmatrix}$$

### Determinant

Mathcad will also symbolically calculate the determinant of a matrix. To do so, select the entire matrix and then choose Symbolics/Matrices/Determinant. In this example, the determinant is found to be 211:

$$\begin{bmatrix} 2 & 3 & 5 \\ 7 & 2 & 4 \\ 8 & 11 & 6 \end{bmatrix}$$

211

## 6.6 SYMBOLIC INTEGRATION

Mathcad provides a number of ways to integrate and differentiate functions. In this chapter, we will focus on symbolic, or analytic integration, leaving numerical integration for the next chapter. The integration and differentiation operators are found on the *Calculus Palette*, which is available from the Math Palette.

In this section, we will use a simple polynomial as a demonstration function and the same polynomial throughout to allow us to compare the various integration and differentiation methods, except where multiple variables are required to demonstrate multivariate integration. The polynomial will be $12 + 3x - 4x^2$, and a multivariable function, the formula for the volume of a cylinder, $\iiint r\,dr\,d\theta\,dl$ (with $0 \leq r \leq R$, $0 \leq \theta \leq 2\pi$, $0 \leq 1 \leq L$), will be used to demonstrate multivariable integration and differentiation.

### Indefinite Integrals

**SYMBOLIC INTEGRATION USING THE INDEFINITE INTEGRAL OPERATOR**

The most straightforward of Mathcad's integration methods uses the *indefinite integral operator* from the Calculus Palette. When you click on the button for the indefinite integral operator, the operator is placed on your worksheet with two empty placeholders, the first for the function to be integrated and the second for the integration variable.

$$\int \blacksquare d\blacksquare$$

To integrate the sample polynomial, enter the polynomial in the first placeholder and an *x* in the second:

$$\int (12 + 3 \cdot x - 4 \cdot x^2) dx$$

Complete the integration using the "evaluate symbolically" symbol, the →. This symbol is entered by pressing [Ctrl-.] (Hold down the Control key while pressing the period key.) The result is

$$\int (12 + 3 \cdot x - 4 \cdot x^2) dx \rightarrow 12 \cdot x + \frac{3}{2} \cdot x^2 - \frac{4}{3} \cdot x^3$$

*Reminder:* The integration variable is a dummy variable. You can put any variable you want in that placeholder. However, if you write the polynomial as a function of x and integrate with respect to y, Mathcad will perform the integration, but the result will not be very interesting:

$$\int (12 + 3 \cdot x - 4 \cdot x^2) dy \rightarrow (12 + 3 \cdot x - 4 \cdot x^2) \cdot y$$

   Alternatively, you can select the entire expression and then choose Simplify from the Symbolics menu:

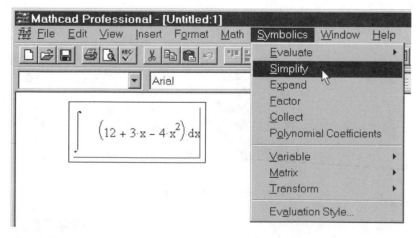

The result will be placed below the integral operator by default:

$$\int (12 + 3 \cdot x - 4 \cdot x^2) dx$$

$$12 \cdot x + \frac{3}{2} \cdot x^2 - \frac{4}{3} \cdot x^3$$

You can modify the placement of the result by using the Symbolics/Evaluation style menu options.

*Note:* Mathcad does not add the constant of integration you might expect when integrating without limits. Mathcad shows the functional form of the integrated expression, but you have to add your own integration constant if you want to evaluate the result. The integrated result is an editable equation region, so adding the constant is no problem:

$$12 \cdot x + \frac{3}{2} \cdot x^2 - \frac{4}{3} \cdot x^3 + C$$

**SYMBOLIC INTEGRATION WITH MULTIPLE VARIABLES**

You can use the indefinite integration operator to integrate over multiple variables. Simply use one indefinite operator symbol for each integration variable. The second integration operator goes in the first operator's function placeholder, and so on. To integrate over three variables say, ($r$, $\theta$, and $l$), we'll use three integration operators:

$$\iiint \blacksquare \, d\blacksquare \, d\blacksquare \, d\blacksquare$$

Note that there is now only one function placeholder (before the first d), but three integration variable placeholders. In the computation of the volume of a cylinder, the function placeholder contains only an $r$:

$$\iiint r \, d\blacksquare \, d\blacksquare \, d\blacksquare$$

And the integration variables are $r$, $\theta$, and $l$:

$$\iiint r \, dr \, d\theta \, dl$$

You instruct Mathcad to evaluate the integral with the $\rightarrow$ operator:

$$\iiint r \, dr \, d\theta \, dl \rightarrow \frac{1}{2} \cdot r^2 \cdot \theta \cdot l$$

Not quite the result you anticipated, perhaps? The expression was integrated as an indefinite integral. The $\pi$ that you normally see in the formula for the volume of a cylinder comes from the integration limits on $\theta$. This will become apparent later, when we integrate this function with limits (using the definite integral operator).

**SYMBOLIC INTEGRATION USING THE SYMBOLICS MENU**

Symbolic integration using the Symbolics menu is an alternate method for integrating with respect to a *single variable* that does not use the indefinite integral operator at all. Instead, you enter your function, e.g.,

$$12 + 3 \cdot x - 4 \cdot x^2$$

and then select the variable of integration, one of the x's in this example:

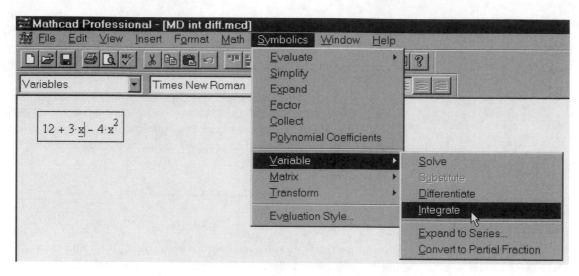

To perform the integration, use the Symbolics menu (Symbolics/Variable/Integrate) to obtain

$$12 + 3 \cdot x - 4 \cdot x^2$$

$$12 \cdot x + \frac{3}{2} \cdot x^2 - \frac{4}{3} \cdot x^3$$

The result (again, without the constant of integration) is placed below the original function. This approach is very handy, but is useful only for indefinite integrals with a single integration variable.

**PRACTICE!**

Use Mathcad's indefinite integral operator to evaluate these integrals (starting with the obvious):

**a.** $\int x \, dx$.

**b.** $\int (a + bx + cx^2) dx$.

**c.** $\int\int 2x^2 y \, dx \, dy$.

**d.** $\int \frac{1}{x} dx$.

**e.** $\int e^{-ax} \, dx$.

**f.** $\int \cos(2x) \, dx$.

### Definite Integrals

Mathcad evaluates definite integrals using the *definite integral operator* from the Calculus Palette. Definite integrals can be evaluated in a number of ways:

- Symbolic evaluation with variable limits.
- Symbolic evaluation with numeric limits.
- Symbolic evaluation with mixed (variable and numeric) limits.
- Numerical evaluation (requires numeric limits)

## DEFINITE INTEGRALS: SYMBOLIC EVALUATION WITH VARIABLE LIMITS

The definite integral operator comes with four placeholders—the function and integration variable placeholders and two limit placeholders:

$$\int_{\blacksquare}^{\blacksquare} \blacksquare \, d\blacksquare$$

To evaluate the polynomial integrated from $x = A$ to $x = B$, simply include the limits in the appropriate placeholders:

$$\int_{A}^{B} (12 + 3 \cdot x - 4 \cdot x^2) \, dx$$

You instruct Mathcad to evaluate the integral either by using the symbolic evaluation symbol ($\rightarrow$) or by choosing Simplify from the Symbolics menu. In either case, the result is

$$\int_{A}^{B} (12 + 3 \cdot x - 4 \cdot x^2) \, dx \rightarrow 12 \cdot B - \frac{4}{3} \cdot B^3 + \frac{3}{2} \cdot B^2 - 12 \cdot A + \frac{4}{3} \cdot A^3 - \frac{3}{2} \cdot A^2$$

## DEFINITE INTEGRALS: SYMBOLIC EVALUATION WITH NUMERIC LIMITS

To evaluate an integral with numeric limits, you can place the numbers in the limit placeholders, as, for example,

$$\int_{-1}^{2} (12 + 3 \cdot x - 4 \cdot x^2) \, dx \rightarrow \frac{57}{2}$$

or assign values to variables before the integration and use the variables as limits, as in

$$A := -1 \qquad B := 2$$
$$\int_{A}^{B} (12 + 3 \cdot x - 4 \cdot x^2) \, dx \rightarrow \frac{57}{2}$$

## DEFINITE INTEGRALS: SYMBOLIC EVALUATION WITH MIXED LIMITS

It is fairly common to have a numeric value for one limit and want to integrate from that known value to an arbitrary (variable) limit. Mathcad handles this type of integration as well:

$$\int_{-1}^{C} (12 + 3 \cdot x - 4 \cdot x^2) \, dx \rightarrow 12 \cdot C - \frac{4}{3} \cdot C^3 + \frac{3}{2} \cdot C^2 + \frac{55}{6}$$

In the preceding example, the known limit was evaluated and generated the $55/6$ in the result. The unknown limit was evaluated in terms of the variable C. This result can then be evaluated for any value of C.

*Note:* When evaluating an integral from a known limit to a variable limit, it is common to use the integration variable as the variable limit as well. Thus, for the preceding example, we would have

$$\int_{-1}^{x} (12 + 3 \cdot x - 4 \cdot x^2)\, dx$$

Mathcad will not evaluate this expression. For Mathcad, the integration variable (the x in dx) is a dummy variable, but the limits are not. In Mathcad, you cannot use the same symbol to represent both a dummy variable and a limit variable in a single equation.

## MIXED LIMITS WITH MULTIPLE INTEGRATION VARIABLES

To obtain a formula for the volume of any cylinder, we would integrate the cylinder function over the variable r from 0 to some arbitrary radius R, over θ from 0 to 2π (for a completely round cylinder), and over l from 0 to an arbitrary length L. The result is the common expression for the volume of a cylinder:

$$\int_{0}^{L} \int_{0}^{2 \cdot \pi} \int_{0}^{R} r\, dr\, d\theta\, dl \rightarrow R^2 \cdot \pi \cdot L$$

Note the order of the integration symbols and the integration variables. Mathcad uses the limits on the inside integration symbol (0 to R) with the inside integration variable (dr), the limits on the middle integration operator (0 to 2π) with the middle integration variable (dθ), and so forth.

## DEFINITE INTEGRALS: NUMERICAL EVALUATION

Numerical evaluation of an integral does not really fit in this chapter on symbolic math, but it is the final way that Mathcad can evaluate an integral. To request a numerical evaluation, use the equal sign instead of the → symbol:

$$\int_{-1}^{2} (12 + 3 \cdot x - 4 \cdot x^2)\, dx = 28.5\ \blacksquare$$

You would normally see the result to 20 decimal places (by default), but this result is precisely 28.5. Note that the result includes a units placeholder. Units can be used with numerical evaluation (and with the limits on symbolic integration as well.)

## PRACTICE!

Use Mathcad's definite integral operator to evaluate these expressions:

**a.** $\int_{0}^{4} x\, dx$.

**b.** $\int_{1}^{3} (ax + b)\, dx$.

**c.** $\int_{-3}^{0} \frac{1}{x}\, dx$.

**d.** $\int_{0}^{\pi} \int_{0}^{2\ cm} r\, dr\, d\theta$.

## APPLICATION:   ENERGY REQUIRED TO WARM A GAS

Warming up a gas is a pretty common thing to do, partly because we like to live in warm buildings and partly because we tend to burn things to warm those buildings. Combustion always warms up the combustion products. It is common to need to know how much energy is required to warm a gas.

The amount of energy needed to warm a gas depends on the amount of the gas, the heat capacity of the gas, and the temperature change of the gas. Also, heat capacities of gases are strong functions of temperature, so the relationship between heat capacity and temperature must be taken into account. All of this is included in the equation

$$\Delta H = n \int_{T_1}^{T_2} C_p \, dT$$

where    $\Delta H$ is the change in enthalpy of the gas, which is equal to the amount of energy required to warm the gas if all of the energy added to the gas is used to warm it (i.e., if the energy is not used to make the gas move faster, etc.),

n is the number of moles of gas present (say, 3 moles),

$C_p$ is the heat capacity of the gas at constant pressure,

$T_1$ is the initial temperature of the gas (say, 25°C),

$T_2$ is the final temperature of the gas (say, 400°C).

Since heat capacities change with temperature, the relationship between heat capacity and temperature is often given as an equation. For example, for $CO_2$, the heat capacity is related to the temperature by the expression:[1]

$$C_p = 36.11 + 4.233 \cdot 10^{-2} T - 2.887 \cdot 10^{-5} T^2$$
$$+ 7.464 \cdot 10^{-9} T^3 \qquad \text{J/mole °C}$$

and the equation is valid for temperatures between 0 and 1500°C.

We can use Mathcad to integrate this expression and determine the amount of energy required to warm 3 moles of $CO_2$ from 25 to 400°C.

$$n := 3$$
$$\Delta H := n \cdot \int_{25}^{400} (36.11 + 4.233 \cdot 10^{-2} \cdot T$$
$$- 2.887 \cdot 10^{-5} \cdot T^2 + 7.464 \cdot 10^{-9} \cdot T^3) \, dT$$
$$\Delta H = 4.904 \cdot 10^4$$

The energy required is 49 kJ.

*Note:* This problem was worked without units for two reasons:

1. The units on the various terms in the heat capacity equation are complicated.

2. Mathcad doesn't have °C as a built-in unit, and the $T$'s in this heat capacity equation must be in °C.

## 6.7  SYMBOLIC DIFFERENTIATION

You can evaluate derivatives with respect to one or more variables using the *Derivative* or *Nth Derivative* buttons on the Calculus Palette. For a first derivative with respect to a single variable, you can also use Variable/Derivative from the Symbolics menu.

**FIRST DERIVATIVE WITH RESPECT TO ONE VARIABLE**

When you click on the Derivative button on the Calculus Palette, the derivative operator is placed on the worksheet:

$$\frac{d}{d\blacksquare}\blacksquare$$

The operator contains two placeholders, one for the function, the other for the differentiation variable. To take the derivative of the sample polynomial with respect to the variable x, the polynomial and the variable are inserted into their respective placeholders:

$$\frac{d}{dx}(12 + 3 \cdot x - 4 \cdot x^2)$$

[1] From *Elementary Principles of Chemical Processes* by R.M. Felder and R.W. Rousseau, 2nd ed., Wiley, New York (1986).

You tell Mathcad to evaluate the derivative either by using the $\rightarrow$ symbol, producing

$$\frac{d}{dx}(12 + 3 \cdot x - 4 \cdot x^2) \rightarrow 3 - 8 \cdot x$$

or by selecting the entire expression and then choosing Simplify from the Symbolics menu, resulting in

$$\frac{d}{dx}(12 + 3 \cdot x - 4 \cdot x^2)$$
$$3 - 8 \cdot x$$

*Note:* Mathcad does not have a "Derivative evaluated at" operator. To evaluate the result at a particular value of x, simply give x a value before performing the differentiation:

$$x := -1$$
$$\frac{d}{dx}(12 + 3 \cdot x - 4 \cdot x^2) \rightarrow 11$$

As an alternative to using the Derivative operator from the Calculus Palette, you can enter your function, select one variable (one of the x's in the polynomial example),

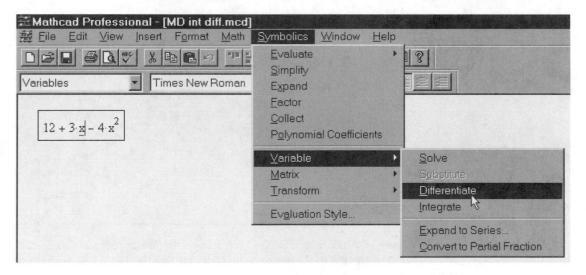

and differentiate the function with respect to the selected variable using Symbolics/ Variable/Differentiate from the Symbolics menu. The result will be

$$12 + 3 \cdot x - 4 \cdot x^2$$
$$3 - 8 \cdot x$$

This method works only for evaluating a first derivative with respect to a single variable.

**HIGHER DERIVATIVES WITH RESPECT TO A SINGLE VARIABLE**

For higher derivatives, use the Nth Derivative operator from the Calculus Palette. This operator comes with four placeholders, but you can only use three:

$$\frac{d^{\blacksquare}}{d\,\blacksquare^{\blacksquare}} \qquad \textit{linked}$$

When you add the power to the right placeholder in the denominator, the same power will appear in the numerator of the derivative operator. You cannot type directly into the placeholder in the numerator. In this example, we'll use a power of 2 to take the second derivative of the sample polynomial:

$$\frac{d^2}{d\blacksquare^2}\blacksquare$$

The two remaining placeholders are for the function and the differentiation variable:

$$\frac{d^2}{dx^2}(12 + 3\cdot x - 4\cdot x^2) \to -8$$

**DIFFERENTIATION WITH RESPECT TO MULTIPLE VARIABLES**

Use multiple derivative operators to evaluate derivatives with respect to multiple variables. For example, the indefinite integral of r with respect to r, θ, and 1 yields this result:

$$\iiint r \, dr \, d\theta \, dl \to \frac{1}{2}\cdot r^2 \cdot \theta \cdot 1$$

If we take the result and differentiate it with respect to r, θ, and 1, we should get the original function back:

$$\frac{d}{dl}\frac{d}{d\theta}\frac{d}{dr}\left(\frac{1}{2}\cdot r^2\cdot\theta\cdot 1\right) \to r$$

The original function is simply r, all by itself.

As a more interesting example, consider the ideal gas law, and take the derivative of pressure with respect to temperature and volume:

$$P = \frac{n\cdot R\cdot T}{V}$$

$$\frac{d}{dT}\frac{d}{dV}\left(\frac{n\cdot R\cdot T}{V}\right) \to -n\cdot\frac{R}{V^2}$$

**PRACTICE!**

Try using Mathcad to evaluate these derivatives:

a. $\dfrac{d}{dx}x^2$.

b. $\dfrac{d}{dx}(3x^2 + 4x)$.

c. $\dfrac{d^2}{dx^2}x^3$.

**d.** $\dfrac{d}{dx}\dfrac{d}{dy}(3x^2 + 4xy + 2y^2)$.

**e.** $\dfrac{d}{dx}\ln(ax^2)$.

**f.** $\dfrac{d}{dx}\cos(2x)$.

## APPLICATION:   ANALYZING STRESS–STRAIN DIAGRAMS

A fairly standard test for new materials is the tensile test. In essence, a sample of the material is very carefully prepared and then slowly pulled apart. The pressure on the sample and the elongation of the sample are recorded throughout the test. We will consider data from a composite material in this example, but to allow for comparison, first consider a tensile test on a metal sample.

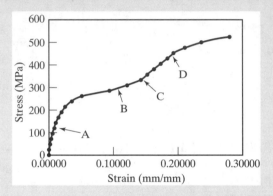

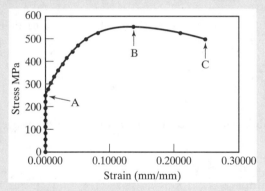

Note the units on strain: mm/mm. This is millimeters of elongation divided by the original length of the sample. The test begins with no stress and no strain. As the pulling begins, the metal starts to stretch. From the origin of the graph to point A, the stretching is reversible: If the pulling pressure were released, the metal would return to its original size. Beyond point A, some of the stretching is irreversible. Point B is called the material's *ultimate stress*—the highest stress that the material can withstand without breaking. Beyond point B, the stress actually goes down as the sample pulls itself apart under the applied stress. At point C, the sample breaks.

The stress–strain curves for composite materials have a different shape, because of the way the materials respond to stress. There are many different com-

posite materials with vastly different mechanical properties, so their stress–strains curve could be very different, but the curve shown in the preceding figure illustrates some interesting features.

The big difference between this curve and the previous one is the presence of a second hump. Between the origin and point B, the curve looks a lot like an ordinary stress–strain curve, and then the second hump starts appearing at about point C. The explanation for this behavior is that the first hump represents mostly the matrix (surrounding the fibers) responding to the stress. The matrix then cracks and separates from the fibers, and the stress is transferred to the fibers between points B and C. From point C on, you are seeing the stress–strain response of the fibers.

There are a couple of analyses we can perform on these data:

a.   Estimate Young's modulus for the matrix and the fibers.

b.   Calculate the work done on the sample during the test.

### Young's Modulus

Young's modulus is the proportionality factor relating stress and strain in the linear sections of the graph between the origin and point A and (sometimes visible) between points C and D. Because the material is a composite, neither of the values we will calculate truly represents Young's modulus for the pure materials, but they will help quantify how this composite material behaves under stress.

The linear region near the origin includes approximately the first four or five data points. Young's modulus for the matrix can be calculated from the change in stress and the measured change in strain:

$$Y := \frac{\text{Stress}_3 - \text{Stress}_0}{\text{Strain}_3 - \text{Strain}_0} \qquad Y = 5.929 \cdot 10^4 \quad \text{<<MPa}$$

Similarly, Young's modulus relating stress to strain in the region between C and D includes points 15–18:

$$Y_{\text{fiber}} := \frac{\text{Stress}_{18} - \text{Stress}_{15}}{\text{Strain}_{18} - \text{Strain}_{15}}$$

$$Y_{\text{fiber}} = 1.012 \cdot 10^4 \quad \text{<<MPa}$$

### Work

A little reshaping can turn a stress–strain diagram into a force–displacement diagram. The area under a force–displacement diagram is the work done on the sample.

Stress is the force per unit cross-sectional area of the sample. If the sample tested is L = 10 mm by W = 10 mm, the area and force on the sample can be computed as

$$A := L \cdot W$$
$$F := \text{Stress} \cdot A$$

To obtain a displacement, *x,* we need to multiply the strain by the original sample length (or height; the samples are usually vertical when tested). If H = 10 mm as well, then

$$x := \text{Strain} \cdot H$$

We can now replot the stress–strain diagram as a force–displacement graph. The result will look like this:

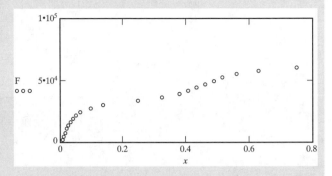

The area under this graph is the work, but in order to use Mathcad's integration operator, we need a function relating force to displacement, not data points. In the last chapter, we saw how to fit a polynomial to data. That's what we need here.

*Note:* In the next chapter, integration methods using the data points themselves will be covered.

Accordingly,

$$f(x) := \begin{bmatrix} x \\ x^2 \\ x^3 \\ x^4 \\ x^5 \end{bmatrix} \qquad b := \text{linfit}(x, F, f)$$

$$\overrightarrow{F_p := (b_0 \cdot x + b_1 \cdot x^2 + b_2 \cdot x^3 + b_3 \cdot x^4 + b_4 \cdot x^5)}$$

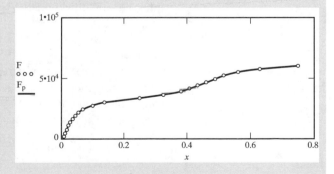

From the preceding graph, it looks like the fifth order polynomial fits the data nicely. But Fp is a vector of values; we still need a function. Hence,

$$F_{\text{func}}(x) := b_0 \cdot x + b_1 \cdot x^2 + b_2 \cdot x^3 + b_3 \cdot x^4 + b_4 \cdot x^5$$

This function can be integrated using the definite integration operator from the Calculus Palette. As the preceding graph shows, the upper limit on x is almost 0.8. The actual value can be found by using the max( ) function on the x vector:

$$\text{Work} := \int_0^{\max(x)} F_{\text{func}}(x)\, dx$$

$$\text{Work} = 3.069 \cdot 10^4$$

That's the work, but what are the units? F was determined from stress (MPa) and area (mm²), and x came from strain (mm/mm) and length (mm). This work has units of MPa·(mm³). We'll convert them:

$$\text{Work} := \text{Work} \cdot \text{MPa} \cdot \text{mm}^3$$

$$\text{Work} = 30.695 \cdot N$$

*Note:* The integration operator can handle units, but the linfit( ) function does not. That's why this problem was worked without units.

## SUMMARY

In this chapter, we looked at Mathcad's symbolic math capabilities—its ability to work directly with mathematical expressions, rather than numerical results. We saw that Mathcad's symbolic math features are housed in two areas and are used in slightly different ways. For example, you can solve for a variable in an equation from either the Symbolics menu or the Symbolic Keyword Palette. With the Symbolic Keyword Palette, there is a "live operator," so that if you make changes to the worksheet, the solve operation will be automatically recalculated, and you specify the variable you want to solve for as part of the operation. In order to solve for a variable using the Symbolics menu, you first select the variable of interest and then use the menu: Symbolics/Variable/Solve. The result is placed on the worksheet, but there is no live operator, so the result will not be automatically recalculated if the worksheet changes. Both approaches are useful.

You also saw that Mathcad can replace (substitute) every occurrence of a variable with another mathematical expression and can factor common terms out of complex expressions. You can use symbolic math to find a common denominator using the simplify operation. Mathcad can manipulate expressions in a number of other ways as well, as described in the following summary.

You learned that Mathcad can do matrix math operations symbolically, as well as integrate and differentiate expressions.

## MATHCAD SUMMARY

**OPERATIONS UNDER THE SYMBOLICS MENU:**

Before using the Symbolics menu, you generally need to select the part of an expression you want to operate on. For example, you need to select a variable in an expression before using any of the Symbolics/Variable operations.

| | |
|---|---|
| Symbolics/**Simplify** | Evaluates common math operations (e.g., square root) to try to simplify an expression. |
| Symbolics/**Expand** | Multiplies out powers and polynomials, expands numerators of fractions. |

| | |
|---|---|
| Symbolics/**Factor** | Reverses the expand operation: simplifies polynomials, pulls a common expression out of multiple terms. |
| Symbolics/**Collect** | Tries to rewrite a set of summed terms as a polynomial. |
| Symbolics/**Polynomial Coefficients** | If the selected expression can be written as a polynomial, returns the polynomial coefficients. |
| Symbolics/**Variable/Solve** | Solves an expression for the selected variable. |
| Symbolics/**Variable/Substitute** | Replaces each occurrence of the selected variable with the expression in the Windows clipboard. |
| Symbolics/**Variable/Differentiate** | Returns the first derivative of the expression with respect to the selected variable. |
| Symbolics/**Variable/Integrate** | Integrates the expression with respect to the selected variable—does not add a constant of integration. |
| Symbolics/**Variable/Convert to Partial Fractions** | Expands an expression into a sum of expressions with denominators containing only linear and quadratic terms and with no functions of the selected variable in the numerator. |
| Symbolics/**Matrix/Transpose** | Interchanges rows and columns in the matrix. |
| Symbolics/**Matrix/Invert** | Inverts the matrix using symbolic math operations, rather than decimal numbers—this preserves accuracy by avoiding round-off errors, but the resulting fractions can get unwieldy. |
| Symbolics/**Matrix/Determinant** | Calculates the determinant of a matrix using symbolic math operations. |
| Symbolics/**Evaluation Style . . .** | Opens a dialog box which allows you to change the way the results of the calculations are presented. |

**OPERATIONS USING THE SYMBOLIC KEYWORD PALETTE**

With the Symbolic Keyword Palette, the symbolic evaluation operator → is used and any variables or expressions that must be specified in order to perform the operation are entered into placeholders as needed. You do not need to select a variable or a portion of the expression before performing the symbolic operation.

| | |
|---|---|
| **solve** | Solves the expression for the specified variable. |
| **simplify** | Evaluates common math operations to try to simplify an expression. |

| | |
|---|---|
| **susbtitute** | Replaces each occurrence of the specified variable with the specified expression. |
| **factor** | Pulls the specified variable out of all terms in an expression. |
| **expand** | Evaluates powers and polynomials involving the specified variable; expands numerators of fractions involving the variable. |
| **coeffs** | Returns the polynomial coefficients, if there are any, for the specified variable. |
| **collect** | Tries to rewrite summed terms as a polynomial in the specified variable. |
| **parfrac** | Expands an expression into a sum of expressions, with denominators containing only linear and quadratic terms and with no functions of the selected variable in the numerator. |
| $\mathbf{M^T} \rightarrow$ | Transposes the matrix (interchanges rows and columns in the matrix). |
| $\mathbf{M^{-1}} \rightarrow$ | Inverts the matrix using symbolic math operations. |
| $\mathbf{|M|} \rightarrow$ | Calculates the determinant of a matrix using symbolic math operations. |

**OPERATIONS USING THE CALCULUS PALETTE:**

| | |
|---|---|
| **Indefinite Integral** | Integrates the expression in the function placeholder with respect to the variable in the integration variable placeholder. If the symbolic evaluation operator $\rightarrow$ is used after the integral, the integral is evaluated symbolically. Mathcad does not add a constant of integration. If an equal sign is used after the integral, the integral is evaluated numerically. |
| **Definite Integral** | Integrates the expression in the function placeholder with respect to the variable in the integration variable placeholder, using the specified limits. (The dummy integration variable cannot be used in a limit.) If the symbolic evaluation operator $\rightarrow$ is used after the integral, the integral is evaluated symbolically. If an equal sign is used after the integral, the integral is evaluated numerically. |
| **Derivative** | Takes the derivative of the variable in the function placeholder with respect to the variable in the differentiation variable placeholder. If the symbolic evaluation operator $\rightarrow$ is used, the derivative is evaluated symbolically. If an equal sign is used, the derivative is evaluated numerically. To evaluate the derivative at a particular value, assign the value to the differentiation variable before taking the derivative. |
| **Nth Derivative** | Takes second- and higher-order derivatives. |

# Problems

### 6.1 SOLVING FOR A VARIABLE IN AN EXPRESSION

In Chapter 2, we used the equation

$$A = 2 \cdot \pi \cdot r^2 + 2 \cdot \pi \cdot r \cdot L$$

for the surface area of a cylinder. The equation is written using the symbolic equality, [CTRL=].

a. Use the solve operation on the Symbolic Keyword Palette to solve for the L in this equation.
b. Use the expression returned by the solve operation to determine the cylinder length required to get 1 m² of surface area on a cylinder with a radius of 12 cm.

### 6.2 SYMBOLIC INTEGRATION

Evaluate the following indefinite integrals symbolically:

a. $\int \sin(x) \, dx$.

b. $\int \ln(x) \, dx$.

c. $\int [\sin(x)^2 + \cos(x)] dx$.

d. $\int \frac{x}{x+b} \, dx$.

*Note:* In part c, notice how Mathcad indicates the sine-squared term: `sin(x)²`, not `sin²(x)`.

### 6.3 DEFINITE INTEGRALS

Evaluate the following definite integrals. Use either symbolic or numeric evaluations.

a. $\int_0^\pi \sin(\theta) \, d\theta$.

b. $\int_0^{2\pi} \sin(\theta) \, d\theta$.

c. $\int_{-3}^0 \frac{x}{x-3} \, dx$.

d. $\int_0^\infty e^{\frac{-t}{4}} \, dt$.

*Note:* The numerical integrator cannot handle the infinite limit in part d; use symbolic integration. The infinity symbol is available on the Calculus Palette.

### 6.4 INTEGRATING FOR THE AREA UNDER A CURVE

Integrate $\int y \, dx$ to find the area under the curves represented by these functions:

a. $y = -x^2 + 16$      between $-2 \le x \le 4$

b. $y = e^{\frac{-t}{4}}$      between $0 \le t \le \infty$

c. $y = e^{\frac{-t}{4}}$      between $0 \le t \le 4$

### 6.5 INTEGRATING FOR THE AREA BETWEEN CURVES

Find the area between the curves represented by these functions:

$$y = -x^2 + 16$$
$$y = -x^2 + 9$$

between $-3 \leq x \leq 3$

### 6.6 ENERGY REQUIRED TO WARM A GAS

At what rate must energy be added to a stream of methane to warm it from 20°C to 240°C?

**DATA:**

Methane flow rate:    20,000 mole/min (these are gram moles)

Heat capacity equation:[2]    $C_p = 34.31 + 5.469 \cdot 10^{-2} T + 0.3661 \cdot 10^{-5} T^2$
$- 11.00 \cdot 10^9 T^3$    J/mole (C)

### 6.7 WORK REQUIRED TO COMPRESS AN IDEAL GAS AT CONSTANT TEMPERATURE

One equation for work is

$$W = \int P \, dV$$

For an ideal gas, pressure and volume are related through the ideal gas law:

$$PV = nRT$$

a.  Use Mathcad's ability to solve an expression for a variable to solve the ideal gas law for pressure $P$.
b.  Substitute the result for $P$ from part a into the work integral.
c.  Determine the work required to compress 10 moles of an ideal gas at 400 K from a volume of 300 liters to a volume of 30 liters. Express your result in kJ. (Assume that cooling is provided to maintain the temperature at 400 K throughout the compression.)
d.  Does the calculated work represent work done on the system (the 10 moles of gas) by the surroundings (the outside world) or by the system on the surroundings?

### 6.8 DESIGNING AN IRRIGATION SYSTEM

Problem 2.4 introduced center-pivot irrigation systems and described these systems in a general fashion. An essential element of such systems is their ability to distribute the water fairly evenly. Because the end of the pipe covers a lot more ground than the pipe near the center, water must be applied at a faster rate at the outside of the circle than near the center to apply the same number of gallons per square foot of ground.

a.  Use Mathcad's symbolic math capabilities to integrate

$$Area_{ring} = \int_0^{2\pi} \int_{R_i}^{R_o} r \, dr \, d\theta$$

to obtain a formula for the area of a ring with inside radius $R_i$ and outside radius $R_o$.

[2] From *Elementary Principles of Chemical Processes* by R.M. Felder and R.W. Rousseau, 2nd ed., Wiley, New York (1986).

b. At what rate must water be applied to provide one inch (depth) of water
  i. to the innermost ring: $R_i = 0, R_o = 20$ feet.
  ii. to the outermost ring: $R_i = 1300$ feet, $R_o = 1320$ feet.

c. Write a Mathcad function that accepts the inside and outside radii and the desired water depth as inputs and returns the flow rate required to provide one inch of water. Use your function to determine the water flow rate for $R_i = 1000$ feet, $R_o = 1020$ feet, depth = 2 inches.

### 6.9  YOUNG'S MODULUS

In the Mathcad applied example on stress–strain curves, values of Young's modulus for the matrix and the fiber were determined using algebra. An alternative approach would be to take the derivative of a function fit to the stress–strain data and evaluate the derivative in the linear regions of the stress–strain curve.

  Let

$$
f(x) := \begin{bmatrix} x \\ x^2 \\ x^3 \\ x^4 \\ x^5 \end{bmatrix} \qquad b := \text{linfit}(\text{Strain}, \text{Stress}, f) \qquad b = \begin{bmatrix} 5.951 \cdot 10^4 \\ -4.006 \cdot 10^6 \\ 1.195 \cdot 10^8 \\ -1.542 \cdot 10^9 \\ 7.184 \cdot 10^9 \end{bmatrix}
$$

be a fifth-order polynomial fit to the stress–strain curves.

  Use Mathcad's derivative operator to differentiate the polynomial and then evaluate the derivative at strain values of 0.001 and 0.048 to find the values of Young's modulus for the matrix and the fibers, respectively.

### 6.10  CALCULATING WORK

The stress–strain data for the metal sample mentioned in the Mathcad applied box have been abridged and reproduced as follows:

| STRAIN (mm/mm) | STRESS (MPa) |
| --- | --- |
| 0.00000 | 0 |
| 0.00028 | 55 |
| 0.00055 | 110 |
| 0.00083 | 165 |
| 0.00110 | 221 |
| 0.00414 | 276 |
| 0.01324 | 331 |
| 0.02703 | 386 |
| 0.04193 | 441 |
| 0.06207 | 496 |
| 0.13793 | 552 |
| 0.20966 | 524 |
| 0.24828 | 496 |

a. Convert the following stress–strain diagram to a force–displacement graph. The sample size is 10 mm × 10 mm × 10 mm.

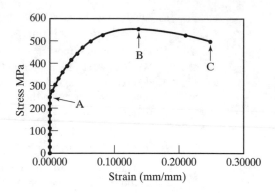

b. Fit a polynomial to the force-displacement data. (A 5th-order polynomial with no intercept works well.)

c. Integrate the polynomial to determine the work done on the sample during the tensile test.

# 7

# Numerical Techniques

## ENGINEERING IN MEDICINE

Medical science has developed dramatically in the past generation, and with the increased understanding of the inner workings of the human body in health and disease comes the ability to apply that knowledge to try to improve the human condition. Engineers from every discipline can play a very significant role in this enterprise. Many bodily processes are traditional areas of engineering study, but usually with a slight twist or complicating factor. For example, most engineers are very familiar with fluid flows in tubes, but blood is a nonNewtonian fluid, in pulsatile flow, in nonrigid tubes. Each of these factors complicates the study of blood flow in the human body, but the engineer's knowledge of steady, Newtonian flow in rigid tubes provides a good foundation for the study of the more complex systems. Similar examples can be cited in other traditional fields of study, such as heat transfer (mechanisms for maintaining the body's temperature), mass transfer (carbon dioxide transfer from the blood in the lungs), reactor dynamics (controlled release of drugs into the body), mechanics (artificial limbs, improved athletic performance), and materials science (biologically inert materials for implants). In each of these areas engineers will work together, along with medical

## SECTIONS

- 7.1 Iterative Solutions
- 7.2 Numerical Integration
- 7.3 Numerical Differentiation
- Summary

## OBJECTIVES

*After reading this chapter, you should be able to:*

- To learn to use Mathcad's powerful iterative solver.
- To learn how to perform an integration on a data set, by:
  - Fitting the data set with a function, and integrating the function, or
  - Integrating using the data points directly.
- To learn how to perform differentiation on a data set, by:
  - Fitting the data set with a function, and differentiating the function, or
  - Differentiating using the finite difference approximations on the data points.

professionals, to expand our understanding of how our bodies work and to apply this knowledge to improve health care.

As only one example, designing an artificial limb requires a knowledge of anatomy and mechanics to design in the right motions, a knowledge of physiology and circuit theory to understand the electrical signals in the body, and a knowledge of control systems to use the signals to control the limb. Where the circuitry, the prosthetic, and the body come in contact, materials must be carefully chosen to meet mechanical, electrical, and biological constraints. This is definitely a field for team players, and the opportunities for engineers to make significant contributions in the field of medicine have never been greater.

## 7.1 ITERATIVE SOLUTIONS

Equations (or systems of equations) that cannot be solved directly occur often in engineering. For example, in order to determine the flow rate in a pipe with a given pressure drop, the friction loss must be known. But the friction loss depends on the flow rate. Thus, in order to calculate the friction loss, you must know the flow rate. But to calculate the flow rate, you must know the friction loss. To solve this very common problem, it is necessary to guess either the flow rate or the friction loss. If you guess the friction loss, you would calculate the flow rate and then calculate the friction loss at that flow rate. If the calculated friction loss equals the guessed friction loss, the problem is solved. If not, guess again.

Mathcad provides a better way to solve problems like this: the *iterative solver*. As a simple example, consider finding the value of x that satisfies the equation

$$x^3 + 12x - 21 = 0$$

The $x^3$ suggests that there will be three solutions, but there could be duplicate roots or imaginary roots. In this example, two of the roots are imaginary. We'll try to find the one real root.

### Using the Worksheet
### for Trial-and-Error Calculations

You can simply do trial-and-error calculations in the Mathcad workspace. For example, if we try x = 0, the expression $x^3 + 12x - 21$ yields –21. Since –21 ≠ 0, the guessed value of x is incorrect. We might then try x = 1:

$$x := 1$$
$$x^3 + 12 \cdot x - 21 = -8$$

This result is closer to zero than the first attempt, so we're moving in the right direction, but the guessed x is still too small. Try x = 2:

$$x := 2$$
$$x^3 + 12 \cdot x - 21 = 11$$

The equation is still not satisfied, but this guess was too big. Try x = 1.5:

$$x := 1.5$$
$$x^3 + 12 \cdot x - 21 = 0.375$$

We're getting close, but x = 1.5 is a little high. With a few more tries, you'll find that a value of x = 1.48 comes very close to satisfying this equation.

*Note:* Iterative solutions always attempt to find values that "nearly" solve the equation. The process of choosing ever-closer guess values could go on forever. To decide when the solution is "close enough" to stop the process, iterative methods test the calculated result against a preset tolerance. For Mathcad's iterative solver, the two sides of an equation are evaluated using the computed value, and the difference between the two values is called the error. When the error falls below the preset tolerance, Mathcad stops iterating and presents the result. You can change the value of the tolerance from the default value of 0.001 to a larger number for less accurate solutions or (more likely) a smaller value for more accurate solutions. Very small tolerance values, such as $10^{-15}$, may make it hard for Mathcad to find a solution because of computer round-off error.

### Automating the Iterative Solution Process

Mathcad provides a better iterative solver than manual trial and error. Mathcad's approach uses an *iterative solve block*, since you can have Mathcad solve multiple equations simultaneously. The solve block is bounded by two keywords: `given` and `find`. The equations between these two words will be included in the iterative search for a solution. Before the `given`, you must provide an initial guess for each variable in the solve block. The iterative solve block for the preceding cubic example, with an initial guess of `x = 0`, would look like this:

$$x := 0$$
$$\text{given}$$
$$x^3 + 12 \cdot x - 21 = 0$$
$$x := \text{find}(x)$$
$$x = 1.4799$$

The equation between the `given` and `find` has been indented for readability. The line

$$x := \text{find}(x)$$

terminates the solve block and assigns the solution (returned by the `find()` function) to the variable x. Here the x variable was used to hold both the initial guess and the computed solution. This is common, but not necessary; you could assign the solution to any variable.

You can check the solution by using the computed value in the equation:

$$x := 1.4799$$
$$x^3 + 12 \cdot x - 21 = 0$$

You can adjust the displayed precision of any result by double-clicking on the displayed value and changing the number of displayed digits, but Mathcad will always drop trailing zeros. The zero on the right side of the equation is actually zero to at least three decimal places. (By default, Mathcad shows three decimal places.) The computed solution definitely satisfies the equation.

Keep in mind the following comments on using iterative solve blocks in Mathcad:

- Finding a solution does not imply that you have found "the" solution or all solutions. You should always try different initial guesses to check for other solutions. For the sample equation, Mathcad can solve for the three solutions symbolically. (Try it.) The results are pretty ugly, but the other two roots are imaginary: $-0.74 \pm 3.694i$
- Solve blocks do support units, but if you are solving for more than one variable, each iterated variable must have the same units. If the variables in your problem do not all have the same units (flow rate and friction loss, for example), you must solve the set of equations without any units on any variable.
- You must provide an initial guess for each iterated variable.

*Use a QuickPlot to find good initial guesses.*
   Create an X–Y Plot (from the Graphics Palette or by pressing [Shift-2]), enter your function on the $y$-axis and the variable in the function in the $x$–axis placeholder. (If the function has a term that cannot be performed on a matrix (e.g., $x^3$), then use the *vectorize* operator to force element-by-element evaluation.) Adjust the axis limits to see the plot, and look for zero-crossings. The curve will cross $y = 0$ for each root. For the sample equation, only one root near $x = 1.5$ is visible, since the other roots are imaginary. A value of 1.5 would be a good initial guess for the iterative solver.

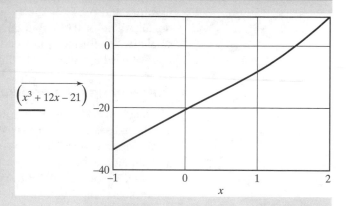

PRACTICE!

Use Mathcad's iterative solver to find solutions for each of the following expressions. For each expression, how many solutions should there be? Use different initial guesses to search for multiple solutions.

**a.** $(x - 3) \cdot (x - 4) = 0$

**b.** $x^2 - 1 = 0$

**c.** $x^3 - 2x^2 + 4x = 3$

**d.** $e^{3x} - 4 = 0$

**e.** $\sqrt{x^3} + 7x = 10$

Here's a typical pump-sizing problem:

What size pump (HP) is required to move water at an average velocity of 3.0 ft/s through a 5000-foot-long pipe with a 1-inch inside diameter? Assume that the viscosity of water is 0.01 poise at room temperature and the pump has an efficiency of 0.70.

Anytime you are designing a piping system, you will need to estimate the friction in the system, since friction can be responsible for much of the pressure drop from one end of the pipe to another. Because of this friction, you need a pump to move the fluid, and you

must calculate how big the pump must be—so you have to estimate the friction losses . . . to estimate the pressure drop . . . to calculate the size of the pump.
   There are many contributing factors to pipe friction: valves, bends in the pipe, rough pipe, a buildup of deposits in the pipes, etc. We will consider only the simplest situation: a clean, horizontal, smooth pipe with no valves or bends. For most flows in such a pipe, the friction factor $f$ can be calculated using the von Karman equation,

$$\frac{1}{\sqrt{\frac{f}{2}}} = 2.5 \ln\left(N_{Re}\sqrt{\frac{f}{8}}\right) + 1.75$$

## NOMENCLATURE

| | |
|---|---|
| D | Inside pipe diameter. |
| $V_{avg}$ | Average velocity of the fluid in the pipe. |
| $\rho$ | Density of the fluid. |
| $\mu$ | Viscosity of the fluid. |
| L | Length of the pipe. |
| $g_c$ | Gravitational constant: 32.174 ft $lb_m$ $lb_f^{-1} s^{-2}$ in English units or 1 (no units) in SI. |
| $\eta$ | Efficiency of the pump (no units). |
| $P_p$ | Pump's power rating (HP or kW). |
| $\dot{m}$ | Mass flow rate of fluid in the pipe. |

The von Karman equation is valid for smooth pipes (e.g., PVC pipe, not steel pipe) and Reynolds numbers greater than 6000. The Reynolds number is defined as

$$N_{Re} = \frac{DV_{avg}\rho}{\mu}$$

Once you know the friction factor, you can calculate the pressure drop in a horizontal pipe from

$$\Delta P = 4f\frac{L}{D}\frac{\rho(V_{avg})^2}{2g_c}$$

Once you have the pressure drop, you can determine the energy per unit mass required to overcome friction, $h_f$:

$$h_f = \frac{\Delta P}{\rho}$$

And you can determine the pump power required as

$$\eta\,P_P = h_f\,\dot{m}$$

With Mathcad, the problem is solved like this:

### INFORMATION FROM THE PROBLEM STATEMENT:

$$V_{avg} := 3\cdot\frac{ft}{sec} \qquad L := 5000\cdot ft \qquad D := 1\cdot in$$

$$\mu := 0.01\cdot poise \qquad \eta := 0.70$$

### COMMONLY AVAILABLE DATA:

$$\rho := 1000\cdot\frac{kg}{m^3} \qquad \textit{Water density}$$

### DEFINITION OF gc:

$$g_c := 1 \qquad \textit{Define in SI, let Mathcad handle units}$$

### CALCULATE THE REYNOLDS NUMBER:

$$N_{Re} := \frac{D\cdot V_{avg}\cdot\rho}{\mu} \qquad N_{Re} = 23226$$

*Because $N_{Re} > 6000$, von Karman Equation can be used.*

### SOLVE FOR THE FRICTION FACTOR:

$$f := 0.001 \qquad \textit{Guessed starting value for the iterative solver}$$

given

$$\frac{1}{\sqrt{\frac{f}{2}}} = 2.5\cdot\ln\left(N_{Re}\cdot\sqrt{\frac{f}{8}}\right) + 1.75$$

$$f := \text{find}(f)$$
$$f = 0.0062 \qquad \textit{Calculated friction factor}$$

### SOLVE FOR PRESSURE DROP:

$$\Delta P := 4\cdot f\cdot\frac{L}{D}\cdot\frac{\rho\cdot(V_{avg})^2}{2\cdot g_c} \qquad \Delta P = 6.158\circ atm$$

$$\Delta P = 90.502\circ psi$$

### SOLVE FOR ENERGY PER UNIT MASS REQUIRED TO OVERCOME FRICTION:

$$h_f := \frac{\Delta P}{\rho} \qquad h_f = 623.986\cdot\frac{N\cdot m}{kg}$$

$$h_f = 208.756\cdot\frac{ft\cdot lbf}{lb}$$

### SOLVE FOR MASS FLOW RATE:

$$A_{flow} := \pi\cdot\left(\frac{D}{2}\right)^2$$

$$m_{dot} := V_{avg}\cdot A_{flow}\cdot\rho \qquad m_{dot} = 1.668\cdot10^3\cdot\frac{kg}{hr}$$

$$m_{dot} = 3.677\cdot10^3\cdot\frac{lb}{hr}$$

**SOLVE FOR REQUIRED PUMP POWER:**

$$P_P := \frac{h_f \cdot m_{dot}}{\eta}$$

$$P_P = 0.413 \circ k$$

$$P_P = 0.554 \circ hp$$

Surprised by the result? It doesn't take much of a pump just to overcome friction in a well-designed pipeline. (It takes a lot more energy to lift the water up a hill, but that wasn't considered here.) If the pipeline is not designed correctly, the friction losses can change dramatically. That's the subject of Problem 7.1.

## 7.2 NUMERICAL INTEGRATION

Numerical integration and differentiation of functions are very straightforward in Mathcad. But many times the relationship between your dependent and independent variables is known only through a set of data points. For example, in Chapter 5 we used a data set representing a relationship between temperature and time. (That data set will be presented again shortly.) If you wanted to integrate the temperature data over time, you have two choices:

* Fit the data with an equation, and then integrate the equation.
* Use a numerical integration method on the data set itself.

Both approaches are common, and both will be described in this section.

### Integration

**INTEGRATING FUNCTIONS NUMERICALLY**

If you have a function, such as the polynomial relating temperature and time that was obtained in Chapter 5, then integrating temperature over time from 0 to 9 minutes is easily performed using Mathcad's definite integral operator. Using the data arrays and the regression statements from before we have

|   | 0 |
|---|---|
| 0 | 0 |
| 1 | 1 |
| 2 | 2 |
| 3 | 3 |
| 4 | 4 |
| 5 | 5 |
| 6 | 6 |
| 7 | 7 |
| 8 | 8 |
| 9 | 9 |

Time =

|   | 0 |
|---|---|
| 0 | 298 |
| 1 | 299 |
| 2 | 301 |
| 3 | 304 |
| 4 | 306 |
| 5 | 309 |
| 6 | 312 |
| 6 | 316 |
| 8 | 319 |
| 9 | 322 |

Temp =

$$F(x) := \begin{bmatrix} 1 \\ x \\ x^2 \end{bmatrix}$$

$$b := \text{linfit}(\text{Time}, \text{Temp}, F)$$

$$b = \begin{bmatrix} 297.721 \\ 1.742 \\ 0.113 \end{bmatrix}$$

$$\int_0^9 (b_0 + b_1 \cdot t + b_2 \cdot t^2)\, dt = 2.777 \cdot 10^3$$

The symbol t was used instead of Time in the integration. The choice is irrelevant, because the integration variable is a dummy variable. Units were not used here. The integration operator does allow units on the limit values, but since linfit() does not support units, the problem is more easily solved without units.

**PRACTICE!**

Evaluate the following integrals, and check your results using the computational formulas shown at the right.

- Area under the curve y = 1.5x from x = 1 to x = 3. (A trapezoidal region.)

$$\int_1^3 1.5\ x\ dx \qquad\qquad A_{\text{trap}} = \frac{1}{2}(y_{\text{left}} + y_{\text{right}}) \cdot (x_{\text{right}} - x_{\text{left}})$$

- Volume of a sphere of radius 2 cm.

$$\int_0^{2\ \text{cm}} 4\pi r^2\ dr \qquad\qquad V_{\text{sphere}} = \frac{4}{3}\pi R^3$$

- Volume of a spherical shell with inside radius $R_i = 1$ cm and outside radius $R_o = 2$ cm.

$$\int_{1\ \text{cm}}^{2\ \text{cm}} 4\pi r^2\ dr \qquad\qquad V_{\text{shell}} = \frac{4}{3}\pi (R_o^3 - R_i^3)$$

---

**APPLICATION:   DETERMINING THE VOLUME OF LIQUID IN A CYLINDRICAL TANK**

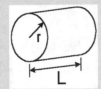

It is common to need to know how much product you have stored in a partially filled, horizontal, cylindrical tank—but the calculation is not trivial. We can use Mathcad's ability to integrate functions to solve this problem.

### Some Fundamentals

- The integral $\int_a^b f(x)dx$ represents the area between the curve f(x) and the x-axis.
- If the f curve is above the x-axis, the calculated area will have a positive sign. A negative sign on the area implies that the curve lies below the x-axis.
- A circle of radius r and centered at the origin, can be described by the function $x^2 + y^2 = r^2$.
- A horizontal line (representing the level of liquid in the tank) is described by the function y = constant. We will relate the constant to the depth of liquid in the tank later in this example.

### Case 1: The Tank Is Less than Half Full

When the tank is less than half full, we can compute the volume by multiplying the cross-sectional area of the fluid (shown shaded in the circle at the left in the figure that follows) by the length of the tank, L. The trick is determining the cross-sectional area of the fluid.

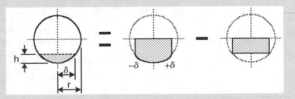

The shaded area in the center circle represents the area between the circle and the x-axis. Note that when the tank is less than half full, there is fluid between $-\delta$ and $+\delta$. We can integrate the formula for the circle between $-\delta$ and $+\delta$ to compute the shaded area in the center circle. Call this area $A_1$.

The shaded area in the rightmost circle represents the area between the function describing the level of the liquid and the x-axis. The integration limits are again $-\delta$ and $+\delta$. Call this area $A_2$. Subtracting $A_2$ from $A_1$ gives the desired cross-sectional area of the fluid in the tank. All that remains is to carry out these integrations, but first we need to know how $\delta$ depends on the level in the tank, h, and the tank radius r.

There is a right triangle involving the level of the liquid and the origin of the axis, shown at the right of the axis. Using the Pythagorean theorem, we can relate the lengths of the sides of the triangle:

$$(h-r)^2 + \delta^2 = r^2$$

Solving for $\delta$ yields the first required Mathcad function:

$$\delta(h, r) := \sqrt{r^2 - (r-h)^2}$$

The integral for the area $A_1$ is then written as a function of r and h as well:

$$A_1(h, r) = -\left[ \int_{-\delta(h,r)}^{\delta(h,r)} \left(-\sqrt{r^2 - x^2}\right) dx \right]$$

Here, the function representing the circle was solved for y, and a negative sign was introduced to calculate the y values below the x-axis. (Since Mathcad's square root operator always returns the positive root, we need to change the sign to obtain the negative y values.) Hence, we have

$$y = -\sqrt{r^2 - x^2}$$

Also, the computed area is below the x-axis, so it will have a negative sign. A minus sign has been included in the function to cause it to return a positive area value.

The integral for $A_2$ is obtained by integrating the function representing the level at liquid in the tank. If the liquid depth is h, then the level is at a (negative) y value of h - r:

$$A_2(h, r) := -\left[ \int_{-\delta(h,r)}^{\delta(h,r)} (h-r) \, dx \right]$$

Again, a minus sign was added to cause the function to return a positive area.

The cross-sectional area of fluid in the tank is then

$$A_{\text{fluid}}(h, r) :=$$
$$-\left[ \int_{-\delta(h,r)}^{\delta(h,r)} \left(-\sqrt{r^2 - x^2}\right) dx - \int_{-\delta(h,r)}^{\delta(h,r)} (h-r) \, dx \right]$$

or, simplifying slightly,

$$A_{\text{fluid}}(h, r) := -\int_{-\delta(h,r)}^{\delta(h,r)} \left[ \left(-\sqrt{r^2 - x^2}\right) - (h-r) \right] dx$$

And the volume in the tank is simply the area times the length:

$$V_{\text{fluid}}(h, r, L) :=$$
$$L \cdot \left[ -\left[ \int_{-\delta(h,r)}^{\delta(h,r)} \left[ \left(-\sqrt{r^2 - x^2}\right) - (h-r) \right] dx \right] \right]$$

## Case 2: The Tank Is More than Half Full

When the tank is more than half full, the procedure is similar:

$$A_{\text{fluid}} = A_{\text{total}} - \int_{-\delta}^{\delta} f_{\text{circle}}(x) \, dx + \int_{-\delta}^{\delta} f_{\text{level}}(x) \, dx$$

The function relating $\delta$ to r and h is unchanged, and since the areas are abve the x-axis, we don't have to worry about changing the signs. The result is the following function for the volume of the liquid in the tank:

$$V_{\text{fluid}}(h, r, L) :=$$
$$L \cdot \left[ \pi \cdot r^2 - \int_{-\delta(h,r)}^{\delta(h,r)} \left[ \left(\sqrt{r^2 - x^2}\right) - (h-r) \right] dx \right]$$

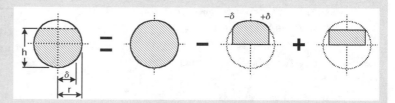

### Creating a General Function for Either Case

Mathcad's `if()` function can be used to automatically select the appropriate formula:

Here, if `h < r`, then the first formula is used; otherwise the second formula is used. Since both functions work for `h = r` (a half-full tank), deciding which formula to use at that point is arbitrary.

$$V_{\text{tank}}(h, r, L) := L \cdot \text{if}\left[(h < r), \left[-\int_{-\delta(h,r)}^{\delta(h,r)} [(-\sqrt{r^2 - x^2}) - (h - r)]\, dx\right], \left[\pi \cdot r^2 - \int_{-\delta(h,r)}^{\delta(h,r)} [(\sqrt{r^2 - x^2}) - (h - r)]\, dx\right]\right]$$

### Integrating Data Sets

**Integration via Curve Fitting**   One approach to integrating a data set is to first fit an equation to the data and then integrate the equation. This was demonstrated in the previous example. A polynomial was fit to the temperature–time data and then the polynomial was integrated using Mathcad's definite integral operator.

**Integrating without Curve Fitting**   An alternative to curve fitting is to simply use the data values themselves to compute the integral. This is fairly straightforward if you recall that the integral represents the area between the curve and the *x*-axis when the data points are plotted. (See the following figure.)

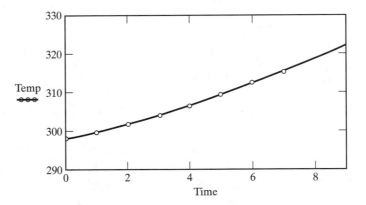

Any method that computes the area under the curve computes the value of the integral. A number of methods are commonly used. One of the simplest divides the area under the curve into a series of trapezoids. The area of each trapezoid is calculated from the data values, and the sum of the areas represents the result of the integration. Since there are 10 data points, there will be nine trapezoids to cover the entire time range. We will keep track of these nine regions by defining a range variable

$$i := 0 \ldots 8$$

Or we could define the range variable in more general terms as

$$i := 0 \ldots (\text{last (Time)} - 1)$$

We then need a function that computes the area of the leftmost trapezoid:

$$A_0 := \frac{1}{2} \cdot (\text{Temp}_0 + \text{Temp}_1) \cdot (\text{Time}_1 - \text{Time}_0) \qquad A_0 = 298.7$$

We can now generalize this equation to obtain a function capable of calculating the area of any of the nine trapezoids:

$$A_i := \frac{1}{2} \cdot (\text{Temp}_i + \text{Temp}_{i+1}) \cdot (\text{Time}_{i+1} - \text{Time}_i)$$

$$A = \begin{bmatrix} 298.7 \\ 300.424 \\ 302.643 \\ 305.164 \\ 307.916 \\ 310.862 \\ 313.974 \\ 317.235 \\ 320.629 \end{bmatrix}$$

Finally, we sum the area of all of these trapezoids to estimate the total area under the curve. This summation is carried out by using Mathcad's *range variable summation operator* from the Calculus Palette:

$$\sum_i A_i = 2.778 \cdot 10^3$$

The result compares well with that computed by using numerical integration of the polynomial in the preceding example. Again, this calculation was performed without using Mathcad's units capability, but units could have been used.

## A TRAPEZOIDAL RULE FUNCTION

We can push this process one step further and write a function that will perform trapezoidal rule integration on any data set:

$$\text{trap}(x, y) := \sum_{i=0}^{\text{length}(x)-2} \frac{y_i + y_{i+1}}{2} \cdot (x_{i+1} - x_i)$$

$$A_{\text{total}} := \text{trap}(\text{Time}, \text{Temp})$$

$$A_{\text{total}} = 2.778 \cdot 10^3$$

In the `trap()` function, the range variable is replaced by defined limits on the summation (and Mathcad's standard *summation operator* is used), and the `length()` function is utilized to determine the size of the array, from which the number of trapezoids can be computed. The expressions

`length(x) - 2`     used in the `trap()` function and

`last(x) - 1`     used in the previous example

are equivalent as long as the array origin is set at zero, which is assumed in the `trap()` function, since the summation starts at zero.

## PRACTICE!

Create a test data set, and then use the `trap()` function to integrate `y = cos(x)` from `x = 0` to `x = π/2`. Vary the number of points in the data set to see how the size of the trapezoids (over the same `x` range) affects the accuracy of the result. Then check your result using Mathcad's symbolic integrator.

- Create the test data set:

$$N_{pts} := 20$$
$$i := 0 .. (N_{pts} - 1)$$
$$x_i := \frac{\pi}{2} \cdot \frac{i}{N_{pts} - 1}$$
$$y_i := \cos(x_i)$$

- Integrate by using the `trap()` function, and vary the number of points in the data set.
- Use symbolic integration to evaluate $\int_0^{\pi/2} \cos(x)\, dx$.

## APPLICATION:  CONTROLLED RELEASE OF DRUGS

When a patient takes a pill, there is a rapid rise in the concentration of the drug in the patient's bloodstream, which then decreases with time as the drug is removed from the bloodstream, often by the kidneys or the liver. Then the patient takes another pill. The result is a time-varying concentration of drug in the blood. In some situations there may be therapeutic benefits to maintaining a more constant (perhaps lower) drug concentration for prolonged periods of time. For example, a chemotherapy drug might be active only at concentrations greater than 2 mg/L. The pills for this drug might be designed to raise the concentration in the blood to 15 mg/L, to try to keep the concentration above 2 mg/L for as long as possible. If you could keep the concentration of a cancer-fighting drug from falling below 2 mg/L for a month or more, it might do a better job of killing the cancer cells. If you could also reduce the maximum concentration from 15 mg/L to perhaps 10 mg/L, the

side effects of the drug might be reduced. In this example, we will consider an implanted "drug reservoir" for chemotherapy. This drug reservoir is little more than a plastic bag containing a solution of the drug. The shape, materials of construction, and volume of the bag, as well as the concentration of the dissolved drug, can all be varied to change the drug release characteristics. This example considers only the volume and drug concentration in the reservoir.

For preliminary testing of the release characteristics, human subjects would not be used. Instead, the computer model used to generate the following graph assumes that the drug is being released into a body simulator (a 50–liter tank) with a slow (1 mL/min) feed of fresh water and removal of drug solution at the same rate. Three tests were simulated, with the drug reservoir volume and concentration adjusted to give a maximum drug concentration 10 mg/L in the simulator. The results

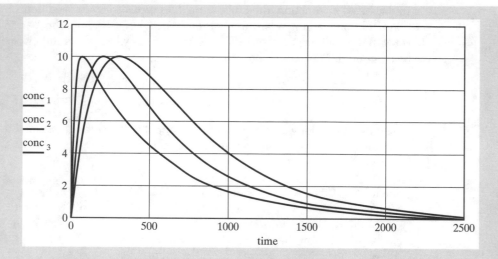

The results are shown in the graph (concentration in mg/L, time in hours):

The $conc_1$ curve was produced using a small reservoir containing a high drug concentration. $Conc_3$ used a larger reservoir with a much lower drug concentration. The curves show that, by varying the reservoir volume and concentration, the active period (concentration above 2 mg/liter) of the drug can be adjusted from approximately 800 hours (about 1 month) to almost 1400 hours (nearly 2 months), without ever causing blood concentrations to exceed 10 mg/L. While this simple drug delivery system is a long way from delivering a good, constant concentration of the chemotherapy drug, it does demonstrate that it is very possible to change the way drugs are administered. By designing better drug delivery systems, we may be able to improve the performance of some drugs and the quality of life of patients.

## Total Drug Release

With the concentration-vs.-time data, and knowing the flow rate of fluid through the simulator, we can determine the total amount of drug that is released from the reservoir. Multiplying the time by the volumetric flow rate gives the volume that has passed through the simulator. The concentrations can then be plotted against volume (liters). This is shown in the following graph, where

$$Q := 60 \qquad \text{ml/hr}$$

$$vol := \frac{time \cdot Q}{1000} \qquad \text{liters}$$

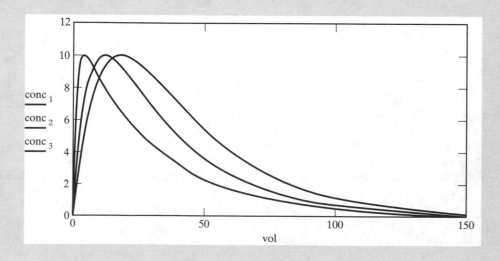

The area under each curve represents to amount of drug released from that reservoir in 2500 hours. The `trap( )` function can be used to perform the integrations:

| | | |
|---|---|---|
| $D_1 := \text{trap}(\text{vol}, \text{conc}_1)$ | $D_1 = 343$ | mg |
| $D_2 := \text{trap}(\text{vol}, \text{conc}_2)$ | $D_2 = 446$ | mg |
| $D_3 := \text{trap}(\text{vol}, \text{conc}_3)$ | $D_3 = 546$ | mg |

## SIMPSON'S RULE INTEGRATION

Simpson's rule is a popular numerical integration technique that takes three data points, fits a curve through the points, and computes the area in the region below the curve. This operation is repeated for each set of three points in the data set. The common formula for Simpson's rule looks something like

$$A_{\text{total}} = \frac{h}{3} \sum_{\text{all regions}} (y_{i-1} + 4y_i + y_{i+1})$$

where the unusual summation over "all regions" is necessary because an integration region using Simpson's method requires three data points. So, using Mathcad's default array indexing, we see that points 0, 1, and 2 make up the first integration region, points 2, 3, and 4 make up the second region, and so on. The number of integration regions is approximately half the number of data points. The distance between two adjacent points is h. The use of Simpson's rule comes with two restrictions:

- You must have an odd number of data points.
- The independent values (usually called x) must be uniformly spaced, with $h = \Delta x$.

We will look at a way to get around these restrictions later, but first we will try an example of applying Simpson's rule when the conditions are met. First we will create a data set containing seven values and strong curvature:

$$i := 0 .. 6$$
$$x_i := 1 + i$$
$$y_i := 1 + \cos(x_i)$$

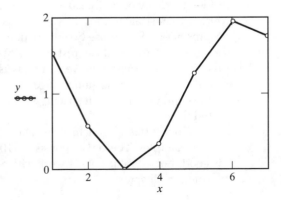

Then we calculate h (from any two x values, since h must be constant) and create a range variable j that will keep track of the index of the point at the center of each integration region:

| INTEGRATION REGION, POINT NUMBERS | CENTRAL POINT |
|---|---|
| 0, 1, 2 | 1 |
| 2, 3, 4 | 3 |
| 4, 5, 6 | 5 |

$$h := x_1 - x_0 \qquad h = 1$$
$$j := 1, 3 .. 5 \qquad j$$

| |
|---|
| 1 |
| 3 |
| 5 |

Next we apply Simpson's rule to determine the area under the curve, again by using the range variable summation operator:

$$A_{\text{Simpson}} := \frac{h}{3} \cdot \sum_{j} (y_{j-1} + 4 \cdot y_j + y_{j+1})$$

$$A_{\text{Simpson}} = 5.814$$

Now we can compare the results with trapezoidal rule integration and exact integration of the cosine function:

$$A_{\text{trap}} := \text{trap}(x,y) \qquad\qquad A_{\text{trap}} = 5.831$$

$$A_{\text{exact}} := \int_1^7 (1 + \cos(x))\, dx \qquad A_{\text{exact}} = 5.816$$

Simpson's method came a lot closer to the exact result than trapezoidal integration did—it usually does. Because Simpson's rule connects data points with smooth curves rather than straight lines, it typically fits data better than the trapezoidal rule does. But Simpson's rule has those two restrictions that make it useless in many situations. Is there a way to get around these restrictions? Yes, there is: You can use a cubic spline to fit any data set with a smooth curve and then use cubic spline interpolation to compute a set of values that covers the same range as the original data, but has an odd number of data points and uniform point spacing. After that, you can use Simpson's rule on the interpolated data.

To test this approach, we will use the temperature–time data employed in the previous examples. These data consist of 10 uniformly spaced values. The uniform spacing is good, but 10 values won't work with Simpson's rule.[1] A spline fit to the data was performed in Chapter 5:

---

[1] Another common way to get around the odd-number-of-data-points restriction is to use Simpson's rule as far as possible and then, if there is an even number of points, finish the integration by using a trapezoid for the last two points.

|   | 0 |
|---|---|
| 0 | 0 |
| 1 | 1 |
| 2 | 2 |
| 3 | 3 |
| Time = 4 | 4 |
| 5 | 5 |
| 6 | 6 |
| 7 | 7 |
| 8 | 8 |
| 9 | 9 |

|   | 0 |
|---|---|
| 0 | 298 |
| 1 | 299 |
| 2 | 301 |
| 3 | 304 |
| Temp = 4 | 306 |
| 5 | 309 |
| 6 | 312 |
| 6 | 316 |
| 8 | 319 |
| 9 | 322 |

$$\text{vs} := \text{cspline(Time, Temp)}$$

Then we can use the `interp()` function to find temperature values at 11 points over the same time interval, 0 to 9 minutes:

$$i := 0 .. 10 \qquad \textit{eleven values}$$

|   | 0 |
|---|---|
| 0 | 0 |
| 1 | 0.9 |
| 2 | 1.8 |
| 3 | 2.7 |
| 4 | 3.6 |
| 5 | 4.5 |
| 6 | 5.4 |
| 7 | 6.3 |
| 8 | 7.2 |
| 9 | 8.1 |
| 10 | 9 |

$$t_i := \frac{9 \cdot i}{10} \qquad t =$$

$$\text{Temp}_{\text{interp}_i} := \text{interp(vs, Time, Temp, } t_i)$$

|   | 0 |
|---|---|
| 0 | 298 |
| 1 | 299.225 |
| 2 | 301.003 |
| 3 | 303.093 |
| 4 | 305.401 |
| 5 | 307.893 |
| 6 | 310.538 |
| 7 | 313.32 |
| 8 | 316.25 |
| 9 | 319.24 |
| 10 | 322.358 |

$$\text{Temp}_{\text{interp}} =$$

Now we use Simpson's rule on t and $\text{Temp}_{\text{interp}}$ instead of `Time` and `Temp`.

$$j := 1, 3 .. 9$$
$$h := t_1 - t_0$$
$$A_{\text{Simpson}} := \frac{h}{3} \cdot \sum_j \left( \text{Temp}_{\text{interp}_{j-1}} + 4 \cdot \text{Temp}_{\text{interp}_j} + \text{Temp}_{\text{interp}_{j+1}} \right)$$
$$A_{\text{Simpson}} = 2.777 \cdot 10^3$$

The result compares well with that obtained from the trapezoidal integration, which is not surprising for this data set, since it does not show a lot of curvature. (There is not a lot of difference between connecting the points with lines or curves for the data set, so there is little difference between the results computed by the two methods.)

## 7.3 NUMERICAL DIFFERENTIATION

### *Evaluating Derivatives of Functions Numerically*

If you have a function, such as

$$y = b_0 e^{b_1 t}$$

Mathcad can take the derivative. If you use the live symbolic operator $\rightarrow$ to evaluate an expression symbolically, Mathcad will use its symbolic processor and give you another function:

$$\frac{d}{dt}(b_0 \cdot e^{b_1 \cdot t}) \rightarrow b_0 \cdot b_1 \cdot \exp(b_1 \cdot t)$$

Or if the values of $b_0$, $b_1$, and $t$ are specified before evaluating the derivative, Mathcad's symbolic processor will calculate a numeric result:

$$b_0 := 3.4$$
$$b_1 := 0.12$$
$$t := 16$$

$$\frac{d}{dt}(b_0 \cdot e^{b_1 \cdot t}) \rightarrow 2.7829510554706259326$$

The extreme number of significant figures is a reminder that Mathcad solved for the value using the symbolic processor. The default number of digits displayed is 20.

On the other hand, if you use the "numerical evaluation" symbol (a plain equal sign, =), then Mathcad will use its numeric processor to calculate the value of the derivative:

$$b_0 := 3.4$$
$$b_1 := 0.12$$
$$t := 16$$
$$\frac{d}{dt}(b_0 \cdot e^{b_1 \cdot t}) = 2.783$$

If you use the numeric processor, you must specify the values of $b_0$, $b_1$, and $t$ before Mathcad evaluates the derivative.

### *Derivatives from Experimental Data*

If the relationship between your variables is represented by a set of values (a data set), rather than a mathematical expression, you have two choices for trying to determine the derivative at some specified point:

- Fit the data with a mathematical expression and then differentiate the expression at the specified value.
- Use numerical approximations for derivatives on the data points themselves.

## USING A FITTING FUNCTION

Curve fitting was covered in Chapter 5, so the process is only summarized here:

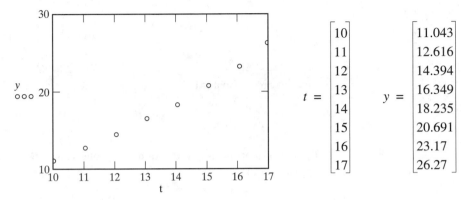

$$t = \begin{bmatrix} 10 \\ 11 \\ 12 \\ 13 \\ 14 \\ 15 \\ 16 \\ 17 \end{bmatrix} \qquad y = \begin{bmatrix} 11.043 \\ 12.616 \\ 14.394 \\ 16.349 \\ 18.235 \\ 20.691 \\ 23.17 \\ 26.27 \end{bmatrix}$$

The data are expected to fit the exponential model

$$y = b_0 e^{b_1 t}$$

which can be rewritten in linear form as

$$\ln(y) = \ln(b_0) + b_1 t.$$

We can then use linear regression and a bit of math to determine $b_0$ and $b_1$.

$$\text{in} := \text{intercept}(t, \overrightarrow{\ln(y)}) \qquad \text{in} = 1.187$$
$$\text{sl} := \text{slope}(t, \overrightarrow{\ln(y)}) \qquad \text{sl} = 0.123$$
$$b_0 := e^{\text{in}} \qquad b_0 = 3.276$$
$$b_1 := \text{sl} \qquad b_1 = 0.123$$

Once we have a mathematical expression, we can evaluate the derivative at $t = 16$ using either the symbolic or numeric processor, as described earlier. The results of using the numeric processor are as follows:

$$b_0 := e^{\text{in}} \qquad\qquad b_0 = 3.276$$
$$b_1 := \text{sl} \qquad\qquad b_1 = 0.123$$
$$t := 16$$
$$\frac{d}{dt}(b_0 \cdot e^{b_1 \cdot t}) = 2.861$$

## USING NUMERICAL APPROXIMATIONS FOR DERIVATIVES

The derivative physically represents the slope of a plot of the data at a specified point. You can approximate the derivative at any point by estimating the slope of the graph at that point. Just as there are several ways to estimate the slope, there are several ways to compute numerical approximations for derivatives. Since array index values are used in these calculations, here are the data (again), along with the array index values:

$$i = \begin{bmatrix} 0 \\ 1 \\ 2 \\ 3 \\ 4 \\ 5 \\ 6 \\ 7 \end{bmatrix} \qquad t = \begin{bmatrix} 10 \\ 11 \\ 12 \\ 13 \\ 14 \\ 15 \\ 16 \\ 17 \end{bmatrix} \qquad y = \begin{bmatrix} 11.043 \\ 12.616 \\ 14.394 \\ 16.349 \\ 18.235 \\ 20.691 \\ 23.17 \\ 26.27 \end{bmatrix}$$

One way to estimate the slope at point $i = 6$ (where $t = 16$) would be

$$\left. \frac{dy}{dt} \right|_{i=6} \approx \frac{y_7 - y_6}{t_7 - t_6}$$

If that equation is valid, then the following equation is equally valid, both are approximations:

$$\left. \frac{dy}{dt} \right|_{i=6} \approx \frac{y_6 - y_5}{t_6 - t_5}$$

The first expression uses the point at $t = 16$ and the point to the right ($i = 7$ or $t = 17$) to estimate the slope and is called a *forward finite difference approximation for the first derivative* at $i = 6$. The term *finite difference* is used because there is a finite distance between the $t$ values used in the calculation. Finite difference approximations are truly equal to the derivatives only in the limit as $\Delta t$ goes to zero.

The second expression uses the point at $t = 16$ and the point to the left ($t = 15$) to estimate the slope and is called a *backward finite difference approximation for the first derivative* at $i = 6$. You can also write a *central finite difference approximation for the first derivative* at $i = 6$:

$$\left. \frac{dy}{dt} \right|_{i=6} \approx \frac{y_7 - y_5}{t_7 - t_5}$$

Central differences tend to give better estimates of the slope and are the most commonly used. Applying this equation to calculate the derivative at point $i = 6$ in the data set, we find a derivative value of $2.79$:

$$\text{slope}_{16} := \frac{y_7 - y_5}{t_7 - t_5}$$
$$\text{slope}_{16} = 2.79$$

There are also finite difference approximations for higher order derivatives. For example, a *central finite difference approximation for a second derivative* at $t = 16$ can be written (assuming uniform point spacing i.e., $\Delta t$ constant) as

$$\left. \frac{d^2 y}{dt^2} \right|_{t=16} \approx \frac{y_{17} - 2\, y_{16} + y_{15}}{(\Delta t)^2}$$

**PRACTICE!**

Use central and forward difference approximations to estimate $\frac{dy}{dx}$ at $x = 1$. Try both the clean and noisy data sets.

$$x := \begin{bmatrix} 0.0 \\ 0.5 \\ 1.0 \\ 1.5 \\ 2.0 \\ 2.5 \\ 3.0 \end{bmatrix} \qquad y_{\text{clean}} := \begin{bmatrix} 0.00 \\ 0.48 \\ 0.84 \\ 1.00 \\ 0.91 \\ 0.60 \\ 0.14 \end{bmatrix} \qquad y_{\text{noisy}} := \begin{bmatrix} 0.24 \\ 0.60 \\ 0.69 \\ 1.17 \\ 0.91 \\ 0.36 \\ 0.18 \end{bmatrix}$$

A polynomial can be fit to the noisy data as follows:

$$f(x) := \begin{bmatrix} x \\ x^2 \\ x^3 \end{bmatrix} \qquad b := \text{linfit}(x, y_{\text{noisy}}, f) \qquad b = \begin{bmatrix} 1.434 \\ -0.588 \\ 0.041 \end{bmatrix}$$

Try using the differentiation operator on the Calculus Palette to evaluate

$$\frac{d}{dx}(1.434x - 0.588x^2 + 0.041x^3)$$

at $x = 1$.

*Note:* The derivative values you calculate in this Practice! box will vary widely. Calculating derivatives from noisy data is highly prone to errors, and you should try to avoid doing this if possible. If you must take derivatives from experimental data, try to get good, clean data sets.

## SUMMARY

In this chapter, you learned to use several standard numerical methods in Mathcad, including an interative solve block and numerical integration and differentiation. The numerical integration techniques involved using Mathcad's integration operators (from the Calculus Palette) when you were working with a function, and numerical techniques like trapezoidal or Simpson's rule integration when you were working with a data set. Similarly, Mathcad's differentiation operators apply when you need to take the derivative of a function, and finite difference methods were discussed for evaluating derivatives when you have a data set.

## MATHCAD SUMMARY

**ITERATIVE SOLUTIONS:**

Given    The keyword that begins an iterative solve block. Remember to specify an initial guess value before using the "given".

Find()    The key word that closes an iterative solve block and the function that performs the iteration and returns the solution. Remember to assign the value returned by find( ) to a variable.

**INTEGRATION:**

of a function    Use Mathcad's integration operators from the Calculus Palette.

of a data set    Trapezoidal and Simpson's rules can be used to approximate the integral, or you can fit a function to the data and then integrate the function.

**DIFFERENTIATION:**

| of a function | Use Mathcad's differentiation operators from the Calculus Palette. |
|---|---|
| of a data set | Finite differences can be used to estimate the values of the derivative, or you can fit a function to the data and then differentiate the function. |

# Problems

## 7.1  ITERATIVE SOLUTIONS

Use a solve block (given/find) to find the roots of these equations. (You may want to use a QuickPlot to find out how many roots to expect.)

a.   $(x - 5) \cdot (x + 7) = 0$

b.   $x^{0.2} = \ln(x)$

c.   $\tan(x) = 2.4x^2$   search for roots between $-2 < x < 2$

## 7.2  FRICTION LOSSES AND PRESSURE DROP IN PIPE FLOWS

In the Mathcad Applied section, the friction loss in a well-designed pipeline was determined. What if the pipeline is not well designed? That's the subject of this problem.

When you are moving water in a pipeline, the flow velocity is typically around 3 ft/s—the value that was used in the sample problem. This is a commonly used velocity that allows you to move a reasonable amount of water quickly and without too much friction loss. What happens to the friction loss and the required pump power when you try to move water through the same pipeline at a velocity of 15 ft/sec?

## 7.3  REAL GAS VOLUMES

The Soave–Redlich–Kwong (SRK) equation of state is a commonly used equation to relate the temperature, pressure, and volume of a gas under conditions when the gas behavior cannot be considered ideal (e.g., moderate temperature and high pressure). The equation is

$$P = \frac{RT}{(\hat{V} - b)} - \frac{\alpha a}{\hat{V}(\hat{V} + b)}$$

where $\alpha$, $a$ and $b$ are parameters specific to the gas, R is the gas constant, P is the absolute pressure, T is absolute temperature, and

$$\hat{V} = \frac{V}{n}$$

is the molar volume (volume per mole of gas).

For common gases, the parameters $\alpha$, $a$, and $b$ can be readily determined from available data. Then, if you know the molar volume of the gas, the SRK equation is easy to solve for either pressure or temperature. However, if you know the temperature and pressure and need to find the molar volume, an iterative solution is required.

Determine the molar volume of ammonia at 300°C and 1200 kPa by

a.   using the ideal gas equation.

b.   using the SRK equation and an iterative solve block.

For ammonia at these conditions:

$$\alpha = 0.7007$$

$$a = 430.9 \text{ kPa} \cdot \text{L}^2/\text{mole}^2$$

$$b = 0.0259 \text{ L/mole}$$

### 7.4  REQUIRED SIZE FOR A WATER RETENTION BASIN

In urban areas, as fields are turned into streets and parking lots, water runoff from sudden storms can become a serious problem. To prevent flooding, retention basins are often built to hold excess water temporarily during storms. In arid regions these basins are dry most of the time, so designers sometimes try to build in alternative uses. A proposed design is a half-pipe for skateboarders that can hold 100,000 cubic feet of water during a storm. The radius of the half-cylinder needs to be scaled to fit the skateboarders, and a radius of 8 feet is proposed.

a. What is the required length of the basin to hold the 100,000 ft³ of storm water? (There may be several short sections of half-pipes to provide the required total volume.)

b. If the basin is filled with water to a depth of 4 feet after a storm, what volume of water is held in the basin?

### 7.5  WORK REQUIRED TO STRETCH A SPRING

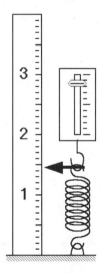

The device shown in the accompanying figure can be used to determine the work required to extend a spring. This device consists of a spring, a spring balance, and a ruler. Before stretching the spring, its length is measured and found to be 1.3 cm. The spring is then stretched 0.4 cm at a time, and the force indicated on the spring balance is recorded. The resulting data set is shown in the following table:

| MEASUREMENT (CM) | UNEXTENDED LENGTH (CM) | EXTENDED LENGTH (CM) | FORCE (N) |
|---|---|---|---|
| 1.3 | 1.3 | 0.0 | 0.00 |
| 1.7 | 1.3 | 0.4 | 0.88 |
| 2.1 | 1.3 | 0.8 | 1.76 |
| 2.5 | 1.3 | 1.2 | 2.64 |
| 2.9 | 1.3 | 1.6 | 3.52 |
| 3.3 | 1.3 | 2.0 | 4.40 |
| 3.7 | 1.3 | 2.4 | 5.28 |
| 4.1 | 1.3 | 2.8 | 6.16 |
| 4.5 | 1.3 | 3.2 | 7.04 |
| 4.9 | 1.3 | 3.6 | 7.92 |

Work can be computed as the integral

$$W = \int F \, dx$$

where $x$ is the extended length of the spring.

a.  Calculate the work required to stretch the spring from an unextended length of 0 cm to 3.6 cm. Watch the signs on the forces in this problem. Force is a vector quantity, so there is an associated direction.

b.  Is the force being used to stretch the spring in the same direction as the movement of the spring or in the opposite direction?

## 7.6  WORK REQUIRED TO STRETCH A NONLINEAR SPRING

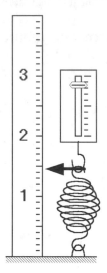

| EXTENDED LENGTH (CM) | FORCE (N) |
|---|---|
| 0.0 | 0.00 |
| 0.4 | 0.15 |
| 0.8 | 0.41 |
| 1.2 | 0.72 |
| 1.6 | 1.07 |
| 2.0 | 1.46 |
| 2.4 | 1.89 |
| 2.8 | 2.35 |
| 3.2 | 2.83 |
| 3.6 | 3.33 |

Springs come in a variety of sizes and shapes. The shape can sometimes affect the performance of the spring. The spring shown in the preceding figure pulls easily at first, but gets stiffer the more it is stretched. (See accompanying table.) It is a nonlinear spring. Calculate the work required to stretch this spring

a.  from an extended length of 0 cm to 1.6 cm.

b.  from an extended length of 2.0 cm to 3.6 cm.

## 7.7  WORK REQUIRED TO EXPAND A GAS

In problems 7.5 and 7.6 work was calculated as

$$W = \int F \, dx$$

But force divided by area is pressure, and length times area is volume, so work can also be found as

$$W = \int P \, dV$$

| VOLUME (ML) | PRESSURE (ATM) |
|---|---|
| 1.3 | 4.50 |
| 1.7 | 3.44 |
| 2.1 | 2.79 |
| 2.5 | 2.34 |
| 2.9 | 2.02 |
| 3.3 | 1.77 |
| 3.7 | 1.58 |
| 4.1 | 1.43 |
| 4.5 | 1.30 |
| 4.9 | 1.19 |

This form is handier for dealing with gas systems like that shown in the accompanying figure. As the piston is lifted, the pressure in the sealed chamber will fall. By monitoring the change in position on the ruler and knowing the cross-sectional area of the chamber, we can calculate the chamber volume at each pressure. Care must be taken to allow the system to equilibrate at room temperature before taking the readings. The pressure and volume after equilibrium are listed in the accompanying table.

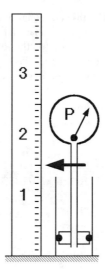

a.   Calculate the work required to expand the gas from a volume of 0.3 mL to 3.9 mL.

b.   Is this work being done by the gas on the surroundings or by the surroundings on the gas?

## 7.8 CALCULATING SPRING CONSTANTS

The extension of a linear spring is described by Hooke's law,

$$F = k\,x$$

where x is the extended length of the spring (i.e., the total length of the stretched spring minus the length of the spring before stretching) and k is the spring constant. The spring constant quantifies the "stiffness" of the spring. Hooke's law can also be written in differential form, as

$$\frac{dF}{dx} = k$$

For a linear spring, dF/dx is a constant, the spring constant. For a nonlinear spring, dF/dx will not be constant, but taking this derivative at various spring extensions can help you see how the spring characteristics change as the spring is pulled.

Use the data from Problems 7.4 and 7.5 to compute

a.   the spring constant for the linear spring (Problem 7.4).

b.   the derivative dF/dx as a function of x for the nonlinear spring (Problem 7.5). Use a central difference approximation for the derivative whenever possible, and create a plot of dF/dx vs. x.

## 7.9 THERMAL CONDUCTIVITY

Thermal conductivity is a material property related to the material's ability to transfer energy by conduction. Good conductors, like copper and aluminum, have large thermal conductivity values. Insulating materials should have low thermal conductivities to minimize heat transfer.

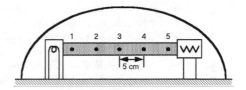

The preceding figure illustrates a device that could be used to measure thermal conductivity. A rod of the material to be tested is placed between a resistance heater (on the right) and a cooling coil (on the left). Five (numbered) thermocouples have been inserted into the rod at 5-cm intervals. The entire apparatus is placed in a bell jar, and the air around the rod is pumped out to reduce heat losses.

To run the experiment, a known amount of power is sent to the heater, and the system is allowed to reach steady state. Once the temperatures are steady, the power level and temperatures are recorded. A data sheet might look like the following:

| Rod Diameter: | 2 cm |
| TC Spacing: | 5 cm |
| Power: | 100 watts |

| TC # | TEMP. (K) |
| --- | --- |
| 1 | 348 |
| 2 | 387 |
| 3 | 425 |
| 4 | 464 |
| 5 | 503 |

The thermal conductivity can be determined from Fourier's law,

$$\frac{q}{A} = -k\frac{dT}{dx}$$

where $q$ is the power being applied to the heater and $A$ is the cross-sectional area of the rod.

*Note:* The term q/A is called the *energy flux* and is a vector quantity—that is, it has a direction as well as a magnitude. As drawn, with the energy source on the right, the energy will be flowing in the -x direction, so the flux in this problem is negative.

a. Use finite difference approximations to estimate dT/dx at several locations along the rod, and then calculate the thermal conductivity of the material.

b. Thermal conductivity is a function of temperature. Do your dT/dx values indicate that the thermal conductivity of the material changes appreciably between 348 and 503 K?

## 7.10 CALCULATING WORK

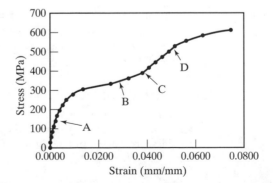

In the last chapter, there was a note in the Mathcad Applied: Stress–Strain Analysis box to the effect that an alternative method of integrating a force–displacement graph is available to calculate work. The alternative method is numerical integration using a function such as trap(). The stress–strain data (shown in the accompanying graph) for a composite material have been converted to force–displacement data, abridged, and tabulated as follows:

| F (N) | x (mm) |
|-------|--------|
| 0 | 0.000 |
| 5500 | 0.009 |
| 8300 | 0.014 |
| 13800 | 0.023 |
| 16500 | 0.033 |
| 22100 | 0.051 |
| 24800 | 0.066 |
| 30300 | 0.137 |
| 33100 | 0.248 |
| 38600 | 0.380 |
| 41400 | 0.407 |
| 46900 | 0.461 |
| 49600 | 0.488 |
| 55200 | 0.561 |
| 57900 | 0.628 |
| 60700 | 0.749 |

# Index